San Francisco's Lost Landmarks

James R. Smith

CRAVEN
STREET
B O O K S
Fresno, California

Published by
Craven Street Books
An Imprint of Linden Publishing
2006 S. Mary St., Fresno, CA 93721
(559) 233-6633 / (800) 345-4447
CravenStreetBooks.com

Craven Street Books titles may be purchased in quantity at special discounts for educational, fund-raising, business, or promotional use.
Please contact Special Markets, Craven Street Books, at the above address, toll-free at 1-800-345-4447or by e-mail: Info@QuillDriverBooks.com

Printed in the United States of America
ISBN 1-884995-44-6

7986

Craven Street Books project cadre:
Doris Hall, Dave Marion, Stephen Blake Mettee

Library of Congress Cataloging-in-Publication Data

Smith, James R.
San Francisco's lost landmarks / by James R. Smith.
p. cm.
Includes bibliographical references.
ISBN 1-884995-44-6
1. San Francisco (Calif.)—History. 2. San Francisco
(Calif.)—History—Pictorial works. 3. Historic sites—California—San
Francisco. 4. Historic sites—California—San Francisco—Pictorial works.
5. San Francisco (Calif.)—Social life and customs. I. Title.

F869.S357.S64 2005
979.4'61—dc22

2004023982

MIX
Paper from
responsible sources
FSC
www.fsc.org   FSC® C011935

This book is dedicated to all San Franciscans, an indomitable people determined to seek their own path, and to my mother, Ruth Elaine Johnson Smith, who had the courage to marry one of them.

Contents

Acknowledgements

While I take full responsibility for the content of this book, I couldn't have done it by myself. Those history writers who put pen to paper prior to the writing of this book led the way and I'm indebted to them. Not that I took all for fact but they provided a starting place and yes, inspiration. The San Francisco Public Library's Main Branch has been my primary source for research and research support, especially the Herb Caen Magazines and Newspapers Center and the San Francisco History Center on the sixth floor. Pat, Selby, and Susan each provided kind, patient support in spite of my hurried requests and myriad questions. The California Historical Society and the San Francisco Museum and Historical Society have each played a key role in the creation of this book, as has the Virtual Museum of the City of San Francisco and the San Francisco Genealogy website SFGenealogy.com; many thanks to Pamela Storm Wolfskill and Ron Filion for retaining history as a major part of that site. I also owe Ron for his serious research and transcriptions (http://www.zpub.com/sf50/sf/), which he so willingly shared.

A number of people have shared their expertise in areas that are less than well documented. Claudine Chalmers, author of Splendide Californie, 2002, and a number of articles on the French in early California, provided invaluable information and guidance on that topic, including the history of the Poodle Dog restaurant. Her website is www.FrenchGold.com for those interested in the subject. Cal Lalanne, grandson of Calixte Lalanne of the nineteenth century Old Poodle Dog and owner of the final incarnation, kindly offered insight into his family and their restaurants. In the same manner, John T. Freeman offered guidance through the maze of the various Chutes locations. His in-depth article on that topic just appeared in The Argonaut-Journal of the San Francisco Museum and Historical Society, Vol. 14 No. 2, Winter 2003. Bill Roddy shared his experiences in San Francisco during the thirties, both directly and through his www.AmericaHurrah.com website. Additionally, a large number of kind folks offered images, anecdotes and histories to help personalize this history. My warmest thanks to all of them.

Ruth Grady Skewis was quick to recall or research incidents and places from her life in "da Mish," the Mission District of San Francisco. She also provided encouragement and some great editing. Matt O'Neil and wife Mary Ellen also shared their memories, especially of the restaurants and the Golden Gate International Exposition. My dad's best friend, Bud Clark, shared stories of growing up in San Francisco. Friendships like that come once in a lifetime, if one is lucky. My sincere thanks to all!

John Freeman is owed special recognition for clarifying the history of The Chutes and for his input on Playland. James Jarvis pointed out the exact location of the Cobweb Palace which I have since verified.

Finally, I owe my family a great debt of gratitude for its support and encouragement as well as their tolerance. My wife Liberty stuck by me through the whole process, overlooking the busy hours and offering her great editing skills and suggestions, as well as urging me on. No man deserves to be this lucky.

Introduction

San Francisco's Lost Landmarks: A City in Perpetual Transition offers an opportunity to look back at earlier times, lives, and lifestyles. Little comparison is made to what the city is now and as you'll find, the tone remains as neutral as possible except in a couple of instances. No attempt was made to judge those times or these—San Francisco is unique in that it is for the most part amoral but not immoral. It has always been a "live and let live" place populated by people who dare to take risks.

San Francisco's city emblem, the phoenix, is as applicable today as always. The city continually renews and reinvents itself. I meet people who tell me they won't go to the city any more because it's become so dark and sinful; yes, it has changed and not necessarily for the better. Yet it's no more dark or sinful than it ever was. Part of that is media sensationalism and part the sanitation of old memories, and I'm as guilty of the latter as anyone else. Yes, the city had changed, but the factor of change is ongoing, because it, more than any other city in the world, embraces change.

So please take this book as a fun look backward, with stories and illustrations of the days, events, and places that we have built on. History doesn't have to be serious, so enjoy and take from this what you will.

Sand dunes like these covered most of the western side of San Francisco, as well as a good part of the remainder. —*Photo courtesy of San Francisco History Center, San Francisco Public Library*

Chapter 1

The Original Land and Shores: Sculpting a City

In 1847, American San Francisco was not exactly ideal for the local inhabitants. The hills were too steep for daily walking and for heavily laden, horse-drawn wagons. The sand, marshland, shallow lakes and meandering streams were obstructions to a well-planned city. The shallow coves and mudflats were barriers to efficient handling of ships' cargos and indeed made it difficult to anchor those ships. Any one of them could be found stranded at low tide and if they built up suction in the mud, they might swamp before breaking loose at the onset of a rising tide. Rocks and small islands in the bay were impediments to shipping traffic. More than a few ships had their hulls ripped out by a rocky peak, like Blossom Rock, lying just submerged at low tide. However, the city's natural contours, boundaries, and features were considered merely a work in progress to the Americans who took the city and state from Mexico.

These are truly lost landmarks, for it's difficult to even imagine what the city once looked like, given the enormity of change. Tracking that change requires a great deal of map work as well as some imagination.

The Gold Rush of 1849 changed the landscape and shores of San Francisco radically. Within the first few years after the madness began, tidelands and coves were filled in, hills were torn down, marshlands were covered, and streams were diverted to underground runs. Between 1846 and 1856, the face of the peninsula was modified almost beyond recognition. No city ever changed its appearance as quickly as early San Francisco.

John S. Hittell, in *A Guide Book to San Francisco, 1888,* (The Bancroft Company), wrote,

> The site of land upon which the city was built consisted, in 1849, of steep ridges and deep ravines. The nearest level and dry land was at the Mission. The place in its natural condition, was unfit for occupation by a dense population, and immense changes were made by cutting down hills, filling up hollows, and converting the mud flats and anchorage in front of the town, as it then was, into land. The city contains more than four hundred acres of "made ground" and a large part of the business is done where the water stood in 1850. The bay shore then came up west of Sansome Street, California to Jackson and a large ship called the *Niantic* was drawn up and normally fixed in 1849 on the northwestern corner of Sansome and Clay, a point about half a mile distant from the present waterfront. The change in the level of the ground has amounted in many places to fifty feet, or more, and railroads were built to carry the hills down to the bay. Happy Valley, Spring Valley, and St. Ann's Valley were destroyed by transporting the hills that enclosed them or by raising the level of the low ground. Spring Valley was at the northeastern corner of Taylor and Clay Streets and was at least fifty feet below the present level. A little spring there was claimed, with the idea that by digging, enough water could be obtained to supply the city, in the days when the fluid was brought from Sausalito in a water-boat and peddled around at twenty-five-cents a bucket from water carts.
>
> Notwithstanding all that has been done to reduce the steepness of the natural grades of streets and lots, including the transfer of 20,000,000 cubic yards of earthy material, San Francisco is still remarkably hilly, and may properly be termed "The Hundred-hilled City."

The cycle of fill, level, and growth continued through World War II. It took more than one hundred years before the people and government said, "Enough!" Even today, there is pressure to just fill a little more or to carve out a bit of a hill.

Woodcut of pre-Gold Rush San Francisco—1848. —*Library of Congress*

Woodcut view of Yerba Beuna Cove in 1849. The ships begin to accumulate. —*Library of Congress*

WALK AROUND THE COASTLINE—MID-NINETEENTH CENTURY

The only way to grasp the magnitude of change to the San Francisco peninsula is to look back before the city, state, and federal governments, as well as the locals, started remolding the area. Yerba Buena, as the little settlement that would become San Francisco was known, had a population of 497 in 1847. This swelled to nearly 30,000 by 1849. This amazing growth put tremendous pressure on the city resources. What would become San Francisco began a massive metamorphosis.

Starting on the western Pacific Ocean side, the beach was pretty much as it is now, minus the roads, improvements, and the attempts to prevent the erosion of the beaches. It is hard to fight the Pacific and that holds true up to Fort Point and the Golden Gate (which was named long before the bridge was built). Inland from the beach, Lake Merced remains remarkably intact, with the notable exception that the outlet creek no longer runs to the ocean. Above Lake Merced, a great sand bank extends east from Ocean Beach a couple of miles inland.

The bay side from Fort Point marks a major shift in the landscape. Protected from the wind and ocean waves and sculpted by tides and streams, the bay shore presents a scalloped look of points and coves. A small double bay runs from Fort Point to Black Point (site of Fort Mason), punctuated in the middle by Sandy Point. That section, where Chrissy Field and the Marina District now stand, was nothing more

View of Black Point (just west of North Beach) from Telegraph Hill—1866. —*Library of Congress*

than a sand bank with brackish lagoons, creeks, and marsh behind it in the mid-nineteenth century. Heading eastward into the bay is North Beach, a gently sloping sand beach terminated by North Point, the point of land jutting out northeast of Telegraph Hill. The north shores fail to provide anchorage close to the land, forcing ships to sail around to the hospitable eastern side of the peninsula.

Yerba Buena Cove provides the first available shelter for ships, as it did for the early residents. That harbor serves the little town of Yerba Buena, extending from the cove and wending around the hills to Mission Dolores. The hills jut up from the harbor, and homes fill the small valleys and dot the lower slopes of Telegraph Hill, Nob Hill, and Rincon Hill. Rincon Point, set aside as a military reservation, marks the bottom of Yerba Buena Cove.

South Beach—yes, there was a South Beach—provides an ideal environment for shipbuilding and repair. The gently sloping beach, protected by low sand cliffs, makes it easy to drag a boat out of the water and to launch it again. The moon-shaped beach extends between Rincon Point and Steamboat Point to the south.

South Beach was the center for ship and boat building and repair. —*Library of Congress*

Looking out at Steamboat Point from South Beach in 1866. —*Library of Congress*

Mission Bay, just below Steamboat Point, offers access to the Mission region via Mission Creek. The creek runs near Mission Dolores, emptying midpoint into the bay. Only shallow-draft boats can use the tidal bay, and any boat can be stranded by a low tide. Inland rolling sandhills, pastures, marshland, creeks, and ponds make up the landscape. The area is called Potrero Nuevo or "new pasture," because it was originally pastureland set aside for use by the local inhabitants, according to Spanish law. This area includes Potrero Hill, which terminates at Potrero Point in the bay, and marks the bottom of Mission Bay. Potrero Nuevo terminates at Islais Creek.

Potrero Viejo, "old pasture," starts below Islais Creek and was added to the Bernal land grant that extends from there to modern day Hunters Point (a long finger of land) and Bernal Heights. The creek defies description and, as such, is optionally referred to as a navigable creek, a bay, a tidal basin, or an non-navigable swamp. The name Islais (pronounced "iss-lis" as in "bliss" and "list") is not Spanish and is said to be the Ohlone Indian word for the wild cherry trees found growing in the area. The inlet, or bay, was called Islais Creek or Islais Creek Bay depending on the speaker's perspective and the tide. It reads about three feet deep at average high tide and it is bare mud at low.

The land below Hunters Point to what is now Candlestick Point, San Francisco's southern border, can be described simply as mudflats, which held little interest for the early locals. Valuable but unusable wetlands, no one even bothered to begin filling them in until the mid-twentieth century.

ISLANDS AND ROCKS

San Francisco Bay quickly evolved into a critical shipping port after the discovery of gold. Nearly

South Beach from Steamboat Point—1866. —*Library of Congress*

Islais Bay and Creek prior to filling the wetland. Note the plank walkways used to access boats at both high and low tides. —*Photo courtesy of San Francisco History Center, San Francisco Public Library*

all of California's wealth funneled through the Golden Gate. The local, state, and federal governments responded quickly to any hazard to navigation. Blossom Rock became the first shipping hazard identified as requiring a permanent solution and the solution turned into a citywide event.

Blossom Rock lay just five feet below the waterline a half-mile northeast of North Point (near Pier 39). It was part of a four thousand-foot crescent consisting of four underwater rocks starting at *Blossom Rock*, then continuing to *Harding Rock*, *Shag Rocks*, and *Arch Rock* and terminating at Alcatraz Island. Ideally placed to waylay or even rip the hull from any unwary ship, Blossom Rock was first named and charted as a navigation hazard by Captain Frederick W. Beechey on the *HMS Blossom*, a British man-of-war visiting San Francisco in 1826. Legend claims the *Blossom* located the rock by striking it, but there is no documentation confirming that event. Regardless, many a ship has encountered the rock, both before it was charted, and since. An East India ship, the *Seringapatam*, ran aground on Blossom Rock in the early 1830s, waiting until the tide turned before she could slide off and continue her voyage. Her teakwood hull saved her from serious damage.

The U.S. Army Corps of Engineers began test explosions on Blossom Rock in early 1867 in the hope that it could be topped off to a depth of twenty-four feet. The Corps determined that the approximately 105- by 195-foot underwater peak could be demolished and proposed a budget of $50,000 to accomplish the task.

Alexis W. Von Schmidt, a civil engineer and builder of the first dry dock in San Francisco, proposed using a similar method to remove the underwater impediment as that used for the dry dock. Von Schmidt asked for $75,000 to accomplish the task. The Corps awarded him the contract, to be paid after assurance that twenty-four feet of clearance had been achieved.

Von Schmidt's team built a square crib at the wharf and then floated it out to the rock. The crib was anchored to the rock and then solid supports were used to fix it rigidly to Blossom Rock. Von Schmidt used the new technology he had devised to build the Hunters Point dry dock, and in October of 1869, he lowered a boiler-iron cylinder nine feet in diameter and thirteen feet tall down to the underwater peak to create a coffer dam, and then sealed it and pumped it dry. His team then inserted a six-foot diameter, seventeen-foot tall pipe inside the first and began the excavation. They excavated downward into the rock to a depth of fourteen and a half feet from the bottom of the dam. From that point, the rock was excavated horizontally to form a cavern sixty feet wide and one hundred forty feet long, with a domed ceiling of twelve feet. Rock columns that had been left for support were replaced with eight-inch by ten-inch wooden beams.

On April 20, 1870, the team began the arrangement of thirty-eight sixty-gallon barrels and seven boiler-iron tanks around the perimeter of the cavern, each one filled with sodium nitrate blasting powder and waterproofed with asphalt. After connecting all with gas pipe and rubber tubing up to the crib on the surface, the underground activity ceased and the cavern flooded with bay water. Von

Blowing up Blossom Rock in San Francisco Bay. —*Author's collection*

Schmidt announced that the rock would be blown on April 23, 1870.

On that day, thousands of spectators, radiating a holiday spirit, gathered on Telegraph Hill to gain a clear view of the great spectacle. Shortly after two in the afternoon, a boat played out the single insulated wire and anchored eight hundred feet away from the crib. The wire was attached to each of the detonators set to the twenty-one and a half tons of explosives. The salt water of the bay served as the return to complete the connection.

At three-thirty that afternoon, a twist of the crank on the magneto-battery initiated an explosion that sent a column of water and rock shooting upward from two hundred to five hundred feet into the air, depending on who did the reporting. The main black column coming up from the cofferdam was surrounded by shorter columns of debris and water that marked the perimeter of the cavern below. Pieces of rock and timber seemed suspended in air before gradually falling back to the bay. The crowds cheered, and the next day newspapers printed enthusiastic accounts of the event.

Soundings indicated that the results were two feet short of the goal. The Army Corps of Engineers refused payment until Von Schmidt could clear the additional depth. Fashioning a floating platform, with a chain operated rake suspended below, Von Schmidt's team scraped the remaining fragments off Blossom Rock and finally achieved the required clearance.

Shag Rocks (1 and 2) and Arch Rock were dealt with after Blossom Rock and were reduced to thirty feet below the surface in 1900. In 1903, Blossom Rock was further reduced to match Shag Rocks and Arch Rock at thirty feet. As ships became larger and drew a deeper draft, additional toppings were required. On August 31, 1932, Blossom Rock was lowered again to forty-two feet below the mean level of low water.

Mission Rock, once proudly standing guard over Mission Bay, suffered a different fate. A convenient anchoring point off the bay, it became a dumping place for tons of ballast, which over the years added measurably to its size. Eventually covered with warehouses and a pier, the China Basin fill encroached on Mission Bay, to within a few hundred yards of the rock. At the turn of the twentieth century, the U.S. Navy disputed ownership by the Mission Rock Company. After thirty-eight years of litigation, the U.S. Supreme Court awarded ownership to the Navy. The Navy then decided they didn't want the island and transferred ownership to Board of State Harbor Commissioners for just under $10,000.

In 1946, plans were made to extend Pier 50 to encompass Mission Rock, creating a super terminal for shipping. The remaining buildings on the island were burned in a massive fire that could be seen from as far as Oakland, and the terminal was built as planned. Mission Rock still exists, but only as a stepping-stone.

Treasure Island remains the exception to the rule. It represents an island built where none existed before. San Francisco wanted to celebrate its two new bridges by hosting the 1939 World Fair but had no suitable land available on which to locate it. The decision made in 1935 to use the San Francisco-Oakland Bay Bridge for access to the fair with a view of the Golden Gate Bridge seemed a natural. The island was to be built on the shoals just north of Yerba Buena Island.

Construction began in early 1936. A series of piles and cofferdams surrounded a four hundred-acre rectangular area. Hydraulic dredging began, but in reverse of the normal method. Instead of removing material, the dredging added it, pumping the bay silt, sand and gravel into the form. The name Treasure Island related to the fill itself, washed down from the gold fields of the Sierra as well as referring to the glitter to be found at the fair. It required twenty-nine million cubic yards of fill dredged from the bay and the Sacramento River Delta as well as fifty thousand cubic yards of loam laid on top after the salt was leached from the fill. Nearly two hundred sixty thousand tons of rock were used to create the containment wall around the island.

By 1938, Treasure Island took shape and before the fill was even dry, the buildings and facilities of the 1939 Golden Gate International Exposition sprouted on the island. A causeway connected Treasure Island to Yerba Buena Island, and in 1939, the fair opened on schedule.

The island was intended to house the San Francisco International Airport after the fair, but World War II intervened. Following the fair, San Francisco traded Treasure Island to the Navy for the land in San Bruno where San Francisco airport now resides. Treasure Island became a naval air base and training center. The year 1993 saw the island returned to the City of San Francisco for civilian use.

THE FILLING OF THE BAY AND THE ABANDONED GOLD RUSH FLEET

The story of early San Francisco is partly a tale of ships coming to anchor in Yerba Buena Cove. The passengers disembarked, the crew offloaded the cargo and then the sailors skulked off to the gold fields to seek their fortunes. The ships rode up and down with the tides, their captains unable to recruit a crew. Eventually, the ships settled into the mud, locked in its grip, never to sail again. Over a short time so many ships lay abandoned that handling newly arriving ships became increasingly difficult. Wharfs were extended between and beyond the abandoned ships, but it was soon realized the best solution would be filling around and over the permanently anchored fleet, extending the eastern edge of San Francisco. That's the story; it's just not the whole story.

In 1848, before the gold madness, and just after California became a United States possession, Brigadier General Stephen W. Kearny, military representative in San Francisco, granted the city ownership of water lots in Yerba Buena Cove. At that time, the tides of the bay ran all the way up to the intersection of Montgomery and First streets. On the south end of the cove, General Kearny added Fremont, Beale, and Front streets to the plan. On the north side, he added Sansome, Battery, and Front streets. Green Street was to extend about five hundred feet into the bay to meet the new Front Street on the north end, with Rincon Point as the southern terminus of

Abandoned ships in San Francisco Harbor—1849. —*Photo courtesy of San Francisco History Center, San Francisco Public Library*

the new grant. Proceeds from the sale of water lots went into city, federal, and, later, state coffers.

Water lots—land parcels that purportedly resided between the high and low water marks—offered an opportunity to build wharves and stores out onto the bay tidelands.

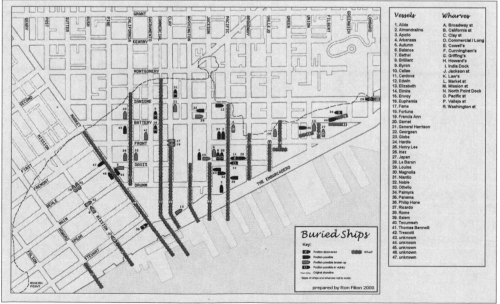

Map of known and suspected locations of ships buried under the Financial District. —*Courtesy of Ron Filion*

The reality was that many of these never saw less than eighteen feet of water. The same plan existed for the Mission Bay area to the south, with the extension of Brannon and Bryant streets through it. Many an investor made a fortune buying these lots and later selling them for immense profits after the Gold Rush began in earnest. James Lick, piano maker and entrepreneur, joined this early crowd. Profits from later land sales, plus his other ventures, quickly made him one of San Francisco's wealthiest men.

South Beach, located just below Rincon Point, paralleled the fate of Yerba Buena Cove. Boat builders and fishermen bought up the original lots but soon developers bought them out to use for industrial sites and shipping.

Suddenly, San Francisco had its own Manifest Destiny—move east. The city and the new state of California recognized the opportunity to gain revenue by selling additional water lots. Within a year, the Front Street property owners were land-locked and two years beyond that the next group locked out the latter. Regardless, each group profited since the city found itself crowded on the northeast corner of the peninsula. Developing west meant dealing with the hills and the dunes. The city marched eastward into the bay.

Ships abandoned in Yerba Beuna Cove, San Francisco, 1849–1850. —*Library of Congress*

Yerba Beuna Cove from Telegraph Hill, ca. 1848. —*Library of Congress*

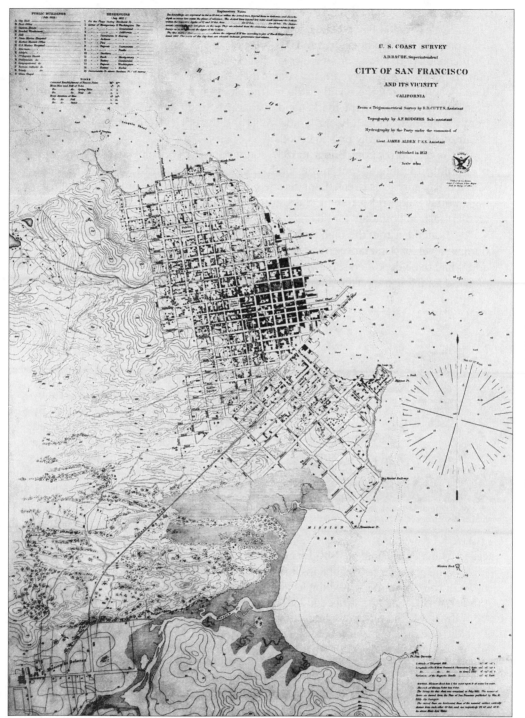

Map of San Francisco in 1853—The map identifies buildings, roads and bay conditions. —*Library of Congress*

While Mission Bay provided an ideal calm water anchorage, traversing by land from one end to the other, north and south, required a serious westward detour due to the incursion of the low-tide shallows landward. The land area to the south comprised San Francisco's new heavy industry zone, where water met rail. The steamboats plied the bay and moored there with cattle for the stockyards and slaughterhouses, grain, fruit, and vegetables for the market and restaurants, and raw materials for everything from the gunpowder factory, the lumber mills and the brick yard to the sugar refinery. Steamboats carried away finished goods.

The creation of Long Bridge in 1867, connecting Potrero Point, just below Steamboat Point to Hunters Point in the south, provided a solution to the detour around Mission Bay and Islais Creek. Long Bridge became an attraction for recreational fishing, Sunday buggy rides, rowing clubs, and small waterside cafes. The bridge also created an eastern boundary for fill and the rush for land began anew.

Located far from the higher-class residential areas, Mission Bay became an ideal dumping site for San Francisco's trash. The city generated massive amounts of garbage and it had to be deposited somewhere. Soon the stench at Mission Bay helped fuel the demand for filling the polluted waterway. The rolling sandhills nearby provided an easy supply of clean fill, and the additional advantage of leveling the landscape. Still, the process progressed slowly until 1906 when Mission Bay became the dump-site of choice for the refuse and ruins left by the earthquake and fire. By 1912, it was completely filled in with the exception of a large channel dug at Mission Creek to allow ship traffic access to the commercial district inland. Mission Creek or Mission Channel is still active and bisects the filled in bay now called China Basin, home of SBC Park and the San Francisco Giants.

Mission Bay in 1853—most abandoned ships were left in Yerba Beuna Cove. Still, Mission Bay didn't escape the city's desire to fill in the bay. —*Library of Congress*

One of the largest incursions into the bay occurred after the earthquake and fire of 1906. The city wanted to exhibit its great recovery as well as celebrate the opening of the Panama Canal, and it needed land for a world fair. A massive lagoon, separated from the bay by a breakwater and situated between Black Point (Fort Mason) and the Presidio offered an ideal location. The Army Corps of Engineers used a liquid-fill technique, using sand and sediment pumped from the bay, as well as rubble from the 1906 quake, to create the area now known as the Marina District. The fill extended from Chestnut to the present day location of the Marina Green and Yacht Harbor just north of Marina Boulevard.

The subsequent Panama Pacific International Exhibition succeeded on a grand scale. When complete, the fair was razed and homes were built. Ironically, the land that celebrated the city's recovery was seismically unstable, due to the sandy fill, and sustained major damage in the 1989 Loma Prieta Earthquake seventy-five years later.

North Beach wasn't immune to change either; it just took longer. Meigg's Wharf was built in 1852 on Francisco between Mason and Powell. At that time, now land-locked Francisco ran along the side of the bay. Meigg's Wharf lasted longer than most, but eventually the city constructed a breakwater beyond the limits of that long pier. They then proceeded to fill it in. It is said today's Fisherman's Wharf sits on the site of Meigg's Wharf. Not so. By 1896, the base of what had been Meigg's Wharf resided five full blocks south of the bay and Jefferson Street, the current northern-most street along Fisherman's Wharf. Telegraph Hill provided much of the fill between Francisco and Jefferson.

North Beach in 1866—Francisco Road skirts the beach, now located far inland due to filling in the shallows. —*Library of Congress*

Hunters Point, a long finger of land, protrudes out into the bay near the south end of the city. Named for an early family of settlers, access to deep water made Hunters Point valuable. Shrimpers, anchovy, and salmon fisherman and shipbuilders all took advantage of easy access to the bay. By 1867, it boasted the first permanent dry dock on the Pacific Coast. Change was slow at the Point. Seafood packinghouses, warehouses, additional dry-docks, and a few wharves, one measuring four hundred sixty-five feet long, made up the bulk of the changes. Hunters Point retained its character until the Navy moved in and took it over.

The winds of war in 1939 dictated a need for military ship-building and repair on the West Coast. The Navy purchased forty-seven acres on the Point, gaining both a foothold and dry-docks. In 1942, all aliens were evacuated, and within a few weeks, the Navy summarily

Tearing down Telegraph Hill—the job proved too expensive, but the face was torn away to help fill the bay. —*Author's collection*

seized the entire Hunters Point neighborhood. An article printed in *The San Francisco News*, March 10, 1942, summarized the situation.

> Immediate expansion of shipyard facilities at Hunters Point on land soon to be acquired by the Navy will force at least 100 civilian families to move, it was revealed by 12th Naval District headquarters today.
>
> The Navy announcement set no deadline for removal, but police, who were asked to serve notice on residents, told them to be prepared to move on 48-hour notice. Indications were, however, that the Navy would not require the removal for at least two weeks.
>
> It was not revealed what machinery the Navy had set up to pay property owners or to provide them with new living quarters. All Hunters Point residents are citizens, aliens having been removed several weeks ago.
>
> We sincerely regret these families must move, but military necessity must come before other considerations, declared Rear Adm. John Wills Greenslade.
>
> The district is defined as the area from the water to Coleman-st and from Fairfax-av to Oakdale-av. It will be a military zone, banned to the public. The 86 homes and 23 business houses in the area have a total value of more than $250,000.

The Navy's action set the stage for a massive filling of the shallows around the point. Hunters Point swelled to 400 percent of its original land area, creating a huge wartime shipyard, and by 1945 employed eighteen thousand people. The area lost any semblance to its original shoreline, redefining a major San Francisco landmark. The shipyards closed in 1974, and by 1980, a portion of the area was set aside for an artist's colony. Today it marks one of the largest colonies in the country, housing over two hundred artists.

The last of San Francisco's major landfills was at Candlestick Point next to the San Francisco/San Mateo county line. The name Candlestick Point originated with the practice of burning abandoned ships off the nearby point. As they burned, they sank into the bay and the burning masts looking like candlesticks. The Navy filled in one hundred seventy acres then failed to develop it due to the end of World War II. Locals continued dumping there, illegally.

Candlestick Park, later called 3Com Park, opened as the Giants home field in 1960, and immediately became the most hated ballpark in baseball history. It was cold beyond reason during the summer with an icy wind blowing in off the bay. If the twenty-degree chill factor didn't drive the fans away, the inconsistent breezes, constantly changing direction, drove the players to tears. Dirt devils blew trash about the field and a pop-up could be carried anywhere. Some players included clauses in their contracts that precluded a trade to San Francisco. The Giants were happy to abandon

"The Stick" to the 49ers football team, moving on to the new SBC Park located in China Basin.

The land outside Candlestick Park was purchased by the state in 1973 and set aside as a park in 1977, becoming the first urban recreation area in California. Today it's a functioning state park favored by windsurfers taking advantage of the stiff breezes on the bay.

TEARING DOWN THE HILLS

If San Francisco wanted to be a proper city, it needed proper roads. San Francisco consisted of two civilian centers in its earliest days: the village of Yerba Buena on Yerba Buena Bay and the Mission Dolores. Travel between them required snaking around the hills and dodging the marshland. Two thoroughfares were planned to correct the situation—Market Street and the Mission Toll Road.

The building of a plank toll road from Mission Bay to the mission (today's Mission Street) proved expensive and time-consuming. Forty-foot piles were driven into the sand and marsh to provide a stable footing. What the builders didn't count on was the depth of some areas of marsh. A pile driven into one section disappeared from sight in one blow from the pile driver. A second pile placed in the hole left behind met the same fate. Whether the marsh was in fact an underground lake or just a deep bog was unknown but setting the footings proved an arduous task.

Civil engineer Jasper O'Farrell provided the first American layout of San Francisco based on the original plan for Yerba Buena done by Jean J. Vioget. O'Farrell began at the present Kearny and Washington streets and extended it to North Beach and west to Taylor Street. Market Street was laid out at a thirty-eight degree angle from Kearny Street—a straight shot between Yerba Buena Cove and Mission Dolores. While this may seem ideal planning, it didn't take into account the hundred-foot-high sandhills that intervened, such as the one at Market and Third streets, later site of the Palace Hotel. Circumnavigating the hill required detouring on Geary and Dupont (now Grant). A series of sandhills running east to west dominated the area.

Most roads were unpaved, suffering the whims of the rains and tides. Private toll roads dominated the small number of paved roads (mostly plank). The busiest roads often were impassible by man and beast. John Williamson Palmer's article, "Pioneer Days in San Francisco," *The Century*, vol. 43, issue 4 (Feb. 1892), describes the city in the winter of 1849 and 1850 as follows:

> The aspect of the streets of San Francisco at this time was such as one may imagine of an unsightly waste of sand and mud churned by the continual grinding of heavy wagons and trucks, and the tugging and floundering of horses, mules, and oxen; thoroughfares unplanked, obstructed by lumber and goods; alternate humps and holes, the actual dumping-places of the town, handy receptacles for the general sweepings and rubbish and indescribable offal and filth, the refuse of an indiscriminate population "pigging" together in shanties and tents. And these conditions extended beyond the actual settle-

ment into the chaparral and underbrush that covered the sandhills on the north and west.

The flooding rains of winter transformed what should have been thoroughfares into treacherous quagmires set with holes and traps fit to smother horse and man. Loads of brushwood and branches cut from the hills were thrown into these swamps; but they served no more than a temporary purpose, and the inmates of tents and houses made such bridges as they could with boards, boxes, and barrels. Men waded through the slough and thought themselves lucky when they sank no deeper than their waists. Lanterns were in request at night, and poles in the daytime. In view of the scarcity and great cost of proper materials and labor, such makeshifts were the only means at hand. [See engraving, "Muddy Street in San Francisco"]

By 1855, a seawall enclosed Yerba Buena Cove, preventing the tides from flooding the streets. Owners of the water lots began filling in their property. The low tide areas between the wharves and stranded ships needed fill. San Francisco's sandhills became that raw material.

While the shallows of the bay provided opportunities for revenue and access to San Francisco Bay as a deepwater port, the city's hills offered the raw materials to fill their dreams. However, using the hills as fill wasn't the only reason for the drive toward leveling the city. The hills also made transportation and travel difficult.

Starting in 1859, David Hewes took on the task of leveling Market Street. Using his "Steam Paddy," a steam-driven shovel so named because it could do the work of a dozen Irishmen, Hewes carved out the street and the land immediately to the north. Sand cars running with a donkey engine on a temporary movable railroad moved the sand to Yerba Buena Cove and filled the marshland south of Market. Market Street finally met its goal—it became the main commercial street of San Francisco.

A Steam Paddy like this sand shovel owned by the railway company did the work of a hundred men. —*Photo courtesy of San Francisco History Center, San Francisco Public Library*

Rincon Hill, overlooking Yerba Buena Cove, later provided more of the fill for that doomed portion of the bay. Based on its view and proximity to the town center, it early became the most distinguished neighborhood in the city. As men made their fortunes, they sent for their families. However, they couldn't ask their wives and children to live in tents and shanties. Mansions sprung up on the hill; some were of timber cut from the redwood forests up north and some reassembled homes originally built on the East Coast. The finest residences on the hill were built between First and Third streets.

Unfortunately for that community, commerce and declining esthetics intervened. China Basin to the south, formerly Mission Bay, attracted unsightly, smoky industries like lumber mills, brickyards, foundries, and the like. It also supported the China shipping trade, spawning convoys of wagons and carts as well as trains coming up from the south bay. It quickly lost the remainder of its dwindling appeal when the city put through the "Second Street Cut," a ravine 100 feet deep like a knife through the heart of the

View down Second Street prior to cutting down the grade. —*Photo courtesy of San Francisco History Center, San Francisco Public Library*

View down Second Street after the cut. Second Street Bridge spans the cut. —*Photo courtesy of San Francisco History Center, San Francisco Public Library*

The excavation of Second Street dividing Rincon Hill. —*Photo courtesy of San Francisco History Center, San Francisco Public Library*

The Latham residence on Rincon Hill—1872. —*Photo courtesy of San Francisco History Center, San Francisco Public Library*

The library inside the Latham residence on Rincon Hill—1872. —*Photo courtesy of San Francisco History Center, San Francisco Public Library*

The exclusive South Park community on Rincon Hill—1866. —*Library of Congress*

Industry spreading at the foot of Rincon Hill made the hill much less desirous as a prestigious community. —*Photo courtesy of San Francisco History Center, San Francisco Public Library*

hill. Earlier, wagons had to go around the hill. Now they could go through it. One home, undercut by the ravine, slid to the bottom. The hill lost its luster. When the invention of the cable car in 1873 enabled easy access to new residences atop Nob Hill, many of Rincon Hill's well-to-do joined the migration to that area.

Immediately following the Second Street Cut, investors attempted legislation to level the rest of the hill. The governor's veto prevented the plan from becoming law but the fight continued for years. In the mid-1930s, San Francisco acquired a portion of Rincon Hill for the footing needed to build the new San Francisco-Oakland Bay Bridge. The need for access to the bridge and the lack of influential homeowners left in the neighborhood cleared the way for the final demise of the hill. Plans were drawn for lowering the streets and leveling the remaining bluffs. Rincon Hill became no more than a bump in the road and was relegated to light industry and warehouses.

Telegraph Hill suffered a less threatening circumstance. Anyone looking at the bare-rock, northeast face of Telegraph Hill might assume that side of the hill had fallen away in an earthquake. Not so. The northeast face of Telegraph Hill lies under North Beach, Fisherman's Wharf, and what once was Yerba Buena Cove. After the soil and sand of the hill was scraped away to reveal bare rock, dynamite was used

The Parrott residence on Rincon Hill prior to the Second Street Cut. —*Photo courtesy of San Francisco History Center, San Francisco Public Library*

Excavating Harrison Street to level the street further divided Rincon Hill. —*Photo courtesy of San Francisco History Center, San Francisco Public Library*

to blast away the rock. Only when it became too difficult and dangerous did the city give up on leveling that great city landmark.

SAN FRANCISCO'S SAND DUNES AND MARSHLAND

Nearly half of San Francisco was originally covered with sand. Some of the sand formed hills like those obstructing Market Street, some settled into lowlands that became marshland such as in the Mission District, but most comprised what the early settlers called the Great Dunes on the west side. Regardless, none of the land in the city was flat, and its form varied according to locale, weather, and the winds. Blowing sand, both fine and coarse, was a curse to the early residents.

Some of the dunes were barren, but most supported a covering of stunted trees, shrubs, plants, and creepers. San Francisco's live oaks, dwarfed by the harsh conditions, never reached their potential. The few pines, spruce, and cypress trees grew nearly horizontal on the west side of the city. There were no wooded areas in the city such as can now be found at the Presidio or in Golden Gate Park. These were all planted in the late nineteenth century. Many native plants existed nowhere else and are now near extinction, maintaining a toehold in the Lobos Creek Dunes and Valley as a part of the Presidio Trust. Some, like San Francisco's long-gone "Shelly Cocoas," were just plain fun.

SHELLY COCOAS

Walter J. Thompson, columnist for the *San Francisco Chronicle*, wrote an article titled "Out Where the 'Shelly-Cocoas' Grew," published in the September 24, 1916, edition. He bemoaned the loss of the native plant habitat from the perspective of his childhood. The term "Shelly Cocoas" must have been a name assigned to the plant by the locals since no record can be found of a plant by that name. Given the description, it's most likely the wild cucumber or more specifically the California manroot, *Marah fabaceus*, native to San Francisco.

Out Where the "Shelly-Cocoas" Grew
—by Walter J. Thompson

Just by way of a foreword, I would say that I spell it "shelly-cocoa" advisedly. I don't admit it is correct. I could show how "shelly-coke" has the backing of authority of weight, but refrain, and maintain that the official orthographical architecture of the word is one of the secrets of boyhood that must be considered inviolate, no matter how old one grows. Wild horses shall not tear it from me. Boyhood's trust and all that it implies is involved.

Also I remark that I am confirmed in the opinion that shelly-cocoas have ceased to exist, like the ichthyosaurus and other things with even worse names belonging to those dear old days before the Pleiades sisters were transformed into stars.

To the old boys of the old town it is not necessary to hold up a shelly-cocoa for identification purposes. We all remember what it looked like, and recall with thrills of joy and pride the days when the city was a kiddy, like ourselves in short pants, and freckled with a magnificent profusion of vacant spaces on its thinly settled slopes, said spaces being the homes of the shelly-cocoa vines. They shared the soil with lupine bushes and stunted oaks, spreading in green patches six and seven feet in size. Every fellow's home had a shelly-cocoa patch annex of varying size, according to location, and out beyond Van Ness Avenue they could be measured off by the acre, until human habitations were not and King Shelly-Cocoa reigned monarch of all he surveyed.

The fruit of the shelly-cocoa vine could have been designed by kind Mother Nature for no other purpose than as an implement of amusement for youth, even as marbles and pegtops. Was there anything more alluring to the eye of a boy than that light green sphere, covered with spines about half an inch long, ranging from an inch and a half to three inches in diameter, the spines, while not stiff or particularly sharp, being full of electricity, which only required contact with the human skin to complete a circuit of radiating thrills and spasms?

And what an exquisite soft, soapy and sticky lather was concealed within the bulb, with an odor which, if not exactly comparable with the spirit of fragrance wafting over the rose-strewn Vale of Cashmere, was markedly of a distinctive character. The shelly-cocoa served a double purpose. When acting in conjunction with a human chin or eye, it titillated the nerves with its electric thrills, and at the same time stirred the tissue of one's olfactory organ to a frenzy of revolt against its atmospherical environment.

Shelly-cocoas and war whoops! They went together in the brave days of yore. The taint of war was in the air. Around the family table the battles of the Rebellion were discussed in detail, and the current literature of boydom told of little else but blood-curdling encounters between painted Indians with uncurbed ambitions, to acquire scalps of palefaces and scouts and trappers whose business in life was to roam around the boundless plains, staked and otherwise, and circumvent the cunning of the predatory savages and tear from their ruthless clutches certain comely damsels who had been nabbed while plucking wildflowers upon the prairie.

To the young San Franciscan this Indian warfare was most appealing, its methods of bang and batter and of direct attack and defense being more understandable than the maneuvering of troops in accordance with a military manual. Many and great were the battles fought on the hillsides where the shelly-cocoas grew, with the spiny bulbs as weapons. King Philip of Pocanoket never displayed more cunning and daring in hurling big Wampanoags through the New England settlements, nor the redoubtable Captain Church more dexterity in chasing them, than did the hillside warriors in factional strife. Confined as it was to the northern side of the city, owing to the refusal of the shelly-cocoas to propagate in the red-rock soil of the Mission, the warfare was between the settlers of the downtown district and the upland Indians. The line of demarcation was the ridge about the line of Jones Street, but the street was not entirely cut through then. Along this frontier were numerous nifty lots sloping down from Washington to Pacific Street. There the tide of war ebbed and flowed.

The downtown Pilgrim Fathers were in big majority, but the Wampanoags of the hills were the best fighters. They had a King Philip, too, in "Ducksy" McGinn, who was mighty in courage and strength. "Ducksy" would plan his campaigns with exceeding care. Preliminary to a planned conflict, every shelly-cocoa patch for blocks around was denuded of its fruit, and arsenals would be established in certain secret spots. Then would the enemy be taunted into attack by certain well-understood methods of aggravation. When the Pilgrims charged up that hill the wily Wampanoags led them along their own trails, and soon would have the Pilgrims in a disastrous ambush. Every shelly-cocoa vine was bare and the air was clouded with the volleys which the Wampanoags sent in. The Pilgrims could not even follow the well-known Beadle movement, "and seeing the enemy approach, he hid behind a tree." There were no trees. They could only run.

It was on the slope running up from Pacific Street at Leavenworth to Washington that the famous battle of Shelly-Cocoa Hill took place. That memorable engagement was sprung as a surprise upon the Wampanoags while King Philip was absent, he having an hours' overtime engagement with his teacher. Up and over the hill poured the Pilgrims loaded with shelly-cocoas and headed by Captain Church, mounted upon his father's heavy-hoofed and formidable dray horse. Cavalry was a new element in the warfare and the Indians gave way in disorder. The enemy held the hillside and the shelly-cocoa patches. Dark was the outlook, when suddenly their feeble war whoops were reinforced by one which had a "Charge, Chester, Charge," ring to it, and up came King Philip Ducksy, armed with an eight-foot fence rail which he swung around like the wing of a windmill. Right for the cavalry he charged, and as Captain Church swept down upon him he dodged and then—whack came the formidable wing on the cavalry's flank. Whack followed whack, and then did the war steed of the doughty Captain place him in the role of John Gilpin as it tore its way toward home. King Philip sounded the advance and the Pilgrims lost no time in following their leader. Oh, the rout was awful! Great was the carnage amid the shrilling of the victors' war whoops. Napoleon at the bridge of Lodi and Sheridan at Winchester's fight faded into insignificance as in-the-nick-of-time battle heroes alongside of the resourceful and brave Ducksy.

Shelly-cocoas were not always in partnership with war whoops. Under the guidance of appreciative youth they were connected with other pursuits more or less useful as well as tending to the enhancement of good feeling among all classes and the growth of uplifting influences. For instance, there was the campaign of education to popularize shelly-cocoas with the grown-up folks. Every inducement was held out to make them take notice of the shelly-cocoa and look kindly upon it. Sister's best young man hastening homeward from the usual Sunday night parlor seance would find his overcoat pockets freighted with juicy shelly-cocoas; Pa, fat and bald headed, would, on leaving after the evening card game, slam his silk hat on hurriedly while a half dozen shelly-cocoas would rattle around inside it like dice in a box; Ma on her busy baking days was reminded of the existence of shelly-cocoas by having one fly through the open window and snuggle down with the fruit in the pie she was building.

But failure croaked like a raven over this field of industry. Strange to say, the older folks could not understand why a shelly-cocoa was born. Such perverseness!

Then there were weird relations between policemen and shelly-cocoas. The spiny bulbs were the abomination of the knights of the star; some of whom even ascribed supernatural qualities to shelly-cocoas; others tried to figure out the tie of affinity between adolescence and the shelly-cocoa. There certainly was some mysterious influence which stirred shelly-cocoas to aggressive action when a policeman approached their haunts. Myriad cases have been reported of shelly-cocoas deliberately tearing themselves loose from their vines and lurking around corners and savagely assaulting a policeman as he turned it, or of leaping upon roofs just to tumble off again and swat a policeman in the neck. It was no use for a policeman to hold up some happy-hearted youth gayly tripping on his way to school, his face wreathed in smiles at the knowledge of how well he knew his lessons for the day. What did he know of the doing of erratic shelly-cocoas?

Attempts to introduce shelly-cocoas into the schools also failed owing to the narrow-mindedness and obduracy of teachers. There was a peaceful and a sentimental aspect to a shelly-cocoa's existence, especially out in the districts where the wig-wams were few and far between and the tribes were not menaced by the strenuous struggles of the border. There the shelly-cocoa had other uses than as a weapon of war. Within the heart of the spiny bulb was an oval-shaped kernel which when dried out hard in the sun like a gourd, was susceptible of a high polish from canary yellow to a rich mahogany, and with copper and brass "Chinee" coins with square holes in the center made up the wampum of the tribes. These dried "shellies" could also be cut up into pretty designs such as baskets, rings or linked bracelets, and necklaces fit to adorn a South Sea princess.

Perhaps you knew that pretty square block of birdcage houses, each set in a garden of roses, called Tuckertown, and which nestled on the slope which caught the slanting rays of the westward falling sun, beginning at Octavia and Washington streets. Perhaps you crossed that ridge like a warrior bold and true homeward-bound from school, and gave a whoop as you gazed admiringly upon the lupine and shelly-cocoa covered vista and saw the belle of Tuckertown swinging on the family gate, just as Dove Eye the Lodge Queen might have loitered around the opening of her chieftain daddy's tepee.

Perhaps you hurled your Davies' *Bourdon* and Swinton's *Outlines*, bound by a strap, to the ground and kicked them gleefully all the way before you until you landed beside Dove Eye and threw a necklace of shelly-cocoa wampum over her shoulders.

Perhaps, I say.

The shelly-cocoa and the golden and purple lupine blossoms are gone forever from all the old hillsides, having given way to the homes of other dwellers who little reck of the romance of the reincarnated Pilgrim Fathers and the Wampanoags and the dimples of winsome Dove Eye that have long since turned to wrinkles. And I have heard these newcomers in Canaan denounce those slopes of dear old San Francisco as dreary, dismal districts where raw winds and damp fogs held high Walpurgian revels. But—

There once lived in the old town an obscure poet whose thoughts over dwelt in "June's palace paved with gold," but whose feet trod the halls of dingy lodging-houses and whose appetite was appeased in "three for a quarter" restaurants. He finally decided to become a prosperous plumber instead of remaining a poor poet. But before bartering his minstrel harp for a plumber's pipe wrench he twanged off a lay called "Where Purple Lupine Grows," in which he lauded the sand dunes, expressing his reverence for the blossom-bedecked hills because of the memory of the days when he wandered over them in company with bonny Dove Eye's sister, who probably later became his bride and the mother of a line of plumbers, and closing:

To some gay gardens are more fair,

But eye cannot impartIdeal of beauty—that is e'er The Standard of the heart.

And the poet-plumber had a lead-pipe cinch on the sentimental situation.

—Article transcription courtesy of Ron Filion [http://www.zpub.com/sf50/sf/sindex.htm]

The north and west sides of the city sported the sandhills while sand blew over the hills and filled the valleys in the southeast. Those valleys soaked up the water from rain runoff and artesian springs to form marshlands, lakes, lagoons, and streams. Just as the Potrero District was ideal for pastureland, the Mission District proved itself ideal for farming. It received more sun than the rest of the city and its softly rolling hills, sandy soil and abundant water made it ideal for row crops, grains, and orchards.

The 1867 San Francisco Municipal Report for Farms cited five thousand acres planted in barley and oats, another eleven hundred acres planted in potatoes, three hundred acres of hay, hundreds of bushels of beans, peas, onions, and beets harvested, as well as ninety tons of turnips and thirty tons of pumpkins and squash produced. Aside from reporting nearly seventy-five hundred horses, the city held within it over four thousand milk cows, more than fifty-six hundred hogs, nearly five thousand chickens, and numerous other farm animals. Orchards and vines accounted for the remainder of the report, with over three thousand fruit trees planted, one hundred raspberry vines, seventy-five grape vines, and thirty thousand strawberry vines producing. San Francisco must have had a hearty appetite for strawberries.

San Francisco's primary crop remained houses and businesses, and soon the Mission District was apportioned with its own street layout and lots for sale. The lakes and lagoons were filled, the artesian wells were tapped and diverted through the storm drains, and the streams were routed to those storm drains as well, all emptying into the artificial Mission Creek and then directly into the bay. The land was leveled and the Mission became a working-class neighborhood for the city's German and Irish immigrants. Not one remnant remains of the fertile land other than the occasional backyard garden, and few people have ever heard of Lake McCoppin that once covered nearly sixteen blocks in the heart of the Mission.

Is the city poorer for all its change? I would say, with apologies to the environment, no. For all its uniqueness, metamorphosis is the nature of San Francisco. We mourn the losses but hail the change that keeps this great city vibrant.

Woodcut of Woodward's Gardens, ca. 1885. —*Author's collection*

Chapter 2

Amusement Parks

WOODWARD'S GARDENS

A visitor to the Mission District of San Francisco sees an impoverished, rundown, somewhat intimidating section of the city. A local recognizes a neighborhood with heart, undergoing rejuvenation. I find the landmarks of my childhood and recall how it looked nearly fifty years ago. What no one sees is evidence of the magic that existed here just over a hundred years ago when Robert Woodward opened his gardens to the public.

Robert B. Woodward earned his fortune in 1849 with sweat and foresight, not in the gold fields of California but by opening a grocery store just off San Francisco's waterfront. Like many a successful businessman, he knew when to say "enough" as the trend changed from a need for staples to a need for services. Woodward started investing his wealth in the burgeoning new economy. Seeing the demand for rooms and meals for those in transit as well as for the more permanent residents, he opened the What Cheer House on Sacramento Street, a hotel and club for men only, which sold good food ala carte and only non-alcoholic beverages. The hotel provided clean and safe accommodations at low prices, an unbeatable combination. The What Cheer House multiplied Woodward's wealth.

In 1857, Woodward retrieved his family from Providence, Rhode Island. He purchased a four-acre tract of land once belonging to General John C. Fremont, located in the Mission District in the heart of the city. That district encompasses the original Spanish town of Yerba Buena, home to Mission Dolores originated by Father Junipero

The front gateway to Woodward's Gardens. —*Photo courtesy of San Francisco History Center, San Francisco Public Library*

Serra. Like many a successful city investor, Woodward build a mansion for his family, but unlike most, he enclosed the spacious grounds and planted magnificent gardens.

The former grocer traveled to Europe in 1861 on an extravagant buying trip that spanned a year and a half. Plants, animals, and artifacts of all types were shipped back to California by the crate loads. During that trip, he developed a taste for art and sponsored an aspiring painter, Virgil Williams, to study in Florence, Italy, and to copy the masterpieces, a common practice of the times. Woodward displayed the results and his other purchases in his home and then in the What Cheer House, soon filling a library and small museum there with attractions from around the world. Copies of famous

Robert Woodward's Gardens just before he went public—1866. —*Library of Congress*

sculptures and busts soon followed the paintings. When display space became an issue, Woodward built a gallery and conservatory on his estate grounds to display his treasures. He longed for public and private museums and galleries in San Francisco to rival those of the East Coast and he set an example for others to follow.

The gardens of his estate soon became Woodward's obsession, and much of the profit from his investments went into them. He opened his estate in November of 1864 to friends and acquaintances with an appreciation for art and elegance. Word spread and requests for visits increased. People stood outside his gates on Sundays hoping to get a glimpse of the glory inside. It took little convincing to encourage him to open his gates to the public. Cooley Altrocchi relates in *The Spectacular San Franciscans*, "One day at the Sunday dinner table Mr. Woodward exclaimed, 'Did you ever see such a crowd of gapers and gazers? I might as well let the public have the run of the grounds.' To which one of his daughters responded, 'Well, why don't you, Father?' The philanthropist pondered this for a moment, and then said, 'Well, that's a thumping good idea. I think I will.'"

By opening his estate to the public, Woodward was ending his private life in San Francisco. After moving his family to his Oak Knoll farm in the Napa Valley, he pre-

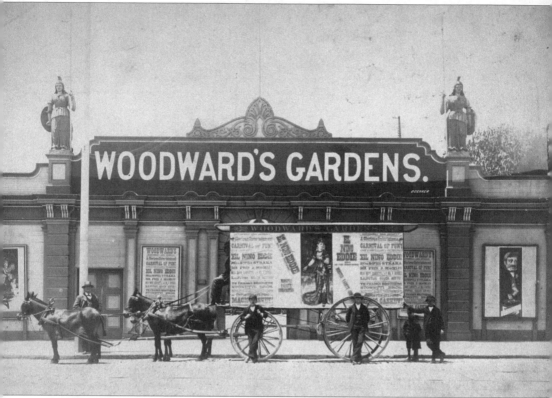

The Main Gate to Woodward's Gardens. Many a kid slipped through thanks to an intentional lax policy. —*Photo courtesy of San Francisco History Center, San Francisco Public Library*

pared Woodward's Gardens for the masses. The Gardens encompassed four city blocks bounded by Mission, Thirteenth, Valencia, and Fifteenth streets. The main entrance stood at the intersection of Mission and Fourteenth streets. Woodward quickly realized he needed more attractions, so he set off for Europe, bringing back hundreds of crates full of the fine, the fascinating, and the odd. He befriended "thousands of skippers and sailor men from the Seven Seas" and they brought him curios from every port. "Beasts, birds, fish, fossils, antique relics, peculiar animal deformities, in great variety, confront the visitor at every turn, affording the student ample opportunity to increase his knowledge, and at the same time, interesting and instructing to a degree, the most superficial observer," stated B. E. Lloyd in his 1876 book, *Lights and Shades of San Francisco*.

Woodward expanded his gateway, topping it with a pair of carved grizzlies and a matched set of statues of the goddess California, the namesake of the state. Kids clamored at the gate even if they didn't have the price of admission. Woodward made it easy for them to slip inside the park. The park included shows, museums, an aquarium, an extensive zoo, and curiosities from around the world, including freaks of natures. Park attractions also included an amphitheater, a dance hall, multiple restaurants, and a theater. Woodward became the "Barnum of the West." A patron saw it all at

Looking northeast from Robert Woodward's house. —*Author's collection*

Woodward's. However, while one newspaper review touted Woodward's fine beer garden and a pitifully uninformed woman wrote back to her church headquarters (copied
in a local newspaper editorial) that beer and whiskey were served more commonly
than water, no alcohol was served there. Like the What Cheer House, Woodward's
Gardens catered to teetotalers.

REMEMBRANCE OF WOODWARD'S GARDENS

We moved, mother and family, out to Twelfth Street about the time
Woodward's Gardens became popular. This place was really a cultural center of
attractions, brought together and maintained by the Woodward brothers,
themselves gentlemen of refinement. Its trees, shrubs, flowers and mosses were
selected and so attractively arranged as to please the most critical patrons and
engage the most casual eyes. The comfort of the animals was made evident to
visitors, and a small gallery of art provided for the relaxation of visitors.

It was in this gallery I first saw a replica of the Naples bronze bust of Dante.
I have never forgotten its effect upon me as I stood alone there, held by its austere
dignity in the half gloom where it was pedestaled—what humility I felt, yet what
strange reflections it stirred.

—Michael Doyle

Though today's residents of the city view that area of the Mission as flat and uninteresting terrain, visitors to that same area in 1866 described a rugged and untamed portion of the city. Crags, mounds, hills, caves, depressions, bogs, and streams made up the base that Woodward carved to create his park. With an eye toward nature, Woodward's Gardens included a conservatory overflowing with exotic trees, plants, and flowers. The sweet aroma, coupled with the warm humid air, created a sense of the tropics. The conservatory had one of the finest collections of ferns in the Western Hemisphere. A small lake hosted all forms of waterbirds at one end in a placid setting of water lilies and cattails. A water park complete with boats and chutes, a skiff ride down a fast moving flume, dominated the other side of the main park. A second lake hosted seals and sea lions, providing an opportunity to observe these animals in a natural setting. Streams and torrents wound through the entire garden area. A stroll in the Deer Park provided scenes that included small tame deer from China and Japan. Walking paths dotted with benches meandered through sculptured gardens and connected the various attractions. Ostriches and goats wandered loose on the grounds. A tunnel ran under Fourteenth Street to provide access to a zoo from the Gardens.

Camels were a novelty in 1880—to ride one was worth writing home about. —*Photo courtesy of San Francisco History Center, San Francisco Public Library*

Woodward's boasted the most complete zoo on the West Coast. A grand enclosure contained the large herbivores such as camels, zebra, buffalo, deer, llama, and kangaroos. A long row of cages held various panthers (mountain lions), jaguars, foxes, and small animals both from North America and around the world. Aviaries housed birds from diverse corners of the globe. Bear pits contained grizzlies and black bears. Families clamored for the opportunity to view creatures they would never otherwise see. Walter J. Thompson, reporter for the *Chronicle* wrote:

> Near by was the bear pit, into which 'Fat' Brown toppled one day to the consternation and positive embarrassment of the bears, who did not recover their nerve until 'Fat' was fished out with a long pole with hook attached. Across the way was the Happy Family, where, by standing too near the bars, Sister Susy lost her hat and back hair to a simian hoodlum of the family, the members of which showed anything but agreeable manners at feeding time.

Ad for Adams animal acts at Woodward's Gardens. —*Author's collection*

The zoo area also included an outdoor pavilion where acrobats from Japan and fire-eaters from Delhi performed for the crowds. Shows of every sort entertained the patrons, including bear wrestling, chariot races, comedy performances, Gilbert and

Staged battles like the Celebrated Sword Contest between Duncan C. Ross and Sergeant Owen Davies in Woodward's Gardens lent an air of excitement to the day. —*Photo courtesy of San Francisco History Center, San Francisco Public Library*

Sullivan plays, and beauty contests thinly disguised as dance reviews. Walter Morosco's Royal Russian Circus wowed the crowds with trapeze acts, acrobatic feats, and tumbling. Heavily painted and feathered Warm Springs Indians, victorious veterans of the Modoc War of 1872, provided examples of tribal dances and music that put fear into young and faint hearts.

The aquarium opened in 1873, with sixteen tanks that held from three hundred to a thousand gallons of salt or fresh water apiece and, for the first time ever, fish and crustaceans survived in saltwater tanks over an extended period. Sea and freshwater fauna and flora were on display, fascinating all viewers. Illumination came from above the tanks lined up on both sides of a forty-foot hall. Animals normally hidden below the waves displayed themselves to the stares of those who had never seen them in their natural state. Crabs, lobsters, and other crustaceans were of particular interest, busily foraging, while making aggressive gestures at each other as they crossed paths. Trout flashed their colors as sport fishermen dreamed of the ultimate catch. Sharks, cod, and perch cruised around the tanks while flounders and rays disguised themselves in the sand. Octopi amazed the throngs with their fluid antics and intelligent eyes. A fish-hatching machine, an early version of a hatchery, created a sensation among park-goers. The aquarium reigned as the most popular exhibit.

Woodward's old home near the entrance became the "Museum of Miscellanies." Gigantic mastodon tusks some ten thousand years old framed the entrance. Mineral samples, fossils, and zoological specimens made up the collection. The mineral display included crystals, volcanic stones, precious and semiprecious gems, and at one point in time, the largest gold nugget ever found. Viewing the nugget cost twenty-five cents extra. Woodward originally paid $25,000 for the nugget that several years later yielded only $23,000 in twenty-dollar gold pieces when smelted and coined. Of course, he made up the difference in the viewing fees charged. The zoological specimens included taxidermy and skins of every sort of animal and bird, as well as fossilized wood, fish, and creatures described as serpents. A rotating panorama displayed stuffed animals in their natural settings. Mischievous children liked to sneak onto one of the panoramas as it rotated away, only to be displayed on that section's next appearance posed with a tiger or bear.

A plush gallery housed Woodward's art collection, a quiet, restful interlude from the excitement of the museum next door. San Francisco's newfound appreciation for art made this a popular stopover. Culture follows money and the city's newfound wealth demanded worldwide status as a center of art and genteel living.

Still, curiosity dominated culture and Woodward searched long and hard for curiosities. He presented Chang from China, an eight-foot-tall giant who paraded the grounds dressed as a mandarin. Patrons lined up beside Chang to compare their height. Woodward hired Admiral Dot, a twenty-five-inch midget said to be smaller than Tom Thumb, who claimed P. T. Barnum had offered him a salary of $12,000 a year to join his circus.

On January 19, 1873, twelve thousand people attended Woodward's Gardens to witness the ascension of Gus Buislay and a small boy in a balloon. Hot air balloons drew large crowds after their successful use in the Civil War. In the corner by the carbarn

Gus Buislay's balloon often bumped the windmill when ascending.
—*Photo courtesy of San Francisco History Center, San Francisco Public Library*

stood a windmill that Buislay often bumped as he soared aloft, hanging on to his big hot-air balloon. Buislay's brother Joseph died in a trapeze accident in the city the next year. The Buislays were a noted French family of gymnasts and trapeze artists who toured the U.S. and Mexico. Buislay descendants remain in Mexico.

General Ulysses S. Grant visited Woodward's Gardens in September of 1879. The former president's tour of the world neared completion and San Franciscans eagerly awaited his arrival from Japan. The wearing of top hats or "tiles" presented too dear an opportunity when he and others gathered for a speech in front of the bear enclosure. San Francisco's rambunctious boys pelted them with large (and rather hard) bouquets of flowers tossed by practiced arms and soon all hats including Grant's were in the bear pit. Not to be outdone, a "pretty buxom girl suddenly broke from the ranks, and, throwing her arms about his neck, made him the victim of an unconditional surrender to an osculatory caress, the smack of which could be heard over in the camel paddock." All was quickly forgiven and the General shook the young hands of all those in a long receiving line and signed hundreds of autographs.

The death of Robert Woodward in late 1879 sounded the death knell for Woodward's Gardens. Wood-ward's sons took over its management but the Gardens slowly declined, lacking Woodward's enthusiasm and showmanship, and finally closed in 1894. Auctions liquidated all the artifacts and animals with much of the statuary, taxidermy, and oddities going to Adolph Sutro's Baths and Museum. Developers graded the land flat and sold it in tracts to provide homes for the working class of San Francisco. It punctuated the end of the century and signaled the end of an era for San Francisco.

The trained bears did their share of tricks but were still wild enough to entertain the crowds. —*Photo courtesy of San Francisco History Center, San Francisco Public Library*

Rear view of Robert B. Woodward's Gardens. —*Photo courtesy of San Francisco History Center, San Francisco Public Library*

All that remains as a reminder that Woodward's Gardens existed is a recently opened bistro on the corner of Mission and Thirteenth streets called Woodward's Gardens and a small brass commemoration plaque mounted on side of the old state armory at the corner of Mission and Fourteenth streets facing the site where Woodward's towering gates once stood.

THE CHUTES ON HAIGHT STREET

Captain Paul Boyton created his Shoot-the-Chutes water ride for the 1893 World's Columbia Exposition (World's Fair). Proving a major success in Chicago, Boyton decided to capitalize on it but didn't want to build or manage rides all over the country. Instead, he sold nonexclusive rights to the name and the ride's design.

Charles Ackerman, a San Francisco railway lawyer, purchased the rights to build the ride in a park on Haight Street between Cole and Clayton streets near the panhandle of Golden Gate Park. The Chutes opened in San Francisco on November 2, 1895 with a single food concession stand and the namesake Shoot-the-Chutes ride. Flat-bottomed boats charged uncontrollably down a 350-foot water flume that rose seventy feet above the water. They hit the pond at speeds up to sixty miles per hour and shot to the end where they were collected back at the platform. Loading up with new passengers, they again began the ride up the inclined track to the platform at top of the ride. There was the occasional mishap when a gondola flipped and deposited the riders in the pond—but then, that was all a part of the fun.

Entry cost a dime for adults; a nickel for kids. The park, located on the city's transit line near Golden Gate Park, "just a short walk from the Children's Playground," offered easy access as well as a replacement for the Midway of the 1894 California Midwinter Exposition at the park. The Chutes began adding more rides and attractions by the following summer. Tintypes pictorializing a visit using a Chutes backdrop & gondola were offered by Jones & Kennett who also worked two locations near Ocean Beach.

The Camera Obscura stood at the top of the ride, housed in a Japanese-style structure. The device used a giant convex lens focused on a mirror to provide a tele-

Chutes on Haight Street looking east, ca. 1895. —*Courtesy of The Bancroft Library, University of California, Berkeley*

scopic panoramic view of the area around the Chutes reflected in the mirror. Just as the boat passengers reached the top, they entered the dark building and were mesmerized by the view reflected on the mirror. With their attention fixed on the mirror, they plunged without notice to the pond below. The Camera Obscura at the Cliff House is a good example of this ancient technology that dates back to 5th century China.

The Scenic Railway, evidently drawing a separate charge from the Shoot-the-Chutes ride, offered a comparably adventuresome attraction. A roller coaster in all but name, it made dips and climbs that surpassed anything in the East, per the park's brochure. The ride circled the perimeter of the grounds, nearly a mile in length. It included an upper and lower track, with only one train allowed on that track at any one time, and a system of lights, signals, and brakes prevented any chance of collision when traversing between the two tracks. Six riders per car made the journey, terminating in an 800-foot tunnel, featuring an electrically lighted scenic diorama of foreign lands on its walls. The brochure stressed the safety of the ride and that set the theme for the park.

Many amusement parks and midways were thinly disguised operations intended to titillate and fleece the public. Not so at the Chutes—it focused on clean family fun to the point of segregating any alcohol served, so women and children could take refreshment without being exposed to drinking. Adjoining the Refreshment Pavilion, the Chutes Café offered ice cream sodas and other refreshments, with no liquor served. The Chutes and its owners maintained a positive moral image during their entire history in the city.

The park also added a miniature railway with a track gauge of only nine inches. Built for the park at half the scale of eastern parks, the six-foot locomotive and tender pulled ten cars, each seating two people. The locomotive was named "Little Hercules," due to its pulling strength.

Chutes also included an English-built merry-go-round, "The Galloping Horses" and a classic American merry-go-round completed the additions for that summer. A building called "The Bewildering London Door Maze" challenged visitors to find their way from entrance to exit, no easy task. If one became hopelessly lost, there were attendants available to guide the lost one out. The shooting gallery offered the opportunity to display one's skills with a .22 rifle. Reports from the rifle shots sounded throughout the park and beyond.

The Chutes Zoo opened in 1896 and included animals from all climes, claiming more than its fair share of carnivores. The zoo's top-liner, Wallace the Lion, drew the crowds. Wallace was touted as the largest, fiercest lion in America. Other zoos offered as high as $5,000 to purchase him. Part of his attraction came from the fact that he had proved untamable, though many a lion-tamer had tried. Other animals available for viewing included a South American jaguar, the Black Bear Brigade, a pair of Indian leopards, kangaroos, wallabies, a brigade of cinnamon bears, and a small pride of lions. The hyena proved a major disappointment; the melancholy beast never laughed. The Congo family, three orangutans, Joe, Sally, and Baby Johanna Congo, joined the fray late, around 1900. The trio aped a human family when seated at the table, with Joe smoking his pipe and Sally sipping tea while Baby Johanna tossed the dishes or played with her doll.

The Darwinian Temple housed a great array of monkeys including Capuchin,

Rhesus, Saponins, Spider, Pigtail, and Dog-face, many available to touch and feed by hand. Glass cases encircling the interior of the structure contained reptiles from around the world.

The Chutes Museum displayed a sad lot. It included all of the zoo animals that died in captivity—stuffed! Rajah, the Bengal tiger, largest of his species, constituted one of the feature attractions of the museum. The brochure, *Chutes and Its Myriad Attractions*, 1901, stated:

> "Here may be seen the three-thousand dollar, long-tailed and longmaned horse,"Beauty."This animal, in life, was one of the chief attractions of the zoo; in death, he is a permanent object of interest, not alone to those who knew him in the zoo, but to those who now see him for the first time. A more beautiful animal never lived.... Also the immense alligator"Jess," over fourteen feet in length, can here be seen, along with numerous other animals of all descriptions that, for too short a period, constituted a part of the live animal collection in the chutes zoo."

The Chutes Theatre opened on June 27, 1897, and claimed to be the largest vaudeville house west of Chicago. Operated year-round, day and night, the auditorium measured 100 feet wide by 130 feet long with seating for 2,000 on the lower floor and another 1,000 in the gallery. The theatre sponsored amateur nights, local performers and vaudeville acts, animal acts, and acrobatic performances, as well as audience-participation events like Cake Walk Night, where those skilled in the art of dancing the cake walk competed for prizes (See *'Scuse me while I Cakewalk* at http://xroads.virginia.edu/~ug03/lucas/cake.html). By 1899, the Chutes began booking name acts like Little Egypt with her"Hoochy Kootchy"act. They also demonstrated Edison's chromatograph. Both shows drew large crowds.

Its rides, theatre, attractions, and restaurant kept the park lively until midnight. Outdoor electric illumination, as well as an illuminated electric fountain, lit up the park at night. An electric tower, similar to the one built for the Midwinter Fair, marked the park's location for those in the surrounding areas. The beacon could be seen for miles.

THE CHUTES AT TENTH AND FULTON

By the turn of the century, the park had outgrown its limited space. The value of the land had appreciated markedly, and was now worth more than the proceeds from the park. San Francisco housing was marching westward and land speculators wanted the property to build the homes clamored for by a growing upper-middle class. Owners Charles Ackerman closed the park on March 16, 1902, tore it down, and rebuilt the amusement mall on leased property located on Fulton Street between Tenth and Eleventh avenues, opening again on May 1, 1902. The new park took advantage of the open spaces in the sand dunes of the Richmond district, expanding its offerings. All of the attractions from the old park found their way to the new site except for the zoo. The restaurant and café still operated in the same manner, with adult beverages kept segregated from the ladies and kids. The park also sported a "sign of the times"—a free "commodious automobile and buggy shed, with an entrance on Tenth Avenue."

Shoot-the-Chutes again took top billing with riders encouraged to look for the Farallon Islands beyond the Golden Gate and even Honolulu, Japan and China from the top of the ride. The new Scenic Railway on its elevated track passed painted tableau-style pictures of remote places including the Alps, Venice, the Blue Grotto of Capri, the Rock Caves of Ellora, India, Egypt, Dixieland and California.

The Chutes on Fulton boasted the first movie house in the city. Named Gillo's Artesto, it offered silent film shorts like Jim Corbett training for an upcoming bout. The audience would watch anything.

Moving pictures—the concept boggled the mind. Then, so did the Mystic Mirror Maze, a house of mirrors guaranteed to put at least one bump on your forehead. If that wasn't enough, Cabaret De Le Mort displayed historic instruments of torture and death.

The Circle Swing created another opportunity for thrills. Basket cars, suspended by cables from a large tower wheel, were spun out by centrifugal force as the wheel turned. The faster the spin, the higher and faster the baskets spun around the tower.

The rowdy new Chutes Pavilion Theater still claimed to be the biggest west of Chicago. Situated on purchased property on the east side of Tenth Avenue, it occupied the south-east corner of Tenth and C (later named Cabrillo) Streets. A great barn-like structure one hundred feet wide by 155 feet long, the theatre seated 2,200 on the main floor and 1,800 in the gallery. Access was via a tunnel under Tenth Avenue or by a bridge over it to the block where it stood on the east side of the grounds. Hosting some of the best shows in the business, the theater ran an ongoing series of acts, performers, and plays. "Shooting the Chutes," a musical comedy featuring the comedian team of Harkwood and Leonzo, played in late September 1905. Al Jolson played the Chutes

Entrance to the Chutes at Fulton and Tenth streets. —*Courtesy of The Bancroft Library, University of California, Berkeley*

Theatre in 1907 in celebration of the city's reconstruction.

The park remained open daily until April 18, 1906. That morning the ground shook and pieces of the park shook themselves apart. San Francisco's Great Earthquake managed to shut the doors at the Chutes for a few weeks, but it bounced back quickly. The city needed time to lick its wounds and the park offered a respite from the rebuilding of the city. The Orpheum's Theatre group leased the Chutes' theatre, bringing large, entertainment-starved crowds out to Tenth Avenue. Their first production opened on May 20, 1906, just a bit more than a month after the cataclysmic event with vaudeville acts and a short movie reel. The Orpheum rebuilt in the Fillmore Theatre district eight months later but their tenure at the Chutes proved lucrative for the Ackerman family.

Shooting the Chutes at the Fulton Street park. —*Author's collection*

The Chutes announced the construction of a roller skating rink on October 21, 1906, to be open before the Christmas holidays. Located on the northeast corner of Fulton and Tenth, it boasted a double floor, intended to soften the noise of the rollers on hardwood. Delayed by heavy rains, by the time it opened on February 9, 1907, the crowds were migrating to the new entertainment district on Fillmore Street. Coney Island Park opened on Fillmore on November 23, 1907, offering direct competition.

Charles Ackerman died the next month, leaving Chutes management to his son Irving, a young Yale-trained lawyer. Irving bought out the Fulton lease and sold it all off. He then purchased the Coney Island Park lease and building, constructing his New Chutes on the block bounded by Fillmore, Turk, Webster and Eddy streets.

The Circle Swing Flying Machine at the Chutes. —*Courtesy of The Bancroft Library, University of California, Berkeley*

THE FILLMORE STREET CHUTES

The Fillmore Chutes opened on July 14, 1909, lacking both a theatre and a zoo. The Coney Island building had shops on the ground floor and apartments on the second and third floors. The opening in the center of this facade led to the lot behind it. Ackerman knew how to run an amusement park and rebuilt the Chutes, bringing the miniature railroad and the Scenic Railway roller coaster from Fulton and adding a carousel. The new Hades ride of-

fered a chance to descend into a dark house of horrors and the Devil's Slide pitched the riders from the heights to the depths of Hell; actually, just the bottom of the ride. He also presented a Flea Circus in the Bug House. In early December, 1909 a zoo, purchased from Victoria, BC made its debut.

Abe Lipman offered while-you-wait postcard photos with a number of backdrops—perhaps sitting behind the wheel of a horseless carriage with multiple backdrops available. Lipman had joined the Chutes in May 1908 when on Fulton. The Photographic Gallery shared its space with the Penny Arcade, where a guest could

View of the Chutes on Fulton from Golden Gate Park.
—*John Freeman Collection*

Chutes on Fulton—new rides included the Devil's Slide and Hades. —*Author's collection*

have a fortune told, hear music on any number of player instruments or view moving-picture exhibitions, all for a penny each.

A new steel and concrete theater was constructed, opening on New Years Eve 1909. In August, 1910, Irving took a chance on a performer from New York who had been black-balled by Flo Ziegfeld. Sophie Tucker was unknown outside of New York, but when she did her one week run at the Chutes Theatre during August 7-13, 1910, she brought down the house. In her ghost-written, sometimes less than accurate, autobiography, *Some of These Days*, she tells of hanging around town, visiting the Barbary Coast joints, where the hot jazz and new dance steps were the craze. Ackerman gave her another week in September and she packed the house every night. Sophie's confidence was re-ignited and she returned to the East Coast, full of new vitality and new rhythms and dance steps she'd learned in the clubs on Pacific Avenue.

Closed for the winter of 1910-1911, the Chutes on Fillmore again underwent a remodeling, reopening on Memorial Day weekend, 1911. The May 26 *San Francisco Chronicle*, stated:

> "The grounds of the Chutes, which has been closed for some months, were thrown open for the summer season yesterday. The water chutes has been taken down altogether, but the tower, from which the boats used to glide, still stands and is utilized as a point of observation. The lake has been filled up and that part of the park which it formerly occupied has been transformed into a beautiful lawn and garden."

At the end of that weekend just after closing at one in the morning on May 29, 1911, a fire started in a faulty water heater in the barber shop and quickly spread. The fire jumped to the roof, spreading to other structures. It destroyed the entire park with the exception of the newly built concrete vaudeville theater. The Fillmore Chutes was gone. San Francisco would not see another permanent amusement park until the unrelated Chutes at the Beach officially opened on October 31, 1921.

The Fillmore site, opened in 1909, lacked the space of the Fulton site but drew large crowds due to its location. —*John Freeman collection*

PLAYLAND AT THE BEACH

Playland at the Beach—San Francisco's last amusement park—entranced three generations. Mention it to a San Franciscan over 50 and you'll get a glazed-over look and a story. "The slides in the fun house—my stomach always dropped over the second hump." "The Missus and I used to dance at Topsy's on Saturday Nights. Half a chicken for four bits and that slide to the dance floor." "Didja hear about the sailor who stood up on the Big Dipper? His head was cut off by a brace and it fell into a lady's lap in a car below." It was the source of dreams, tales, and urban legends though the 1945 story of the sailor, Edward Tobiaski of Chicago, whose head was crushed by a beam, proved to be correct.

Chutes at the Beach was later renamed Playland at the Beach. —*Photo courtesy of San Francisco History Center, San Francisco Public Library*

Playland didn't begin as a planned amusement park. Seal Rocks and the far-off Farallon Islands attracted visitors, as did the Seal Rock House hotel and the Cliff House. Ocean Beach was "The Beach," just as San Francisco is "The City." A few independent concessions sprung up at the end of the trolley line at Ocean Beach. Arthur Looff, whose roots were in Coney Island, New York, ran the now famous merry-go-round, the Hippodrome. John Freidle operated a shooting gallery and a baseball knock down game called Babyland. Knock down a baby, win a prize. The two formed a partnership. Freidle had the money and Looff, whose father built the Hippodrome, the expertise. A dance hall and theater were quick to spring up.

There were ten rides by late 1921, including the Shoot-the-Chutes water ride. That main attraction inspired "The Chutes at the Beach" as the name for the park. In 1922, the famous Big Dipper was born, with its cars traveling its 3,000 feet of track in one minute, seven seconds. The drops were phenomenal, including the long drop, claimed to be eighty feet. That roller coaster ran until 1955, when new safety regulations forced its replacement by a tamer German-built wooden coaster, the Alpine Racer, a Wild Mouse type of ride. The Chutes at the Beach continued to grow.

The Whitney brothers, George and Leo, took over the park in 1929 and renamed the park Playland at the Beach. George had been an early concessionaire and in 1926 became the manager of the park. Ownership of most of Playland was still held by the various concessions, including the Friedle brothers.

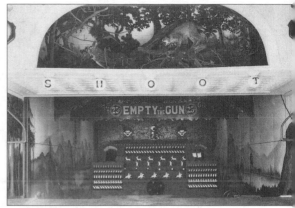

Playland at the Beach grew to nearly one hundred concessions. It soon featured such attractions as the Midway, the Bug House (Fun House), restaurants, and eateries of every type. The Sideshow sported the usual exhibitionists and short acts. It has been claimed that the sideshow was

Playland's Shooting Galley. It hadda be rigged! The real question was, "Who would win, the skunk or the bobcat?" —*Author's collection*

The Roller Coaster at Chutes at the Beach, later renamed Playland. —*Author's collection*

the first to present Major Mite, Clarence Chesterfield Harden, who went on to be a headliner for the Barnum and Bailey Circus. "The Eden of Wonder Museum" was an attraction similar to a modern-day wax museum. The hand-carved figures were not made of wax but a special resin mix. George Whitney took special pride in the scene of "The Last Supper."

The Whitney Brothers' version of Topsy's Roost opened on June 29, 1929 in the

Ocean Beach Pavilion Building, and was another of the adult attractions at Playland. A fried chicken house and dance hall, it served fun as the main entree. In spite of Prohibition, Topsy's was the place to be, accommodating up to one thousand guests at a time. The building housed a large dance floor and tiers of lofts, called roosts. Fried chicken, hot biscuits and waffle fried potatoes served in the roosts were eaten by hand, without utensils. Dancers rode slides from the roosts to the dance floor. Music by Red Lockwood and his Musical Roosters, and later by Ellis Kimball kept the house swinging. A menu from the late-'40s (see following page) illustrates the flavor of an evening at Topsy's Roost.

Charles Coryell on the Fun House Turntable with a group of children from his neighborhood at Playland at the Beach. If you sat dead-center, you could stay on until someone nudged you off. —Photo courtesy of San Francisco History Center, San Francisco Public Library

The year 1929 brought the Great Depression and Playland took it hard. The Whitney brothers began buying up the concessions as they folded. By 1942, the Whitney brothers owned it all, over a million square feet of amusement park. The park survived the Depression under the Whitney brothers' guidance and flourished during World War II and the Post War Era. San Francisco was both an Army and Navy town and became a tourist stop for a country looking for fun after a hard couple of decades. The Beach was on everyone's agenda and Topsy's swung at night.

Playland at the Beach with owner George Whitney showing a life-sized reproduction of Leonardo Da Vinci's "The Lord's Last Supper" to Harold A. Meyer. —Photo courtesy of San Francisco History Center, San Francisco Public Library

RULES OF THE ROOST

LIQUOR SERVICE CHARGE

As we pay a high license fee for the privilege of serving liquor, in case patrons bring liquor with them, or wine, a corkage charge of 25c will be made for each party regardless of how many consume the liquor, except minors who are not in any case permitted to buy or consume liquor on the premises.

Bringing in of Ginger Ale, Rickey, Beer, etc., is strictly prohibited. We charge our full list price for such beverages brought in by patrons.

See Separate Menu for
TOPSY'S SPECIAL $1.00 DINNERS

Served during following hours only: Saturdays, 5:00 p. m. to 8:00 p. m.; Sundays, noon to 9:00 p. m.; other days 5:00 p. m. to 9:00 p. m.

TOPSY SEZ:

Minimum Service Saturday nights and Holidays $1.00 per person after 9 p. m. Minimum charge at all other times 50c per person. No cover charge at any time. All sales subject to State Sales Tax. Checks of $2.50 or more subject to 3% Federal Tax.

Examine check before paying. Kindly report any inattention or overcharge to the floor manager.

Please do not smoke on the dance floor as it is dangerous to others. Dance soliciting is not permitted.

We are not responsible for lost articles left in booths. Use check room on main floor near entrance.

Please remember our delicious Fried Chicken, Hot Biscuits, Waffle Fried Potatoes, etc., are prepared to order. This takes a little time. Enjoy our music and dancing. Your patience will be rewarded. Eat with your fingers, enjoy that chicken, and have a good time.

Phone Skyline 3423 for Reservations or Party Arrangements.

Topsy's Roost is open from noon to 1 a. m. Sundays, and from 5 p. m. to 1 a. m. week days.

We close Mondays . . . Except Holidays

"Yours for GOOD PICKIN'S"

GOOD TIME AND A GOOD TIME

SOUVENIR MENU ~ TAKE ME HOME

Topsy's Roost – S.F.
PLAYLAND at the BEACH
Menu

EAT WITH YOUR FINGERS ~ TOPSY STYLE

COCKTAILS

Oyster	.25
Crab	.25
Fruit	.25

TOPSY'S SPECIALS

HALF FRIED SPRING CHICKEN	.50
CHICKEN TAGLIARINI	.50
CHICKEN PIE ALABAM.	.50
HAM AND EGGS TOPSY	.50
N. Y. SIRLOIN STEAK	.75
CRAB LOUIE	.50
CHICKEN SALAD	.50
Combination Salad	.25
Hearts of Lettuce	.25
Sliced Tomatoes	.25

HOT

Biscuits and Honey	.15
Corn Pones and Honey	.15
Waffle Fried Potatoes	.15
Chicken Broth	.15
Crisp Celery Hearts	.15
Jumbo Olives	.15

DESSERTS

Mammy's Apple Pie	.15
Whitney Bros. Ice Cream	.15
Apple Pie a la Mode	.30
Fruit Jello, or Cobbler	.15

DRINKS

Coffee	.10
Pot of Tea	.15
Milk	.10
Bottled Beers—Local	.25
Eastern Beers	.35

TOPSY'S SPECIAL SANDWICHES

Sugar Cured Ham	.25
Smoked Liverwurst	.25
Club Sandwich	.50
Sliced Chicken	.50
American or Swiss Cheese	.25
Chicken Salad Sandwich	.35

Colored views of Topsy's Roost—Set of 5 post cards 10c. We pay postage of 5 post cards 10c. We pay postage for address cards and drop in Topsy's mail boxes. Ask waiter.

GOOD THINGS TO DRINK

COCKTAILS

Martini	.30
Manhattan	.30
Old Fashioned	.30
Honolulu	.30
Pink Lady	.35
Daiquiri	.35
Side Car	.35
Bacardi	.35
Topsy Southern	.35

MIXED DRINKS

Gin Rickey	.35
Sloe Gin Rickey	.35
Tom Collins	.30
Bourbon Highball	.30
Whiskey Sour	.35
Scotch Highball (Dom.)	.30
Scotch Highball (Imp.)	.35
Singapore Sling	.35
Mint Julep	.40

STRAIGHT

Bourbon Whiskey	.25
Bourbon (6 years old)	.30
Bourbon (18 years old)	.40
Rye Whiskey	.30
Scotch Whiskey (Dom.)	.25
Scotch (Imported)	.35
Fleischmann's Gin	.25

FIZZES

Gin Fizz	.30
Sloe Gin Fizz	.35
Silver Fizz	.35
Golden Fizz	.35
Royal Fizz	.40
New Orleans	.40
Waldorf	.40

LIQUEURS—CORDIALS

Creme de Menthe	.30
Creme de Cocoa	.30
Benedictine (Imp.)	.40
Apricot Nectar	.25
Brandy (Calif.)	.30
Brandy (Imp.)	.40

CALIFORNIA WINES PER GLASS—20c

Port .. Claret .. Angelica .. Sherry .. Chablis .. Burgundy

CALIFORNIA BOTTLED WINES

Dry	1/2 Bot.	Bot.	Sweet, etc.	1/2 Bot.	Bot.
Burgundy	.45	.85	Port	.75	1.25
Claret	.45	.85	Sherry	.75	1.25
Cabernet	.45	.85	Angelica	.75	1.25
Sauterne	.45	.85	Muscatel	.75	1.25
Riesling	.45	.85	Burgundy Carb.	1.75	3.00
Sonoma RUBIO	.45	.85	Moselle Carb.	1.75	3.00
Tipo R Tipo W	.75	1.25	Champagne	2.25	3.75

BEVERAGES

Bottled Beers (Local)	.25	Ginger Ales	.50
Bottled Beers (Eastern)	.35	Lime Rickey	.50
Mineral Water	.50	Orange Rickey	.50

DANCING

Menu back for Topsy's Roost restaurant at Playland at the Beach. Folks sat in roosting boxes and used the slides to get to the dance floor. —Author's collection

The Famous Slides and South Tiers of Roosts and Coops,
Topsy's Roost,—Chutes at the Beach—San Francisco—Whitney Bros., Props.

There Is No Place in the World Like Topsy's—
Chutes at the Beach—San Francisco—Whitney Bros., Props.

A Night at Topsy's Roost—Brightest Spot
in the Gay Life of San Francisco—Whitney Bros., Props.

East Tiers of Unique Roosts—Topsy's Chicken Roost,
Chutes at the Beach—San Francisco—Whitney Bros., Props.

The Show Boat and Levee—Topsy's Roost—
Chutes at the Beach—San Francisco—Whitney Bros., Props.

During the 1950s, Playland assaulted the senses. Activity and lights were everywhere. It sparkled with scenic vistas of every sort: rides flashing by, colorfully lighted exhibits, couples walking arm-in-arm, and flocks of girls and guys stealing glances. Machine vibrations rumbled up through your soles and the rides put your guts in your throat. The smells, oh the smells of fried chicken, cotton candy, fudge, grilled onions, popcorn, taffy, steamed dogs, tamales, and caramel overwhelmed any sense of propriety in diet. The aromas preceded the snap of the skin of a succulent sausage with mustard and onions or the spicy bite of a Bull Pupp enchilada. Later, you consumed an It's-It ice-cream sandwich from The "It" Stand; two big oatmeal cookies surrounding a scoop of vanilla ice cream, all dipped in chocolate.

Playland had its own sounds, sounds still heard in the memories of those who loved it. Laffing Sal's incessant belly laugh overrode the roar of the wooden coaster and its attendant screams. Bells rang and the steam calliope of the merry-go-round competed with the slamming of the bumper cars. Barkers cajoled and the shooting gallery put out staccatos of .22-calibre pops. Beyond that, laughter carried the main beat. People were having fun.

The sixties were not kind to Playland. Better parks emerged in the Southland and people traveled farther for entertainment. A seedy element crept into the park—gangs and predators. Families drifted away from it. Yet, it still held such charm. Dennis Haughey worked at Playland during those years. In a personal correspondence, he wrote the following about his years at Playland at the Beach:

Playland was an excellent place to work for extra money from a second job, or in my case, a source of primary income while attending college. My first day of work was a warm day in the summer of 1966. I started on the Alpine Racer. It was also the day that Sutro Baths burned

Laffing Sal spent her whole career laughing at the guest passing by Playland's Fun House. It was impossible to pass by her without a grin or a snicker. Sal moved to the Santa Cruz Beach and Boardwalk, starting a new career while still holding court at the Musee Mechanique on Pier 45 in San Francisco and at Playland-Not-at-the-Beach in El Cerrito. Multiple Laffing Sals ensured continued laughs at the Fun House. —*David Johnson Collection of San Francisco Photography*

A picture of better days. The Merry-Go-Round closed September 4 1972, after fifty-eight years of operations. The animals were hand carved by Charles I. D. Loof sixty-five years ago. —*David Johnson Collection of San Francisco Photography*

down. Over the next three years, I moved from there to the Tilt-A-Whirl and then on to the rest of the amusements. Eventually I could operate all the rides and finally, become a "break man," a position coveted because the variety of tasks helped prevent the boredom of the many slow, foggy hours when there were few customers. It was an ideal job with minimal demands, a constantly changing cast of characters, and great location. While growing up, I had spent many happy hours there, filled with fond memories. It was great to be a part of making new special moments for others. I had seen the Midway in much better days, and it was sad to see the inevitable slide toward doom, much like the Big Slide in the Fun House, powerless to stop, yet realizing that I should enjoy the ride. So that is what I did. Things were in a progressive state of deterioration. The crowds dwindled, except on those rare warm, sunny days, when people sought relief from the inland heat at Ocean Beach. Such conditions existed on a pair of Sundays in 1967 and 1968, and exploded into rioting. I knew that the end was very near when some of the rides and concessions were brought in by West Coast Shows and their cast of "Carneys." I left in the summer of 1969, returning for the auction in 1971, where an attempt to sell the Merry-Go-Round, piece by piece, was narrowly avoided. It has returned in whole again to Yerba Buena Center, but the fabulous organ tended by an old man named Dave is no more. He would sit there all day Saturday and Sunday, listening for anything amiss because it was like a child to him. That organ and the strains of Laffing Sal combined for an unforgettable cacophony of sound, the signature melody of Playland.

Each ride had something about it that made it unique and certain operational techniques could bring out the best of them. One could make certain cars spin faster for those we wished to give a special ride to, or slower for those who presented a less than friendly attitude, particularly on rides like the Tilt-A-Whirl, Octopus, and Heyday. Sometimes, we would put an extra thrill into a dark ride like Limbo with a tap on the shoulder of a rider in the darkness. The Fun House used six people on a busy day, but there was only one good station. That was operating the air jet, in a seat above the Joy Wheel. From this perch, one could run the Barrel, the Joy Wheel, and use the many levers that would release a blast of air. We remained on the alert for a man wearing a hat or better yet, a woman wearing a skirt. After negotiating the maze of mirrors and revolving obstacles, customers would relax once they made it into the main floor. That is where the first set of jets were. There were others spread around the building. The worst station was at the bottom of the slide, checking to make sure that no one went up with shoes on. The odor could be unbearable on a warm day. Then, there were all those wide-eyed kids on the Merry-Go-Round, clutching the reins while the lights whirled around. They would often get that longer ride when customers were few.

The "Limbo" monster ride at Playland. September 4, 1972. —*Photo courtesy of San Francisco History Center, San Francisco Public Library*

When working the Dodger bumper cars, we would use the special "mechanic's car" that went twice as fast as all the others. That one was used to patrol the floor. After a day of that I would have to control the urge to "hit" another car on the Great Highway while on my way home in my little Fiat, which was not much bigger than a bumper car.

Playland still exists in that best of places, the memory. I took with me a special memento of my days on the midway. I met my wife Mari there. Thirty-plus years later, we are still together on that wild ride called life. What a thrill ride!

—Dennis Haughey, June 2000

Dennis' recollections echo the sentiments of many a San Franciscan. Playland's time was over. George Whitney died in 1958, and the Whitney family sold their interest in the park in 1964. In 1971, the new owners sold Playland to developer Jeremy Ets-Hokin for $66,000,000 . Playland at the Beach operated for the last time on September 4, 1972. Ets-Hokin tore it down shortly afterward and it was replaced 17 years later with high-priced condominiums and apartments with million-dollar beachfront views.

The Fun House at Playland at the Beach. Laffing Sal is in the lower window. —*Photo courtesy of San Francisco History Center, San Francisco Public Library*

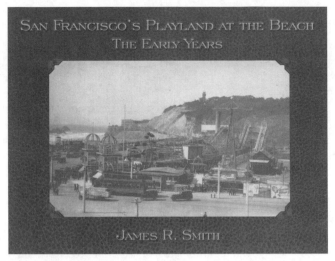

Playland at the Beach: The Early Years by James R. Smith (Craven Street Books, 2010)

San Francisco's Playland at the Beach: The Early Years by James R. Smith (Craven Street Books, Fresno, 2010) offers an in-depth look at the first 25-plus years of Playland at the Beach, soon to be followed by *San Francisco's Playland at the Beach: The Golden Years* chronicling the park until 1972. Both books are lavishly illustrated with photographs never before published.

HERB CAEN'S VIEW ON PLAYLAND

The late Herb Caen, San Francisco's most beloved columnist, said it best on that last day.

Old Playland. I suppose only those who knew it in the glory days will really miss it and part of the glory disappeared when the scary, rickety roller coaster, the Big Dipper, was torn down in the late 1950s, for what is an amusement park without a roller coaster? After a show or on a weekend, we'd ride the Dipper in clouds of shrieks, losing our breath on the first dizzying descent and never finding it again till the end, when it was "Let's go again!" There was the slide that took you into Topsy's Roost to *dance* to Ellis Kimball, the milk bottles that wouldn't fall even when you hit them, Skee Ball (delightful game) and the prizes you gave your girl just in return for her admiring gaze.

Goodbye to all that, to part of our youth, and like that youth, we expected Playland to last forever. It is an odd, sad feeling to have outlived it.

—*San Francisco Chronicle*, September 4, 1972.

Cliff House number three—Sutro's French Chalet Cliff House. The rowdy party days were over. Sutro brought civility to Ocean Beach. —*Author's collection*

Chapter 3
Ocean, Bay & Wharf-side Attractions

MEIGG'S WHARF AND THE COBWEB PALACE

San Francisco in the mid-nineteenth century demanded entertainment. Pockets jingled with gold. The mines, the burgeoning shipping business, the merchant trade and wild speculation fueled a runaway economy. Keyed to a fever pitch, the city wanted to play, to blow off steam. San Franciscans were soon to show the world that they were not only getting rich but knew how to spend their new wealth as well.

Harry Meigg recognized his new wharf on Francisco near Powell Street as an ideal place for the merchant and tourist trade. Always looking for that extra buck, Harry encouraged his old friend Abe Warner, among others, to open a business on Meigg's Wharf. In the city's early days, North Beach began its metamorphosis into the place to be.

Abe opened the Cobweb Palace at the foot of Meigg's Wharf on the north side of Francisco in 1856. His establishment earned its name by the strings of cobwebs hanging from the rafters. Abe admired both spiders and their webs. He refused to sweep them down and chastised anyone who did. "Filibuster" Walker once poked at a web with his cane. Known in the city as much by his floppy slouch hat and long black cape as by his dissertations, William Walker claimed a reputation as a famed Central American orator. "That cobweb will be growing long after you've been cut down from the gibbet," Abe remarked. A Honduran firing squad executed Walker about three years later.

Today, Fisherman's Wharf only hints at what Meigg's Wharf must have been like. The clean smell of the bay intermingled with steamed crabs and shellfish, fresh baked bread, and spices hauled off ships from the Orient. Waves slapped the pilings, stevedores shouted out the contents unloaded from of the ships, and drayers called to their mules as they cracked their whips and rumbled heavy-laden carts off the dock's. Organ grinders, screaming children, and seagulls added to the wild cacophony of noise intermittently punctuated by gunshots.

Crowds gathered at Abe's tavern to view his extensive collection of oddities. The Cobweb Palace displayed scrimshaw of sperm whale teeth and walrus tusks. Totem poles from Alaska adorned the entryway. Wonders from the Orient included Japanese No theater masks. War clubs and the like from the South Pacific and taxidermy of all sorts joined the collection. Abe's live menagerie included trained parrots, monkeys, and various small animals, as well as the occasional bear and kangaroo. One parrot named Warner Grandfather often spouted, "I'll have a rum and gum. What'll you have?" He swore in four languages and enjoyed the freedom of the saloon. An old, crippled sailor sat outside Abe's bar selling peanuts to young couples and children. Meant for tourists, the peanuts often found their way from little hands into the mouths of the parrots and monkeys. All manner of food and leftovers fed the bears. Abe spent almost nothing feeding his animals.

A day of excitement begged a visit to Meigg's Wharf. More than just a hangout for sailors and sea captains, Meigg's Wharf and the Cobweb Palace exuded a carnival atmosphere. On any Sunday, young couples and families strolled on the wharf, taking in the sights, visiting the shops, testing their skill at the shooting gallery, and sampling Abe's free crab chowder. The Palace offered a new experience for the locals and tourists—pier-side dining. The Dungeness crabs were sweet, succulent, and sure to please. Customers dined on simple fare of cracked crab, clam chowder, mussels, and an excellent local French bread.

Abe had a fancy for tawdry paintings of nudes, reputedly collecting over a thousand. Dust and cobwebs obscured most of those hung on the walls. However, Abe was a tidy man, well groomed and of good reputation, the cleanliness of his bar notwithstanding. He held court over all from his usual position behind the bar. Though the drink of choice at Abe's was a hot toddy made of whisky and gin boiled with cloves, he also served the finest liquors and brandies from France.

The ships at Meigg's Wharf disgorged everything a growing new city needed. Ready-built mansions with numbered pieces came from New England round the Horn.

Abe with a few of his friends and customers, in front of the Cobweb Palace shortly before it was demolished. That location today can be found at 444 Francisco Street, nearly five blocks from the Bay where Powell meets Jefferson and the Embarcadero. The City constructed a breakwater enclosing Meiggs Wharf then filled in the cove it created. See page 13. —*Courtesy of The Bancroft Library, University of California, Berkeley*

Pen-and-ink drawing of the interior of Abe Warner's Cobweb Palace. Parrot Warner Grandfather swings amid the webs that could grow as long as six feet. —*Author's collection*

Fresh fruit and vegetables were shipped in from Mexico and Chile. California couldn't feed itself yet, let alone a nation. Spices, chinaware, and fine cloth arrived from the Orient. The local fishing fleet offloaded their abundant daily catch. Lumber ships carrying virgin heart redwood arrived from Northern California towns like Scotia and Eureka. And, the goods San Francisco needed often came via Meigg's Wharf.

Businesses spawned around the wharf taking advantage of the short hauling distances from the ships. Sardine canneries built up just west of the wharf. The bay teemed with sardine and they provided fine protein for hungry miners. Sawmills opened, taking the raw logs to produce not only lumber, but also the fine wooden trim and scrollwork required for an ever more opulent city. Factories, such as Ghirardelli Chocolate, added to the city's flavor. Each ethnic group brought its skills, traditions, and trades, making them wholly San Francisco's.

Abe Warner retired in 1897 at the age of eighty. By then, the state of Meigg's Wharf reflected a serious decline in business. The shipping trade returned to the piers by the new Ferry Building, where the wide Embarcadero Road and new rail lines could quickly dispatch goods. Fancier attractions elsewhere beckoned the crowds. Nickel trolleys bused folks to Sutro's Baths at Ocean Beach where a dime gained

Meigg's Wharf, built in the mid-850s by Harry Meigg.
—*Author's collection*

entry with fifteen cents more to swim indoors. The Baths boasted the world's largest indoor saltwater pool, which held over a million and a half gallons. The structure also housed a mechanical arcade, a theater with ongoing stage productions, three restaurants, and a museum, all under a magnificent Victorian glass-paned roof covering two acres. Awe-inspiring Golden Gate Park with its paved carriage roads and glorious exhibits drew both the elite and the masses. Stunning views of the Pacific and Seal Rock from the French chateau-inspired Cliff House attracted locals and tourists alike. San Francisco now sported a taste for the fine life and the dingy sights around the old wharf simply would not do.

COBWEB PALACE

Michael Doyle wrote a letter to his grandchildren in the 1920s telling about his childhood and early years in San Francisco. In that letter he related the following:

Northerly, I looked down upon the peninsula's head with its two blunt horns, Russian and Telegraph hills, quite bare in those days, between which protruded Meigg's Wharf like a long tongue lapping the waters beyond....

Old Meigg's Wharf—what crowds and family groups it drew together on Sundays and holidays! Here was a free, out-of-door menagerie to which the multitudes, lacking attractions elsewhere, flocked, mostly afoot, to spend a few hours' leisure with its tethered bears, its cages of jumping, swinging, and grimacing monkeys and gorgeous parrots from all climes—birds so richly dyed that it was a natural child's fancy that they must have flown here from some glorious heights far off through rainbows that stained their plumage in passage.

Inside a long, low, and very rough building, whose proprietor had for years collected attractions—curios from all over the world, purchased mainly from sailors, sometimes for a drink or two of liquor. Such, as well as candies, cakes, nuts, and the like, being sold to visitors, more than maintained the place for many years. Much of the sweet things sold was doled out from the fingers of little folk back to the always greedy captive creatures outside, and this amusement materially reduced the bills for upkeep.

SUTRO HEIGHTS

Adolph Sutro built his home on a rocky ledge overlooking the Cliff House and Seal Rocks just south of Point Lobos and north of Ocean Beach. The grounds consisted of a spacious turreted mansion, a carriage house, and various outbuildings, all set in expansive gardens. The parapet that separated the grounds from the cliff edge offered the best view of the Pacific Ocean in the city. The vista overlooking Ocean Beach, Seal Rocks and the Golden Gate with the Farallones in the distance proved awe-inspiring. Observers watched great ships, under sail or steam, enter and depart the harbor. Whales in abundance spouted offshore. The sea lions jousted for the limited real estate on the rocks below.

The estate dominated the area. Sutro spent in excess of a million dollars trying to recreate an Italian garden. Though the statues were plaster rather than marble and required a fresh coat of white paint annually to avoid erosion, the effect was stunning. By 1883, Sutro opened his gardens to the public and allowed people to stroll the grounds for the donation of a dime. That small fee helped to pay the fifteen gardeners he employed to maintain the grounds. A gate attendant collected guests' picnic baskets and the ever-present hot roasted peanuts, returning them to the guests on their departure. It seems Sutro didn't want picnic trash or shells cluttering up his estate. Even a populist had his limits.

Adolph Sutro died in 1898, land rich but cash poor, following his frustrating tenure as mayor of San Francisco. His daughter Emma lived on the estate at Sutro Heights until her death in 1938. When it become too expensive to maintain, the family donated the estate to the City of San Francisco that same year. The city demolished the buildings and removed the statuary with the exception of the winged lions at the gate and a few select pieces. The estate became Sutro Heights Park.

ADOLPH SUTRO'S SAN FRANCISCO

History remembers Adolph Sutro as one of San Francisco's finest citizens and its first populist mayor. A mining engineer, he arrived in the city from Prussia in 1850. Among his early accomplishments, Sutro designed and constructed a tunnel that drained and ventilated the mining shafts of the Comstock in Nevada. Sutro amassed millions from that and other mining endeavors, always as an owner or partner in any project. He sold his shares in the Comstock tunnel in 1880, just before the veins of silver played out. A man of foresight, he acquired fully one-twelfth of San Francisco—all the western dunes and seashore deemed worthless by others. Developing that worthless land increased his fortune many times over. Best remembered for his attractions and gifts to the city, Adolph Sutro remains a city icon.

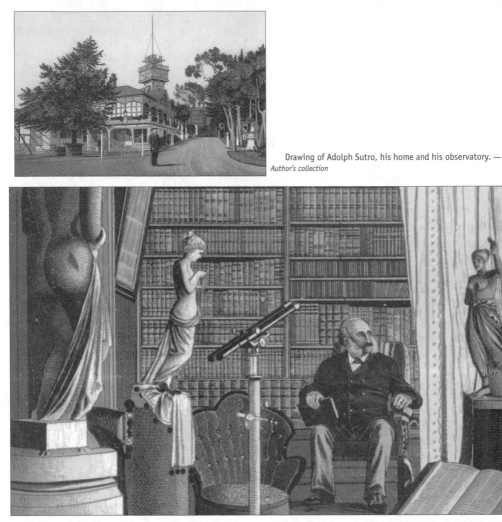

Drawing of Adolph Sutro, his home and his observatory. —
Author's collection

Adolph Sutro in his library at home. —*Author's collection*

Sutro had industrious plans for
his property. He exceeded those
beyond anyone's imagination. —
Author's collection

THE CLIFF HOUSE

The Cliff House still exists but only as a shadow of the legendary landmark that stood before and during the reign of Adolph Sutro. Few people agree on how many Cliff Houses have actually stood at the far end of San Francisco just south of Point Lobos. The majority will say three; the knowledgeable will claim five and some will argue six. It's all

Cliff House number one—this was the first version. —*Library of Congress*

a matter of interpretation, but in fact the Cliff House has been built or rebuilt from nothing three times, extensively expanded once, has undergone one major facelift with an addition and just completed a major renovation. Five is what George Whitney, the last private owner, claimed back in the 1950s. The twenty-first century renovation makes it six.

While an early history states San Francisco pioneer Sam Brannon built the first Cliff House in 1858, that structure was build on Sutro Heights, not on the cliff overlooking Seal Rocks. The Mormon elder built that structure using timbers salvaged from a ship that ran aground on the cliffs below—purchased for the sum of $1,500. Though it bore the same name, it was not one of the progressions of the "Cliff House" at its current location.

Senator John Buckley and C. C. Butler built the first Cliff House on the current site in 1863. Captain Junius Foster assumed it as the lessee and proprietor of the Cliff House Restaurant. High prices and limited access didn't deter San Franciscans—the carriage trade and well-heeled populace had money to spend. A great restaurant and wonderful view made the Cliff House an instant attraction. Feats of daring drew crowds that were happy to pay a dollar a seat to watch the outdoor acts of tightrope walkers or daring swimmers racing past the rocks, braving treacherous riptides. One daredevil, the celebrated Rose Celeste, walked a tightrope from the Cliff House across the ocean waves to Seal Rocks and back.

Captain Foster expanded the Cliff House in 1868. The extensive additions provided an expansive ocean view and promenade as well as two wings on the existing structure. Photos show the old Cliff House nestled safely inside the new—the second Cliff House. It attracted greater crowds and became the meeting place for city and state bosses as well as the seamier crowds from the Barbary Coast. Though it remained the attraction of choice by tourists, including three presidents, the genteel local clients abandoned the Cliff House. It became famous for scandals and antics committed in the upstairs rooms.

This shift disturbed Adolph Sutro, owner of Sutro Heights across the road. Sutro purchased the Cliff House in 1883 and evicted Captain Foster, installing his own man, Mr. Wilkins as manager. The enterprise again drew crowds of local people given its renewed focus on families, good food, and entertainment.

In 1887, the schooner *Parallel*, loaded with dynamite, ran aground on the rock below the Cliff House, demolishing the north wing. That same year, the Cliff House also hosted the world first parachute drop, performed by Thomas Baldwin, who was carried aloft in a hot air balloon. The event was observed by President Benjamin Harrison, among others.

A chimney fire destroyed the second Cliff House on the evening of Christmas day, 1894.

THE CLIFF HOUSE AND THE PARALLEL

On the afternoon of Thursday, January 13, 1887, the ninety-eight-foot schooner *Parallel* left Hay Wharf in San Francisco bound for Astoria, Oregon. She was loaded with kerosene, a cask of dynamite caps, and 1,685 fifty-pound cases (about forty-two tons) of black powder. By Saturday evening, the captain still fought for open sea, tacking against strong headwinds. The *Parallel*, gripped by the tide, slowly approached the Cliff House. Captain Miller ordered his men into the lifeboats and abandoned the ship at 8:30 P.M.

Mr. Wilkins, manager of the Cliff House, telephoned John Hyslop at the Point Lobos signal station an hour later to report that a ship was about to hit the rocks. Descending to the bluff below the signal station, Hyslop saw the ship was heading toward a small cove below the restaurant. Sutro arrived at his restaurant with several of his gardeners and, under the direction of Hyslop, they lowered ropes to the ship below. When no one took the ropes, it was obvious the crew had abandoned the ship. The *Parallel* hit the rocks at 10:30 P.M. and began breaking up.

A life-saving crew arrived on scene but with no one to save, Captain Kroeger, the chief, put two members, Henry Smith and John Wilson, on watch. The crowd that gathered slowly dispersed, leaving just Smith and Wilson. At 12:34 A.M. the cask of dynamite caps detonated, touching off the black powder. The ship exploded in a deafening blast, shooting a great wall of flame and debris up the cliff. The explosion catapulted Smith and Wilson two hundred feet back from their position at the cliff edge. The sound of the blast carried all the way to Oakland and San Jose. The shock wave struck the ship *Commodore* fifteen miles off the Golden Gate. Its crew scrambled to their stations thinking they had struck a reef. Sutro's mansion took considerable damage and houses nearby were nearly torn apart.

People look for souvenirs after the *Parallel* exploded. The Cliff House bar quickly opened in spite of all the broken glass and the northern wing being blown away. The Cliff House was repaired. —*Courtesy of The Bancroft Library, University of California, Berkeley*

Both men caught in the blast had serious injuries, but they survived. The cliff face had forced the blast skyward, although the Cliff House had taken most of the brunt of the blast. The event destroyed the north wing and blew out every window. Doors shot off their hinges and balconies inside and out collapsed. Each room was a mass of debris. Crowds gathered that morning to view the remains. Wilkins, spotting the opportunity, had one of the bars swept out and immediately opened for business. The bar had record sales that Sunday. Souvenir hunters had a field day looking for scraps of the *Parallel*.

Onlookers scrambled on to the remains of the schooner *Parallel* at low tide, looking for souvenirs and posing for photographs.
—*Author's Collection*

Drawing of Cliff House number two—two wings and a deck wrapped around the first Cliff house, ca. 1889. —*Author's collection*

Cliff House number two as seen from Sutro Heights. —*Author's collection*

Sutro paid $75,000 for the construction of the third Cliff House—a French chateau-style, eight-story structure. Completed in February 1896, it boasted a large public dining room and numerous private lunch and dining rooms, a bar, a ballroom, a parlor, an observation tower two hundred feet above sea level and art galleries displaying some of Sutro's fine collections. Although visited by two U. S. presidents, William McKinley and Teddy Roosevelt, the Cliff House still remained a place for the common person to enjoy. Sutro's nickel streetcar line, coupled with fair prices, meant that a workingman could bring his family to share in the luxury, the stunning views, and fine food, all at reasonable prices.

After Adolph Sutro's death, the Cliff House was sold to John Tait of Tait's at the Beach, an earlier successful Ocean Beach resort. On September 7, 1907, the most

The third incarnation of the Cliff House and certainly the most striking. This was the French Chalet design and was one of the most photographed buildings in the city. —*Enhanced print courtesy Head's PhotoTouch.*

Sutro's most-loved Cliff House burned to the ground on September 7, 1907. A remodeling was underway and may have been the cause. —*Library of Congress*

opulent of all Cliff House reincarnations burned to its foundation. A remodeling project was underway at the time and may have been the cause.

Tait rebuilt the Cliff House again with the support of Dr. Emma Merritt, daughter of Adolph Sutro. Steel reinforcing bar and poured concrete meant this version would not suffer the fate of the previous two. With the appearance of a giant gray shoe box, the Cliff House now depended on the local view rather than its own visage to attract customers. Tait reopened the fourth version of the Cliff House on July 1, 1909. In spite of its lackluster appearance, it remained the place to visit for locals and tourists. It still provided a ballroom for dancing as well as fine dining rooms and its one-of-a-kind view.

The Cliff House again shut down in 1918. Located next to Fort Miley, the military had it shut down due to infractions by military personnel. It reopened in December of 1920 under the new ownership of Shorty Roberts, another beach resort owner, famous for Rob-

Cliff House number four—this utilitarian block structure was built in 1909 to replace the opulent French Chalet. —*Author's collection*

erts at the Beach. Unfortunately, prohibition now reigned and a dry Cliff House lacked the previous allure. Roberts shut down all but the coffee shop in 1925.

The Cliff House changed hands twice more, purchased in 1952 by George Whitney, owner of Playland at the Beach, then acquired by the Golden Gate National Recreation Area in 1977. It continues to be a favorite for locals and visitors alike. The last major renovation was completed on September 1, 2004, restoring it to the 1909 neo-classical look. It's definitely worth a visit.

Cliff House number five: Whitney Brothers' attempt to modernize with redwood siding, ca. 1960. Number six? You judge! —*Author's collection*

SUTRO'S BATHS & MUSEUM

The Victorian Age charmed San Francisco. The city loved the grandiose, the ornate, and the obscenely overblown. The new popularity for public baths encouraged Adolph Sutro, flamboyant mayor and leading citizen, to build the Sutro Baths. Completed in 1894 and opened officially in 1896, it debuted as the largest public bath in the world. It had seven pools of various depths, temperatures, and sizes, all but one being saltwater. The largest, an indoor L-shaped, unheated saltwater pool, measured 300 feet long by 175 feet wide. The pools contained a total of 1,685,000 gallons of ocean water. It took one hour to empty or fill them using the action of the high and low tides. The accommodations included 500 dressing rooms and grandstands built for 5,000 spectators. The magnificent Victorian building, roofed in crystal glass (100,000 panes), boasted an ornate Victorian decor with a Grecian temple-like en-

The main facility of Sutro Baths nears completion. —*Courtesy of The Bancroft Library, University of California, Berkeley*

trance, sweeping staircases, and gardens of tropical ferns, palms, and climbers. Sutro Baths covered two acres of the coast at Point Lobos just north of the Cliff House's— in all it could accommodate 25,000 guests.

Sutro built his baths for all the people of San Francisco, not just for the elite. A populist, he wanted all to share the current prosperity and opportunities. His baths included a theater with ongoing stage productions, three restaurants with combined seating of up to a thousand diners, a gymnasium, and a museum. A single modest fee offered

The interior of the baths was a Victorian wonderland. —*Courtesy of The Bancroft Library, University of California, Berkeley*

entry to all. The Sutro Railroad (trolley) made regular runs out to the Beach and the people came in droves. Swimming cost a quarter and it was only a dime for spectators to view the pools and use the remainder of the facility. Sutro's provided bathers with a locker, towel, woolen suit, soap, and showering facilities. The Baths boasted room for 1,600 bathers and maintained 20,000 suits and 40,000 towels.

Swimming at the Sutro Baths elevated aquatic sports and activities to a passion in San Francisco. In a place too chilly for outdoor swimming, now anyone could do so

Indeed, the Sutro Baths were the largest in the world. —*Author's collection*

Adolph Sutro built his estate above the Cliff House on Sutro Heights. —*Author's collection*

in warmth and comfort. At one point in its history, Sutro's carried a gigantic neon sign that proclaimed "Tropical Beach" and indeed, it was, with an abundance of plants and a warm, humid climate. Swimming classes overflowed, kids barreled down to the water in chutes, and splashed in the pools. Competitions of every sort, as well as special exhibitions, took up significant space in the newspapers. Sutro Baths blazed with excitement and the town loved it.

The museum at Sutro's Baths inspired awe and curiosity. Artifacts from around the world and from other eras graced Sutro's museum. Many of the exhibits had the air of a bygone morbidity. The museum's statue of a Chinese man, who had plucked each hair from his body and inserted it into his likeness to accurately copy himself, was featured in Ripley's Believe It or Not! column in the *San Francisco Chronicle*. The museum displayed the travel trunk and assorted clothing of Tom Thumb, the midget of P. T. Barnum fame, and it included a carnival created from toothpicks by a prison inmate at San Quentin State Prison. A real Tucker automobile was on display by the late 1950s. Sutro's Museum even had authentic Egyptian mummies. In order not to leave anything to the imagination, some were unwrapped. These were the cause of children's exclamations during the visit and their nightmares that night.

The museum also sported a large collection of historic amusement machines of from earlier era. Automata, coin-operated musical instruments, penny-arcade machines and mechanical sports games provided amusement for the mechanically obsessed. The automata were amazing including a mechanical carnival, can-can dancers kicking up their legs and pirouetting to a lively tune, pioneers crossing the plains in covered wagons and scenes of Americana, all performing complicated mechanical activities.

The baths struggled financially in the '30s. A skating rink replaced the largest pool in 1937. Thus, San Francisco gained a toehold into winter sports. The city's kids learned to ice skate but the rink never drew the adults. Maintenance costs and dwindling attendance necessitated shutting the baths down in 1952. Sutro's grandson, Adolph G. Sutro, immediately sold Sutro's Baths to George Whitney who by then owned Playland and the nearby Cliff House. Whitney reopened the Sutro Baths, but closed the remaining pools in 1954. Sutro closed for good in early 1966—the land slated for an apartment complex. On June 26, 1966, during the early demolition process, Sutro's Baths burned to its foundations. Rumor claims it was arson, but the fire wasn't worth investigating. What were left are the finest ruins in the city, now part of the Golden Gate National Recreation Area. People still gather to imagine the lost grandeur. Anyone lucky enough to have visited the baths recalls unforgettable memories of one of Adolph Sutro's finest achievements.

The main pool at Sutro's baths. —*Author's Collection*

Sutro built his own trolley line to Ocean Beach and his Baths and Cliff House, then only charged a nickel to use it. —*Photo courtesy of San Francisco History Center, San Francisco Public Library*

MEMORIES OF SUTRO BATHS

The following is a letter to the editor from the *San Francisco Chronicle*, Saturday, October 17, 1998:

Editor—Growing up in San Francisco in the 1930s was wonderful. So there was the Depression. So my mother and I had to live with my grandfather in his house on Herman Street, with my aunt and my balmy uncle, where arguments were a way of life. So what? I could always escape to the Sutro Baths.

For five cents, I rode the 22 Line north on Fillmore to Sutter and transferred to a number 1 or 2, which went out to the beach. The last mile passed through countryside and then we pulled into an old wooden terminal. The first things that assailed our senses were the sea air and a peanut machine that whistled.

I went outside and walked a few feet to the Sutro Baths, a massive Victorian structure that was beginning to show its age. I think I paid 25 cents admission. I was given a swim suit (we could not bring our own) and a meager towel. The suits were not trunks. They covered all of my puny body with straps that went over my shoulders, and they were made of wool with "Sutro Baths" across the front in white letters. As if anybody would have wanted to steal one!

Suit in hand, I went down the stairs through Sutro's museum of tropical plants and stuffed bears, gorillas and lions, all of which looked moth-eaten, to get to the lockers, miles of them, stacked in tiers. An attendant guided me down to one, unlocked the door, and gave me a metal number tag on a cord, which I put on my wrist.

I changed into my woolen suit and raced down the stairs to the baths. There were eight or nine pools with temperatures ranging from hot to ice cold. The biggest pool had a waterwheel. My friends and I climbed stairs to reach it, and then lay down on it while it slowly revolved, dumping us into the pool. Sometimes we got tangled up with girls and they'd start screaming.

The hard part came when I had to leave. I climbed back up to the rows of lockers, went to mine and stood by it, yelling to the attendant to come. You don't know what torture is until you've stood shivering in a wet, cold, wool bathing suit at Sutro Baths.

Gee, it was fun.

—Bill Roddy, America Hurrah, http://americahurrah.com

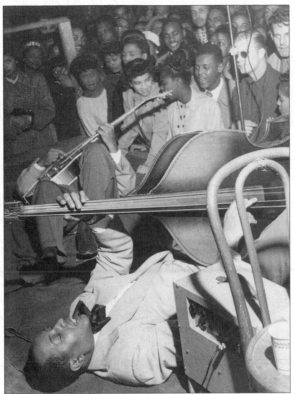

Primalon Ballroom in the 1950s—the band was HOT that night!
—David Johnson collection of San Francisco Photography

Chapter 4

Gambling Houses, Parlors, Clubs, Saloons and Dives

Oh, how the San Francisco locals love celebration, entertainment, and drinking, and the city always provided something for everyone. Ranging from the Barbary Coast dives noted for shanghaiing their patrons to the glittering nightclubs, from the El Dorado Saloon of the Gold Rush to the speakeasies down in South Beach and China Basin, from the Bohemian Club's civic leaders to Finocchio's female impersonators and from the newly rich to the Beat Generation, the city found ways to express itself. The city's nightlife was legendary, and rightfully so.

The discovery and runaway publicity of California's gold created a city like no other. The population exploded, instantly creating a metropolis of unencumbered males and free-flowing cash. The lack of wives, mothers, and girlfriends deprived the population of all forms of family and social life. Preachers came to preach and pews may have filled on Sundays but that covered only a small percentage of the populace and many attended only to atone for their sins of the prior evening. Given a fair bit of jingle in a large number of pockets, San Francisco invented its own social life, centered on clubs, saloons, gaming establishments, and houses of prostitution. Which of those a man attended depended largely on his desires and his available cash or gold. Rudyard Kipling, having arrived in San Francisco in 1889 after a months-long tour of the Orient, found himself aghast at what he experienced at our Golden Gate.

Concerning his experiences, Kipling wrote:

> There is neither serenity nor indifference to be found in these parts; and evil would it be for the Continent whose wardship were intrusted to so reckless a guardian. Behold me pitched neck-and-crop from twenty days of the High Seas, into the whirl of California, deprived of any guidance, and left to draw my own conclusions. Protect me from the wrath of an outraged community if these letters are ever read by American eyes. San Francisco is a mad city, inhabited for the most part by insane people whose women are of remarkable beauty.

Kipling stepped into a place created forty years prior, which exhibited no social mores to speak of while boasting a society created out of facade, pretense, and money and based on the visions of the newly rich (not cultured enough to warrant the term Nouveau Riche).

The Gold Rush Era

Men lacking a wife at home or a lady to court, uprooted, and with no mother, hometown preacher, or tongue waggers to observe their comings and goings found solace in the company of others like themselves, pursuing activities they would never consider in their hometowns. They joined in varied forms of entertainment to pass the evenings and most included the consumption of alcohol. Rich men drank the world's finest liquors at the Lick House, the Palace Hotel or the Occidental. The rest just drank, but don't think they sat around drinking redeye. Cocktails, wine, and champagne comprised most of the drinks served. Mornings started with a gin cocktail, termed a digestive, before breakfast. An encounter with any acquaintance on the street called for a drink at the nearest bar, regardless of the hour. Drinks for the house followed any success and drowning of sorrows was the order of the day. Any reason to drink was a good reason. San Francisco had no interest in temperance.

Drinking establishments included saloons, bordellos, gambling houses, hotel barrooms, and clubs. The ship *Apollo*, anchored and then grounded, became one of the earliest saloons, using an entry initially on planks and later via the new Long Wharf.

Sailors could wet their whistles there without leaving the bay. Other abandoned ships suffered similar fates since real estate and building costs quickly climbed beyond reach. Barrels, planks and sailcloth made up the early bars. Dives like the Whale and Cowboy's Rest represented the lowest establishments, providing shelter for the toughest sailors and San Francisco's criminals alike. Legitimate places like the Balboa, the Foam, the Bowhead, the Grizzly Bear, the Veranda and Sverdrup's provided sailors and miners a decent place to drink for a fair price. Crimping, the conscription of unwilling men, soon reared its ugly head to fill ships' crews and more than a few drunken sailors found themselves aboard strange ships sailing out the Golden Gate.

Early bordellos lacked any amenities other than a tent or a rough wooden shack. Sometimes stationed in cribs similar to animal pens, privacy was at a premium. Women arrived from all points, from South America (all called Chilenos), from the East Coast and Louisiana, from France and other European countries and eventually from China. The women drew hundreds of dollars a night. Few of the women ever saw any of the money collected.

Hubert Howe Bancroft, California's early historian, said, "The first females to come were the vicious and unchaste, who opened and presided at brilliant saloons and house of ill-fame and sat by the gambler and assisted him in raking in his gains and paying his losses. Flaunting in their gay attire, they were civilly treated by the men, few of whom, even the most respectable and sedate, disdained to visit their houses."

When the building boom began, many bordellos paid for lavish surroundings. The upscale "parlor houses" dripped with opulence, installing furnishings of the highest style, with cost no factor. Pretenses, coupled with the shortage of available women, created a societal blessing on the institution that existed nowhere else. High social occasions held in the parlor of a house of ill repute drew the most prestigious guests. Many society matrons of the post Gold Rush era were veterans of the early parlor houses of San Francisco, although they pretended they bore the bluest blood in the city.

One of the earliest and finest parlor houses belonged to Mrs. Irene McCready, paramour of James McCabe, owner of the El Dorado. Mrs. McCready's parlor, located on Portsmouth Square, burned down twice in the fires that periodically devastated

Portsmouth Square and the Empire Saloon, ca. 1851—it didn't take long for San Francisco to find ways to take advantage of the gold flowing in. —*Library of Congress*

San Francisco, but each rebuilding produced a finer facility, financed by her excessive profits. While their businesses prospered, the relation of McCabe and McCready did not. McCabe beat her after one of her jealous tantrums and she, like Delilah, got him drunk (and some say drugged) and shaved not only his head but his whole body as well. The people were as volatile as the times.

Gambling houses like McCabe's El Dorado appeared early in the city's history. After opening in 1849, the El Dorado was housed in a tent renting for forty thousand dollars a year, but a quarter-million dollars changed hands across her tables daily. A large one-room structure quickly replaced the tent and provided private booths, separated by muslin drapes, where any form of shenanigans or planning could occur. The new facility bragged elegantly ornamented and polished rococo furnishings in celebration of newfound wealth. Expensive paintings depicting voluptuous nudes in various poses adorned the walls. A band, orchestra, or soloist played at one end of the house on a raised stage, shared with an orchestrion. That pump-driven instrument, later called a nickelodeon, included a player piano and perhaps some organ pipes (maybe flutes or violin), a mandolin, a snare drum, a bass drum, timpani, a cymbal, and a triangle. An ornate bar, complete with cut glass mirrors, dominated the opposite end of the room.

Gambling tables at the El Dorado sported roulette wheels or card games such as Faro, each table run by a dealer clad in black and white. Gold sat in stacks on the tables in the form of nuggets, dust, and coin, and it flowed between the players and dealers. Most passed toward the dealers, of course. The El Dorado's barman, Jerry

The El Dorado—just the place for high-rollers. Jerry Thomas concocted some of his famous cocktails here. —*Author's collection*

Thomas, portioned out generous measures of bourbon, glasses of champagne, and innovative cocktails. Mr. Thomas, arguably the most famous bartender of the nineteenth century, invented the Tom and Jerry and the flaming Blue Blazer, named for the flame, not a jacket.

Fierce competition prevailed for the patrons' money and gold. Entertainment helped fill the boredom of life without companionship and saloons such as the Bella Union hired Simone Jules, a raven-haired Frenchwoman of striking beauty. The *Alta California* newspaper railed about a woman working in a gambling hall but to no avail. She drew crowds to her tables, turning more profits than any of the men. As more women arrived, attractive barmaids encouraged even more sales. The Bank Exchange offered an air of respectability in an effort to attract newly rich businessmen. Outspending the El Dorado, it hung paintings said to be worth $100,000 and pre-

The Bella Union on Portsmouth Square—one of the earliest and rowdiest joints, it offered drinking, gambling and even a few women. —*Photo courtesy of San Francisco History Center, San Francisco Public Library*

The Bank Exchange—they outspent the El Dorado in a bid for the wealthy clients. —*Photo courtesy of San Francisco History Center, San Francisco Public Library*

sented a décor that included marble floors, a marble topped bar, and fine crystal. The Bank Exchange's barman, Duncan Nichol, claimed Pisco punch as his invention, charging two bits a glass, a high cost for the times. That mixed drink consisted of two jiggers of Pisco, a Chilean or Peruvian brandy, plus a splash of pineapple or lemon juice and perhaps some mineral water. While Americans found straight Pisco undrinkable, Nichol's punch soon became a San Francisco favorite. The exact recipe unfortunately is lost.

Prostitution continued beyond the confines of the American operated saloons and dance halls. Chinatown's famed prostitute Ah Toy bought out her contract through the "generosity" of a few wealthy and prominent white gentlemen. She opened her own house of prostitution in Chinatown on Pike Street (now Waverly Place) just off Clay, and Ah Toy became one of the wealthiest madams in San Francisco, subjecting other young girls to the same life that she had endured upon arriving in the city. Prostitution in Chinatown came in three flavors—lookee, feelee, and doee, usually two bits, four bits, and a dollar respectively. Chinese prostitutes were slaves and made no money of their own. They were usually killed or left to die of disease when they outlived their allure and usefulness, and local preachers and benevolent societies made no headway rescuing these girls who arrived in their preteen years from China. Ah Toy's reign proved short-lived. Brought a number of times before the magistrate for keeping a "disorderly house," she soon left the city. Chinese prostitutes suffered discrimination by law and circumstance, were excluded from medical help and hospitalization, and endured the expected downfalls of the profession. The *Chronicle* claimed Ah Toy died in 1928 in the city of San Jose, just short of her hundredth birthday.

THE ENTERPRISE YEARS

The Gold Rush played out near the end of the Civil War. The easy pickings gave way to hard digging and mechanized methodology, like hydraulic mining. Families headed to California, bringing with them agriculture, manufacturing, and trades. California agriculture differed from that of the rest of the country. Instead of small family subsistence farms, such as those of the homesteaders during the Westward Movement, individual Californians farmed on a huge scale for the marketplace. Pioneers, such as James Lick, planted thousands of acres of orchards. Crops drew cash, not just store credit, and farming became big business in the Golden State. Produce shipped from South America cost dearly, inducing Californians to abandon the gold fields for the cornfields and the pastures.

The opening of the Transcontinental Railroad in 1869 heralded a new era of trade and the creation of wealth based on goods not gold. Construction began on January 8, 1863, and was dependent largely on the importation of hordes of Chinese to perform the dangerous, backbreaking labor that Americans refused. These arrivals from the Celestial Empire fostered the creation of the largest Chinese settlement outside of China and with it an entirely new experience in establishments of leisure. Opium dens and Chinese prostitutes proliferated in the city.

The winter spanning 1871 and 1872 brought the mines and farms into direct conflict. Silt, tailings, and debris carried into the rivers and caused flooding in the Central Valley and overflow of that silt and debris onto farms, especially in Yuba and Sutter counties. The farmers filed suit, and coupled with the floods of 1878, it spelled the end of mining. Judge Phil Keyser ruled that the mines did not have the right to clog the rivers with their tailings and debris. That first ruling spelled the end of big business mining, with an estimated $6,000,000,000 worth of gold left in the hills of California.

The Golden Gate funneled riches into San Francisco as the gateway to the Orient. Trade replaced gold as basis for San Francisco's growing wealth. Shipping, manufacturing, banking, and investments fueled the city's economy. The opening of the Transcontinental Railroad provided reasonably priced trade and transport both east and west. San Francisco controlled the vast majority of the trade between the United States and the Pacific Rim countries including Mexico, South America (primarily Chile and Peru), Japan, China, the Philippines, and Australia. The city held a near monopoly on trade with the Sandwich, or Hawaiian Islands.

San Francisco's inhabitants still primarily came from elsewhere and were still primarily men. Those men left their morality back at home. Some families set up homes in the city, but it remained a city with a disproportionate number of single, unattached males.

The waterfront and Barbary Coast earned reputations as unsavory areas run by crimps, thugs, and criminals. Chinatown opened possibilities of intriguing sin and debauchery previously unimagined by the locals. The number of bars, saloons, gambling houses, dance halls, and houses of prostitution continued to grow. The city maintained its reputation as a wide-open town. Yet, San Francisco yearned for respectability, which inspired the creation of social clubs and other establishments necessary to hold societal affairs. These arose with the trappings of the newly rich. Diversity between the haves and have-nots became most apparent when considering their respective places of socialization.

The Barbary Coast emerged as favorite haunt for sailors, laborers, criminals and during the day, for brave tourists. Originally called Sydney Town for the Australian thugs known as the "Sydney Ducks" running the area, it continued down an increasingly hard path. Crimps like Shanghai Kelly, Jimmy Laflin, Bob Pinner, Horseshoe Brown, and Shanghai Brown all ran saloons known for Shanghaiing sailors and non-sailors alike. Calico Jim, a notorious Chileano, operated a notoriously dangerous place at Battery Point. Others were like German George Reoben, who opened a boarding house for sailors at 37 Pacific Street, maintaining a room, board, and liquor tab for them and then shipping them out on the next ship to cover the resulting tab. Often the drinks included drugs intended to make the subjects easier to handle, and boarding and bar tabs sometimes included trumped-up charges for services or goods never received. Abe Warner's Cobweb Palace was the only truly safe establishment that welcomed sailors. Shanghaiing was a legal practice until the early twentieth century, supported by local politicians and overlooked by upstanding citizens pleased to rid the town of a few undesirables. (Author's note—Don't confuse George Reuben, the author's great-great-grandfather with George Roeben, the crimp, an error made by a number of history writers, including Herbert Asbury. Reuben kept a store, Yankee Notions and

Fine Goods, on San Francisco's California Street during that same period and both men had German-born wives.)

Later in the late nineteenth century, the Barbary Coast hosted clubs, theaters, and melodeons. All were bawdy places inviting rough traffic of the lowest sort. The Billy Goat was one of the worst of the lot, renowned for its odor of unwashed bodies, stale beer, and damp sawdust. Pigeon-toed Sal, a middle-aged Irish woman, owned the Billy Goat and served as its barkeep and bouncer. Cheap drinks attracted the poor and the frugal—extra large mugs of beer for a dime and a big glass of rotgut whiskey for a nickel. Knockout potions emptied the pockets of any who might have a few dollars, adding to Sal's take, and any illegalities met with Sal's approval as long as she received her customary 50 percent cut.

Entertainment, as well as drink, drew the crowds to most places including Denny O'Brien's Saloon on Kearny. O'Brien's facility included a pit where dogfights and the associated betting ensued. Local boys received between a dime and quarter for scrappy wharf rats that were later tossed into the pit with terriers in a battle to the death. Other dives depended on the formula of wine, women, and song with waitresses and singers doubling as prostitutes and drinking companions. Bull Run on Pacific Street, in the area called Hell's Acre, typified the worst of those.

This dive offered a dance hall and bar on the ground floor, with rooms upstairs containing cots or bedrolls for those with fifty cents to a buck for a turn with one of the ladies. "Anything goes here" was the motto of Ned "Bull Run" Allen, the proprietor, and to encourage this, he required all his female employees to drink while working. Their antics when drunk amused the owner and his customers. Any girl who passed out was hauled upstairs and as many as thirty to forty men paid twenty-five cents to a dollar for a turn with the unconscious lass. Half the receipts belonged to the girl but she seldom received her due.

The girls led a hard life and often died young of cirrhosis, tuberculosis, syphilis, pneumonia, or some other disease, if not by the violence inflicted on them by their customers or employers. No one was exempt from the danger of such places. The Bull Run closed after Allen ran amuck in his dance hall, brandishing a large ivory tusk. Patron Bartlett Freel stabbed the berserk Allen with a clasp knife, killing him. The judge at Freel's trial remarked, "Allen's death would work no hardship upon the community" but Freel, a Barbary Coast Ranger himself, still did time in a federal penitentiary. The term "ranger" applied to anyone actively involved in the "business" of the Barbary Coast, including proprietors, barkeeps, thieves, and anyone else involved in that sordid business.

A few blocks away in Chinatown, another vice held sway. Opium dens and the mythical underground tunnels of Chinatown prevailed as the object of attention for do-gooders, racists, politicians directing attention elsewhere, preachers lambasting the "Sodom of the West," and curiosity seekers. In reality, the opium trade barely touched the non-Chinese culture with the exception of down and outers, a few Bohemians and the occasional prostitute. The controlling tongs, Chinese gangs, valued a low profile and had no desire to instigate a purge of Chinatown. Opium largely remained the vice of the city's Chinese.

POST-QUAKE SAN FRANCISCO

The earthquake and resultant fire of April 18, 1906, wreaked great physical and social change on San Francisco. The city hoped to clean up its rampant immorality as well as rebuild its structures. Prior to the trembler, Mayor Eugene Schmitz of the Union Labor ticket personified the rampant graft and greed in the city, aided by the man behind the power, Boss Abe Ruef. They had overlooked the city's municipal needs including a reliable water supply, in favor of lining their own pockets, much through kickbacks from the dives in the Barbary Coast and the French restaurants with entertainment rooms upstairs. The jury convicted Schmitz of taking kickbacks but the state Supreme Court overturned it. In his haste, Federal Prosecutor Francis J. Heney violated the law and trampled Schmitz's rights. Boss Ruef wasn't so lucky and did time. Schmitz's six-year term of office ended in 1911 when "Sunny Jim" James Rolph, a Reformer, took office promising to clean up the city. Sunny Jim kept his word, working to improve political and social conditions in city while serving five terms. Still, cleaning up San Francisco proved no small task.

San Francisco remained the hot spot of the coast. The West Coast movie industry that started in Niles, fifty miles east of the city, migrated to the Los Angeles basin where the sun required for shooting blazed reliably. Unfortunately, Los Angeles lacked entertainment, so the movie magnates, stars, and crews took the train north to San Francisco for luxuries, culture, parties, and entertainment of both the highest and basest sort.

Prostitution, which was legal until 1915, flourished in a city that recognized few limits. Market, Kearny, Broadway and Stockton streets bounded the red light district as defined by city officials. Morton Alley, currently and amusingly named Maiden Lane, packed in more bordellos in its short two blocks than any other area in the city. Visible from an abutting Union Square, the city's emerging retail bright spot, the alley created an affront to moral decency. Prostitutes in various stages of undress beckoned passersby, noisily touting their wares and individual skills. San Francisco's board of supervisors effectively killed the Morton Alley houses by creating an area of exclusion bounded by California, Powell, Kearny and Stockton streets in 1890, and by 1892, it had specifically banned the use of houses on Morton Street (formerly Morton Alley) for prostitution. The reasoning behind this was simple. The ratio of male to female in San Francisco gradually shifted until it had reached parity in 1910. As families became prevalent in the city, that shocking institution created friction for the board. However, unenthusiastic police raids often helped maintain the facade of closure while the bordellos continued operation.

The great earthquake and fire of 1906 permanently shut down the houses on Morton Street. The state's Red Light Abatement Act of 1913 made prostitution illegal in the state and the mayor ordered the police to enforce the prostitution laws. Still, no serious efforts ensued until 1917 when the state Supreme Court upheld the act. After the populace demanded enforcement at a packed meeting held at the Dreamland Skating Rink, the police took action. The force encircled the Barbary Coast on February 14, 1917, Valentine's Day, closing eighty-three houses of prostitution and putting 1,073 ladies out on the streets. Of course, that didn't stop prostitution in the city. It only distributed it. Much of the trade moved to the Tenderloin (bounded by Geary, Mason, Market, McAllister and Polk), a good, middle-class area. Many a house operated freely there as long as city officials received their cut. The famed madam Sally Stanford opened her business at 610 Leavenworth Street in the Tenderloin.

The saloons, night cafes, and gambling houses fared far better than the parlors after the great quake and fire of 1906. Like the phoenix on the city seal, they emerged from the ashes gaudier than ever. Louis Gomez, the owner of the Monterey at 431 Pacific, built the House of All Nations and boasted that his dancing girls represented women of all civilized nations, and he soon discovered that the variety created an enticing attraction. Entertainment drew crowds and music was hot in San Francisco. First ragtime then jazz, caught fire in the city. If a patron of ragtime, or later jazz, wanted the real thing, there was Purcell's, a "hot, colored joint," which opened just after the quake on Pacific Street.

Lew Purcell and Sam King, two ex-Pullman porters started The Ivy on Pacific, but later split up. Renamed Purcell's, the club offered the best music and dancing, and when jazz hit, it boasted the hottest jazz on the West Coast. Integrated before the invention of the term, Purcell's packed them in, colored and white. The "Texas Tommy"

originated there and "Ballin' the Jack" made a name for Pet Bob, Johnny Peters, and the like. Singers like Al Jolson and Sophie Tucker performed here. Jolson took ideas from Purcell's for his road show. Anna Pavlova, the famed Russian ballerina, learned the "Turkey Trot" at Purcell's and took it back to Russia. Jazz may have started in New Orleans, but thanks to Purcell's and African-American music men like Sid LePerotti and Jelly Roll Morton, San Francisco provided the inspiration for composers and band leaders like Art Hickman and Paul Whiteman, who taught it to mainstream America.

Of course, Purcell's was never tame and many went there just to see the nasty dancing and the fights that sometimes escalated into shootings. Spider Kelly's Tivoli Café, next door, saw many a bullet come through a shared wall. Spider Kelley's image suffered little by the occasional interruption from next door. Kelly bought the saloon after he retired as a successful lightweight boxer, touting his past and the violence of those bare-knuckle days. His club staged floor shows that would make today's Las Vegas blush, and the club was recognized by many

Purcell's (earlier named The Ivy) was the first club owned, operated, and performed by African Americans. They brought jazz and the hot new dance steps to San Francisco. —*Author's collection*

Exterior shot of Spider Kelly's club. He appropriated the Tivoli name but this was no theatre. —*Photo courtesy of San Francisco History Center, San Francisco Public Library*

Spider Kelly's bar—the dance floor is empty but not for long. It looks peaceful but Kelly's was one of the rowdiest on the Barbary Coast. —*Photo courtesy of San Francisco History Center, San Francisco Public Library*

Dancing at Spider Kelly's club. In this posed photo, to the left is Little Egypt, famous for her Hoochy Kootchy dance, who appeared during the 1915 Panama Pacific International Exposition. —*Photo courtesy of San Francisco History Center, San Francisco Public Library*

as the lowest, most rotten dive in the whole world. Patrons expected and found the worst drinking, fighting, and whoring on the Coast at Kelley's.

The electric lights of Pacific Street lit up the night fog, and the doors never closed except on Election Day. The Hippodrome led in popularity, followed by The Thalia, a pretentious dance hall, and, of course, Purcell's. All included gambling, music, and girls at twenty cents a dance. The Thalia's girls sold two-dollar dummy keys, keys to their rooms which in fact opened nothing. Still, prosecutors successfully charged Thalia's owner, Terry Mustain, with running a disorderly house. The clubs sold more than just dummy keys. Violence was common but usually only involved Rangers. The Barbary Coast continued to celebrate out of control until 1921 when the police again cordoned it off and shut it down hard. Many of the clubs followed the parlors into the Tenderloin. The Barbary Coast attempted a resurgence at the end of Prohibition, but the effort failed.

THE DEPRESSION AND WAR YEARS

It took the Great Depression to take the wind out of San Francisco's wild ways as the most sinful city in America. The end of the "enterprise years" heralded a change in how the city viewed itself. In place of Sin City, it focused on tolerance and an appreciation of the unique. The vices continued but dimmed considerably as the depression dragged on. Tight wallets and a growing sense of morality put the squeeze on the city's entertainment.

The flourishing music industry, which included musicians, composers, publishers, and recording studios, dried up as well, much of it moving south to support the burgeoning movie industry. The Musician's Union, which had once been the most influential union in the city, dealt increasingly with declining membership and out of work members. Prohibition ended, but the city was drying up.

Some Barbary Coasters, like Portuguese-born Isadore (Izzy) Gomez, considered taking a different tact and Izzy followed his heart. He opened Isadore Gomez' Café in 1930 at 848 Pacific Street, a somewhat rundown café focusing on the new Bohemian movement and its artists. Three principles ruled Izzy's life: "When you don't know what to say, say nothing"; "Life is a long road, take it easy"; and "When you come to a pool of water on that long road, don't make it muddy; maybe you'll pass there again, and you'll be thirsty."

Izzy, wearing his ever-present black fedora, served great food, thick steaks, crisp fried chicken, huge platters of French-fried potatoes, and big salads, all served with good, homemade grappa at two bits a glass, available even during Prohibition. Izzy's became a gathering place for aspiring artists, and famed writer William Saroyan, himself a regular at Izzy's, portrayed and immortalized the place, its characters, and their situations in his play titled *The Time of Your Life*. Gomez prided himself on the fact that no one left his place hungry. He gave away meals to writers, friends, and those down-and-out who caught his eye.

Composer Sterling Sherwin wrote the song *Down at Izzy Gomez*, published in a songbook produced for the 1939 World's Fair held on San Francisco Bay. Izzy's gained international fame and he basked in his good reputation. Unfortunately, Izzy had once served time for running a speakeasy. He diligently, but unsuccessfully, endeavored to erase that black mark up until his death in 1944. Izzy's Café held on for a while afterward but eventually fell to the wrecker's ball.

Tolerance marked the years just before and during the war. As long as a joint kept a low profile, it could survive by being "different." Different just blended into the city's montage. Clubs walked a fine line, trying to remain within the law, but just barely. San Francisco usually looked the other way at cross-dressing shows, first popular due to the shortage of females and later for their novelty. James Evrard included female impersonations in his stage productions as early as 1850. Evrard later served as a San Francisco police officer, rising to the rank of sergeant. The odd club in the Gay '90s would feature men in drag, and sometimes arrests would follow.

In the early 1930s, Finocchio's Café opened as a speakeasy and Bohemian café on Stockton Street. A customer there did a great impersonation of Sophie Tucker to the delight of the patrons, most of those being part of the art and theater scene. Finocchio's continued presenting female impressionists without fanfare until the end of Prohibition in 1933, when the club opened its doors for a full public review. The city police raided the club in early 1936, but Finocchio's persisted, with Joe Finocchio promising to "run it like a regular theater," allowing no mingling of entertainers and customers. The police agreed that if he complied, Finocchio's could remain open. Joe Finocchio and his wife, Marjorie, realizing the club drew more than just the homosexual and transvestite crowd, opened Finocchio's Club at 506 Broadway in North Beach on June 15, 1936. Joe had found his audience and they packed the place. The straight crowd wanted to gawk at those embracing an alternate lifestyle, and for gays Finocchio's provided a gathering place to socialize.

The entertainment value far exceeded the narrow interests of both sides, as talented entertainers presented crowd-pleasing live-voice performances. Finocchio's was a class act, a cabaret-style revue that had to meet the audience's expectations as thoroughly as though the participants were indeed women. It wasn't good enough to be just a guy in drag; each entertainer had to convincingly sing, act, and entertain. Finocchio's became the poster child for a different, more tolerant look at the gay community.

The club remained a major tourist spot during World War II, drawing the military crowd after a short period of being "off-limits," due to regulations concerning drinking hours, rather than the club's content. The club made the short list of must-sees for out-of-town tourists, and locals delighted in bringing their country cousins in for a jaw-dropping show.

Early 1950s souvenir bar menu and ad for the Finocchio—scotch was $1.15, bourbon, gin, vodka, rum and cordials, $1.10. —*Author's collection*

David de Alba at the Finocchio Club—female impersonator and entertainer, de Alba brought Judy Garland back to life. —*David de Alba*

Stars like Frank Sinatra, Bob Hope, Bette Davis, and Tallulah Bankhead, the latter an admitted bi-sexual, stopped by. Some celebrities came just for the fun of seeing themselves portrayed.

By the 1970s, the high tourist attendance and Finocchio's hands-off rules discouraged the gay crowd and they largely went elsewhere. However, the shows continued with enthusiasm. A small band heralded the entrance of the Master of Ceremonies, performed for many years by Carroll Wallace (Frank Weirdt), who couldn't really sing or keep time. It didn't matter—he could hold an audience. The Finocchio Eve-ettes, named for Joe's second wife, Eve, did a chorus number that might include "The March of the Wooden Soldiers." The show included singers, strippers, dancers, comedy acts, and celebrity impersonations. David de Alba became Judy Garland in a convincing impersonation, capturing the look, mannerisms, and voice of the star. Along with his impressions including Boy-Chic, a Latin flirt, David presented singing clown acts, such as Piérrot and Judy's famous Hobo. Other Finocchio greats included Lucian Phelps, who brought the house down with her Sophie Tucker's "Last of the Red Hot Mamas" routine, along with in-ternational dancing star René de Carlo, noted as much for his lavish costumes as his fine dancing, and Cuban stripper Bobby De Castro, who fired up the audience with his routines. Lavern Cummings, the most gorgeous guy in drag, joined Finocchio's in 1956 and stayed for nearly twenty-seven years. Some of the club's performers were gay and some were straight, but through the years, more real stars walked out onto Finocchio's stage than can possibly be listed.

Mona's 440 Club was another that took advantage of the city's tolerance and tourism. Opening in a Columbus Street basement on North Beach in 1936, Mona Sargent's tavern quickly hit the travel sheets as a place "where girls will be boys." The first openly lesbian club, Mona's female waiters and performers wore tuxedos and patrons dressed their roles. Within a couple of years, Mona's moved to 440 Broadway and took the address as part of the club's new name, Mona's 440 Club. Great enter-

Late 1940s ad for Finocchio's. —*Author's collection*

Promotional postcard for the Finocchio Club in the early 1970s. —*Author's collection*

tainment, first local and later national talent, made a night at Mona's an event. Straights loved the opportunity to rub elbows with openly gay patrons, posing for pictures with them when possible. Gladys Bently, the great African-American cross-dressing diva, sang the blues to an enthusiastic audience during the World War II years. Known alternatively as "America's Great Sepia Piano Artist" and the "Brown Bomber of Sophisticated Song," the 250-pound Bently exuded sexuality. Mona's introduced a generation to the lesbian lifestyle in a proud manner.

After twenty-six years, Mona's closed and was replaced by Ann's 440 Club at the same location. Still popular with the lesbian crowd, Ann's brought in male entertainers like Charles Pierce and Lenny Bruce. Johnny Mathis performed there at age nineteen, and his performances at Ann's rocketed him to fame. Other lesbian bars opened and closed, notably Maud's Study, heralded in a movie titled *Last Call at Maud's*. Mona's opened the way for others, socializing the view of alternate lifestyles.

Mona's, Maud's and Finocchio's transgender themes flaunted the sexually exotic in San Francisco's emerging sexual tourism business but they were not alone in that pursuit. Ethnic eroticism also created a large draw. Charlie Low's Forbidden City offered lavish Chinese décor and an exotic atmosphere and hosted all-Chinese revues, including singing acts and strippers. Westerners found the concept of observing Oriental women particularly enticing, and the club quickly became one of the city's most popular. Forbidden City drew celebrities, such as Ronald Reagan and Jane Wyman as seen in *San Francisco Life*, December 1942.

THE FILLMORE JAZZ CLUBS

Before World War II, the small African-American community in San Francisco lived primarily in the Fillmore District, sharing that area with Japanese-Americans and others. The war changed that mix radically—the Japanese-American residents were forced out to internment camps, leaving a void which additional African-Americans filled, taking jobs offered by the war industries. In 1940, the African-American population of San Francisco was 81,048; by 1950, it had jumped to 462,172, though some say the census got it wrong and the population increased by ten times over that decade. The Fillmore neighborhood quickly became a unique cultural region, later called Harlem West, and it strongly supported the emerging blues and jazz clubs.

Jazz clubs in the Fillmore included the Blue Mirror, Jimbo's Bop City, the Primalon, the Long Bar, Jack's of Sutter Street, the Booker T. Washington Hotel Lounge, the New Orleans Swing Club, and Club Alabam. Memorable performers included greats like Charlie Parker, Ella Fitzgerald, Duke Ellington, Count Basie, Billie Holiday, Miles Davis, Dinah Washington, John Coltrane, and Louis Armstrong.

Herb Caen, the *San Francisco Chronicle*'s celebrated columnist, said it best.

> Around 1 A.M., the crowd started filing out, to gather in knots on the sidewalk, yelling, laughing, chattering away. The Young San Franciscans, in the glow of health, the time of their lives. The mood was still as mellow as the weather, as redolent of the city's long history as the foghorn that sounded occasionally. I thought briefly of my own youth, of making the rounds in The City That Was, hitting the after-hours spots, "slumming" (what a word) in Fillmore District jazz joints where a guy named Jimbo served up booze in a thick coffee cup.

West Coast jazz was a little different, a little more structured, but just as hot. The clubs packed them in and the Fillmore became synonymous with jazz and high-living. Performers often jammed all night in the "Mo." The jazz clubs were serious entertainment. Folks dressed up and let the music ease their troubles. The clubs created excitement, but beyond that, they offered a sense of community. These places belonged to the neighborhood.

However, urban renewal began tearing down buildings and disrupting the local color, and the black community and the jazz clubs went into a serious decline. Sixty-four Fillmore District blocks were scheduled for destruction and the population was pushed out toward the East Bay, the Bayview-Hunters Point District, or just stayed in the district to live in the projects, which also were torn down later. By 1961, the first urban renewal effort, the widening of Geary and the building of the Japan Trade Center closed 461 black businesses and displaced 4,000 families. More projects followed, and it seemed nothing had been learned from the disenfranchisement of the Japanese-Americans.

There have been efforts to revitalize the area and create a Jazz Historic District in the Fillmore. When Willie Brown became mayor, this seemed a given. Unfortunately,

Willie was busy and now it's up to Gavin Newsome or his successor—not a hopeful situation.

THE PRIMALON ON FILLMORE STREET

The Primalon was located on Fillmore Street between Turk and Eddy streets. It was formerly a ballroom and later a skating rink. During the fifties, the hottest black jazz musicians played there on weekends. T. Bone Walker, Cootie Williams, and Roy Milton are but a few of the great jazzmen who performed at the Primalon Ball Room. It was about this time, as an emerging photography student at the California School of Fine Arts, when I discovered that musicians made great photo subjects. I took delight in photographing those performers mentioned, and more.

The Primalon was usually crowded with folks from all over San Francisco. Lots of young white kids came to listen to the performances. The Fillmore was the place for jazz performances in late '40s and '50s. There were numerous nightclubs: Jack's after-hours spot on Sutter Street, the Blue Mirror, and the California Supper Club. The Primalon attracted large crowds who came to dig the jazz. Some have observed that the Fillmore District in many ways resembled New York's Harlem scene. Referred to as the "Harlem of the West," efforts are underway to reclaim the Fillmore's jazz legacy of that period.

—David Johnson, photographer

Lost in the music at the Primalon ballroom. —*David Johnson Collection of San Francisco Photography*

THE BEAT ERA—POST WWII

The war years changed San Francisco. Soldiers and sailors who visited and fell in love with the city during the war years packed up their families and moved to the city of their dreams. The rebuilding of Japan and the Orient funneled materials and wealth through San Francisco's port and shipping reached all-time highs. The city focused on business and on making money—at least most did. Some chose to drop out of this new society, beat down by its demands, adopting a Bohemian point of view mixed with a bit of Eastern philosophy. They became the members of the Beat Generation, known derisively as beatniks, a derogatory term coined by San Francisco columnist Herb Caen, much to the chagrin of the objects of his criticisms.

San Francisco factions had adopted Bohemian concepts as early as the 1860s. The Bohemians of the 1950s found a natural fit, especially among the free thinkers of North Beach. Jack Kerouac, Allen Ginsberg, and Lawrence Ferlinghetti entered the nonconformist San Francisco scene in the early and mid-1950s, after centering their philosophy and style in Paris and New York. They fought against the establishment-controlling, intrusive government and corporate greed. The police arrested Ferlinghetti for publishing and selling copies of Ginsberg's poems, "Howl," the Beats' defining document. They declared the poem obscene, but Ferlinghetti prevailed in the courts.

The Beat Generation gathered in humble little clubs such as Enrico Banducci's Hungry i and his friend Bud Steinhoff's Purple Onion on North Beach across the street from each other on Columbus and Jackson. The clubs featured jug wine and offbeat entertainment, including readings, folk singers, minstrels, edgy standup comedy, and anything else that might goad the establishment. The two tiny clubs highlighted and fought for issues like free speech, creating national and international impact.

Both clubs popularized some of the mid-century's greatest talents, such as Barbra Streisand, Maya Angelou, and Robin Williams. Folk music groups and musicians like The Kingston Trio, The Limelighters, Glenn Yarborough, and Rod McKuen drew the college Beats, who suddenly took an interest in guitars and group sings. Comedians like Mort Sahl, Woody Allen, Professor Irwin Corey (World's Foremost Authority), Dick Gregory, Phyllis Diller, and Lenny Bruce amused, entertained, and indoctrinated their audiences. Lenny's famous arrest for obscenity happened at the Hungry i. The Smothers Brothers, Tom and Dick, sang and bantered at the Purple Onion, displaying wit that cut like a razor, satire like barbed wire and brotherly interaction with the sharp sting of sibling rivalry. As did the Smothers Brothers, the Hungry i and Purple Onion redefined political movement and entertainment. The buildings held no importance—what went on inside created landmark changes.

Of course, San Francisco never danced to just one beat. Clubs on North Beach went topless, as the tourists and locals continued their march toward voyeuristic entertainment mixed with drinking. The Condor stood proudly on the corner of Columbus and Broadway as the premier topless club. Carol Doda headlined, first sporting her "thirty-fours" then expanding her act into those notorious "forty-fours." Talent gave way to titillation but full tour buses arrived constantly, as the newspapers kept the public's eye on the antics of San Francisco's foremost headliner. Carol, in a topless bathing suit, and a Condor bouncer, crushed by a hydraulic piano during a sexcapade, provided a counterpoint to the Vietnam War.

THE CURTAIN FALLS

After the late sixties, when the flower children had taken the city by storm, the clubs and taverns began a downward spiral. Popular bars like Henry Africa's took hold for a while, but even its retro-red velvet wallpaper, dark wood trim, Tiffany lamps, and Victorian ferns could no longer hold San Francisco's attention. The North Beach clubs grew sleazier and gradually lost their appeal to all but the most bored tourists. Carol

Doda retired her act in the '80s and the Condor closed, later replaced by a sports bar of the same name. The Hungry i and the Purple Onion booked third-rate entertainers and retreads from the fifties. The "i" later reopened under the same name as a sex-peep show parlor and the Purple Onion now serves head-banger's music to unsuspecting tourists, hoping to rediscover the flavor of San Francisco's Beat era. Finocchio's lost its freshness after dropping the band and live singing in favor of lip-syncing performers. The club gave its last performance on November 27, 1999, when the Finocchio family could no longer afford to renew its lease due to a significant rent increase and sagging attendance. The city lost interest in gathering places, preferring to sit down to watch television and the nightly news.

DAVID DE ALBA AT THE FINOCCHIO CLUB

The Finocchio Club operated on Broadway for sixty-three years, with hundreds of men gracing its stage. David de Alba represents one of the best of those entertainers dazzling the club's audiences during the seventies and eighties with his female impersonation and voice impressions of Judy Garland, Liza Minnelli and others along with his own creation, Boy-Chic. Mr. de Alba kindly shared the following anecdote from his days at the Finocchio Club.

Half an hour before the fourth and last show was to start, Mrs. Finocchio's sister Maria ran upstairs toward our dressing rooms and shouted to Emcee Carroll Wallace that we had no one in the audience and she was going to cancel the fourth show and to announce it to the cast. To Carroll's delight, since we worked very hard on the three previous shows, he blew the whistle and told us to get ready to go home early. Meanwhile, my Finocchio roommate, comedian Russell Reed, looked at me slyly and said in a whisper, "David, don't believe a word from Carroll Wallace. Don't you dare take your makeup off. Carroll is trying to get us in trouble with the house!" The house meant Mr. and Mrs. Joseph Finocchio.

A few minutes passed by and Maria ran upstairs again and shouted, "Carroll, three people just walked in and we have to do the last show after all!" Carroll blew the whistle again, shouted, "Showtime!" and announced the bad news to the cast who, including Carroll, had already removed their wigs and part of their stage makeup.

Meanwhile Russell said to me, "What did I tell you David? It was all Carroll's doing." I told Russell that it was not Carroll's own doing because I heard Maria make the announcement to cancel the fourth show and why would Carroll go through all the trouble to take off his own glue-on wig and makeup? Carroll and Russell did not like each other very much and I never did find out the reason. I heard that at one time Russell worked for Carroll in a revue that he had formed between his Finocchio gigs.

Anyway, as the show opened with The Eve-ettes, (the chorus line named for Eve Finocchio), you could see the expressions on the faces and hear the laughter of the few people in the audience. The Eve-ettes appeared with partial face makeup, no false eyelashes, and their street pants rolled up under their skirts. As they would do a high kick on stage, you could see men's pants instead of girlie-type stage underwear. Even Carroll's own wig was not glued on and looked like it could bounce off his head at any moment.

As the show progressed and the middle and final productions came on, The Eve-ettes' face makeup progressively improved between appearances, repairing it while acts like Lavern Cummings, Russell Reed and I were on. By the last entrance, all were perfectly made-up and gowned, as though nothing had happened.

From then on, there was a note on the blackboard upstairs for the cast that there will always be a fourth show whether there is an audience or not. If the club was empty, it provided an opportunity for any of us singers to break in new arrangements with the band trio headed by Bill Bullard.

Mr. de Alba also opened a hair salon in the Potrero Hill district of San Francisco, gaining fame as the "Stylist to the Stars" for his work with local celebrities, as well as with the stars of Finocchio's. Featured on Bay Area television and in newspaper articles, famed columnist Herb Caen covered a television pilot shoot for the series *Spies,* with Tony Curtis, at the de Alba salon. Mr. Curtis, a female impersonator in the movie *Some Like It Hot*, met with Mr. de Alba, discussing de Alba's career.

Interest remains in the man who brought the image and voice of Judy Garland to life in San Francisco. Mr. de Alba's career remains active, highlighted by an avid online fan club hosted at www.david-de-alba.com.

Fay Templeton toured the country, first with her parents in the John Templeton Company and later with her own companies. She had a great singing voice as well as consummate acting skills. San Francisco was always on her tour agenda. She died here in 1939. Her last major role was in Jerome Kern's *Roberta*.

Chapter 5
Early Theatres & Stage

San Francisco craved and valued its opera houses and theatres from its earliest days. The city began building theatres soon after the start of the Gold Rush, which featured the likes of Lotta Crabtree, Edwin Booth, and Lola Montez. Always in competition with New York and always yearning to appear cultured, the newly rich eagerly supported the promotion and attraction of the finest artists to San Francisco. Enrico Caruso was in town for a series of performances on the morning of the great 1906 earthquake. San Francisco drew the best performers and companies to its fine theatres and opera houses.

No discussion of the great theatrical houses of San Francisco would suffice without touching on those who built them and those who took the stage. The Golden Era of Theatre in the city began in 1850 and continued through the 1860s, when San Francisco boasted and supported mature offerings of the theatre arts. And, other great houses came and went until the great earthquake and fire of 1906 forced a nearly complete renewal of all. Only the Chutes playhouse remained in its original condition after that event.

THE EARLY YEARS—FIRST HALF OF THE GOLDEN ERA

Drinking, gambling, and the associated bawdy music certainly provided diversions, but they weren't enough. Interactive pursuits wear thin and the Forty-niner soul longed to sit back and be entertained. Theatre filled that need as sustenance for the imagination. The earliest record of a theatrical performance heralded readings and songs performed by Stephen Massett in a one-man show at the courthouse on Portsmouth Square held on June 22, 1849. Tickets cost three dollars, and the door receipts

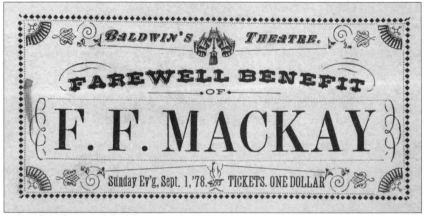

"Benefit performances helped finance travel expenses or cover other financial needs of respected performers."—Author's collection

cleared five hundred dollars. Four ladies attended, taking advantage of the seats reserved for them up front. A businessman, world traveler, and renowned performer, Massett proved that San Francisco could offer a ripe market for theatre.

Performance facilities soon emerged, ranging from bare stages within saloons to the opulent Jenny Lind Theatre, named for the "Swedish Nightingale," who took America by storm, though she never visited San Francisco. No matter—the name alone was magical. Initially, San Francisco theatre consisted of circus acts, musical repertoires, and soliloquies. Washington Hall, San Francisco's first theatre, presented the city's first full play, *The Wife*, performed on January 16, 1850, by actor John B. Atwater and his "Eagle" company, late of Sacramento. The review by the *San Francisco Call* stated, "The only thing worthy of note on that occasion was the high price charged for admission, the large attendance and the poor performance." The play closed after a week and the company disbanded following the treasurer's declaration of the loss of the week's receipts at the "Monte" tables. Washington Hall, later called Foley's Saloon, fell in the fire of May 1850.

Joseph Andrew Rowe toured South America with his circus troupe, and then arrived in San Francisco in late summer of 1849. By October, Rowe presented Rowe's Olympic Circus in an amphitheatre on Kearny Street between California and Sacramento streets. The circus proved profitable but from Atwater's experience, Rowe recognized the opportunity for dramatic performance. On February 4, 1850, Rowe boosted his prices and included plays in his circus, starting with Shakespeare's *Othello*, and followed by the comedy *Bachelor Buttons*. The mix of circus and theatre succeeded. Rowe added more performers and continued until the close of the season, with benefit performances on March 26, 1851.

Benefit performances provided a venue to thank gifted visiting performers or to help a troupe member with a financial need or for a variety of other reasons, including support for the various volunteer firemen's associations, all intended to draw patrons and their dollars or gold. Such performances were common in a city quickly gaining a reputation for generosity.

After selling his original amphitheatre, capable of holding an audience of twelve to fifteen hundred, to his clown, William H. Foley, Rowe built and opened the New Olympic Amphitheatre. Foley had left the troupe earlier in the season to start his own company. That amphitheatre burned down on June 14, 1850, during the third of the great fires that plagued San Francisco during its first few years. Between December of 1849 and June of 1851, the city suffered six great fires, giving rise to the phoenix rising from the flames as the symbol and later the seal of the City of San Francisco. Far from being destroyed, the city renewed itself after each fire, stronger and more ornate. Foley rebuilt his theatre and presented *Rob Roy*, using live horses in a performance declared "spectacular."

Rowe's new amphitheatre continued the proven formula of circus and stage. He also continued to hire and present new actors to the San Francisco stage, including Sarah Kirby (later known as Sarah Stark) and he reintroduced the likes of John Atwater, who now met with better reviews, combining with Miss Kirby in *The Lady of Lyons*. In spite of his local success, Rowe, like many others in San Francisco, tired of routine, taking his company on tour to the Sandwich (Hawaiian) Islands. He returned to San Francisco a wealthy man in 1854. Foley left town shortly after Rowe, and he settled in New Zealand in 1855, building a highly successful career there and in Australia, based on circus and stage. It seems San Francisco wasn't big enough for both Rowe and Foley.

Doctor D. G. "Yankee" Robinson and James Evrard's Dramatic Museum demonstrated the determination that typified San Francisco. The partners began construction just weeks after the second great fire of May 4, 1850, planning to open on June 22. The same fire that destroyed Foley's amphitheatre on June 14 also destroyed the Dramatic Museum eight days before its opening. Undeterred, the pair started over, opening on July 4 with a performance of Robinson's farce *Seeing the Elephant*, which was followed by the presentation of his original song, "The Used-Up Miner." The small theatre only held an audience of four hundred, but the *Pacific News* lauded it as "a cozy little theatre,""a lovely little box of a place," and "a little gem." The *Illustrated California News* described it in detail—just the place for intimacy between actor and audience. The Dramatic Museum stood as the city's first comedy house and set the stage for San Francisco's new form of political ridicule. The city recognized Robinson as one of the two critical figures in San Francisco's early theatrical accomplishments. The other was Tom Maguire.

Tom Maguire, owner of the Parker House hotel and saloon, built his auditorium above the Parker House, naming it the Jenny Lind Theatre. Maguire espoused the art of theatre, although there is no hint he had training in that field. Yet, his management and enthusiasm drove the success of his enterprises as well as the art for nearly the duration of his career in San Francisco. The Jenny Lind began as a showplace, intended to impress as well as present.

Maguire's goal was elegance—elegance in style with elegant performances. He hired James Stark, a skilled hand at theatre, as the director and began the production of *Macbeth, Hamlet, King Lear, Much Ado about Nothing, Richelieu, Pizarro, The Rivals,* and other English classics. His performances met with immediate success at the box office and in the newspaper reviews. The theatre soon took its rightful place at the top, at least until the fire of May 4, 1851, when it burned to the ground. Maguire ordered a second Jenny Lind Theatre built. That theatre opened on June 13, only to burn down again nine

Maguire's Theatre in 1868—Tom Maguire did more for San Francisco theater than any other individual. He died a pauper in New York.
—*Library of Congress*

days later. Undaunted, cigar jammed between his teeth, Maguire began a third Jenny Lind. This one took longer to build, as it was constructed of brick, with fine, yellow-toned sandstone facings shipped from Australia, but Maguire was determined that it would survive the next conflagration and be the finest theatre in the city. The interior glowed in pink shades, offset by gilded trim. It included a balcony, three galleries, one "fitted up in excellent style for respectable colored people," an orchestra pit, and a dress circle. Maguire's new edifice met with resounding acclaim. Veteran actor Walter Leman stated that the third Jenny Lind "rivaled the best theatres in the Atlantic states."

The Jenny Lind Theatre—regardless of all the Jenny Lind references, she never performed in San Francisco. It burned down twice in 1851; this is version 3, ca. 1852. —*Author's collection*

During the same period, Doctor Robinson realized he needed to match the new Jenny Lind in order to compete with Maguire. Fire destroyed his Dramatic Museum and he had leased the new Adelphi, but that theatre failed to match the yet unfinished Jenny Lind. Robinson purchased land on Sansome Street and quickly erected the American Theatre, opening on October 20, prior to the opening of Maguire's new theatre. Rumors of a weak foundation proved true when the structure sank two inches on opening night, but it experienced no further structure problems.

An intense competition ensued between the two owners. Maguire actively drew the audiences and performers away from the American, paying higher wages and cutting ticket prices. By February 1852, Robinson admitted defeat and resigned from the management of the American Theatre. Though sold out most evenings, the Jenny Lind Theatre left Maguire deeply in debt as well. Audiences could be sparse, as on some nights the good folks of the town stayed off the streets after dark, if the Sydney Ducks or members of the Vigilance Societies roamed.

Maguire's acquisition and upkeep of a number of smaller theatres, as well as the high overhead, maintenance, and debt service for the Jenny Lind stretched his finances to the breaking point. He booked special venues, including lotteries for prizes that included jewelry, paintings, and Chinese fabrics, as well as a staged boxing exhibition. All was to no avail, for an impending mechanic's lien on the Jenny Lind forced Maguire to consider his options. In a scheme destined for controversy, he offered his theatre to the city for the sum of two hundred thousand dollars. San Francisco lacked a city hall. After months of considerable debate and heated emotions, the Jenny Lind underwent the necessary remodeling to become San Francisco's first city hall. Maguire received his price and regained his solvency, although the city lost its finest theatre.

His enthusiasm for theatre undimmed, Maguire built yet another house, though not nearly so opulent, focusing on function over facade. San Francisco Hall opened on Christmas Day of 1852, featuring the world-renowned Signora Elisa Biscaccianti. The Signora arrived in San Francisco on March 15, 1852, per the *Daily Alta California*, and was the first prima donna to visit San Francisco. She took the city by storm with her beauty and her voice. Not only the cultured fell under the spell of the coloratura soprano, known as "the American Thrush."

ELISA BISCACCIANTI

Signora Biscaccianti wrote from San Francisco, "I am dreadfully bitter tonight; I feel as if I should like, morally speaking, to smash everything to pieces and 'let go' as the saying is. However as I must let the steam off in some way or other, I will try to do so harmlessly and tell a simple little story, to show how some of the poor nobodies of this world, may come up quite as truly to the heart pitch, as do the so called great and noble. Oh! How often under a rough coat beats a manlier heart than that which ding-dongs under the well cut frock of some fashionable dandy. A man's a man for a' that. The house that night was crammed from pit to cribbing. There were lovely women with flashing eyes and flashing diamonds, attended by model beaux ever ready to roll up their eyes, flirt and sentimentalize, whether they feel it or not; sufficient for the hour is the nonsense thereof. But to my wee story. I had sung many pieces in French, Spanish and Italian, but finally came the turn for the dear, old tune of 'Home Sweet Home.' I do believe one could have heard a pin drop so hushed, so silent was the house; when all at once, a sob, a suppressed sob stole over the audience like a wail of sorrow. All eyes were turned in the direction from which it came. A poor miner, roughly clad with his slouched hat partly cov'ring his bronzed face had entered the pit, and having crept into a corner was leaning on the back of a seat weeping as if his very heart would break.

"Suddenly recollecting himself, and seemingly aware that every one was looking at him, he rose and softly stealing down the aisle left the theater, as if, poor fellow! Ashamed of having loved the dear, old home before so many people.

"I shall never forget the almost religious (silence) which followed that song of mine; it was more to me than the most enthusiastic plaudits that ever rang in my ears; for I knew that there were hearts present too full for utterance. I felt that night when all was over as if, I had done a great, a real good.

Who shall say that by my song of 'Home Sweet Home' I had not drawn a soul from wrong, returning a wandering son to the love of his poor, old mother, who was weeping for him, not knowing through his neglect, whether to mourn him as dead, or as lost only to her.

"May I not believe that I too had had my mission of love and charity."

The Boston-born, multilingual Biscaccianti led the way for other international talents to risk the voyage to San Francisco. Her tour met with unqualified financial and artistic success and the city mourned her departure in January of 1853. News of the financial gains to be had in San Francisco swept the artistic community, and the city soon gained a new reputation as "the actor's El Dorado."

SAN FRANCISCO'S STAR RISES—SECOND HALF OF THE GOLDEN ERA

The period between Atwater's first performance at Washington Hall and the beginning of 1853, with Elisa Biscaccianti's departure, marked the prime of local or journeyman performers. People in the trade worked the city and a few bright stars emerged to the delight of the audiences, but by 1853, San Francisco had earned its place as a port of call for national and international star companies and talent.

San Francisco Hall—later often called the San Francisco Theatre—promised success, but to ensure it, Maguire hired Junius Booth as manager and his former rival Doctor David Robinson as a premier actor. Local actors kept the house lit but the international stars drew the crowds, a feast or famine situation. The time required sailing around the Horn or to brave crossing the Isthmus of Panama created much difficulty in scheduling talent. This situation left the city with either a plethora of actors or a dearth, depending on the vagaries of shipping. Maguire later held the leases for two theaters in the city, two in Sacramento and one each in Stockton, Marysville, and Sonoma, and he scheduled the performers from one theatre to next, controlling both the performances and the performers. Maguire now held a monopoly on the West Coast stage and the complaints flew loud and long. By the 1860s, Tom Maguire gained the less-than-generous title as the "Napoleon of Theatre Managers in California."

A discussion of San Francisco's theatre requires mention of Lola, if only because the name so outshined reality. Lola Montez arrived in San Francisco in May of 1853, and she was immediately escorted to the Bella Union to sing and dance. This she did, though some say she could do neither. Regardless, the miners showered the whip-

Lola Montez brought her famous Spider Dance to San Francisco, receiving critical acclaim for an innovative Spanish-inspired performance. Her volatile temper was world-renowned

wielding "Countess of Landsfeldt" with gold. The American Theatre scheduled her for a performance on May 27, 1853, and for several nights following. The city awaited these performances with great anticipation.

The day following her performance, the *Daily Alta California* printed its account, stating that no one had the patience to wait through the preliminary performances. All awaited Lola.

> The dance was what all had come to see, and there was an anxious flutter and an intense interest as the moment approached which would bring her before the house. She was greeted with a storm of applause, and then she executed the dance, which is said to be her favorite, and has won for her much notoriety. The Spider Dance is a very remarkable affair. It is thoroughly Spanish, certainly, and it cannot be denied that it is a most attractive performance. As a danseuse, Madame Lola is above mediocrity. Indeed, some parts of her execution was truly admirable. We shall endeavor to do her full justice in another notice.

Lola gained notoriety in Europe, America and Australia for whipping editors and critics who gave her poor reviews. In truth, the Spider Dance imitated finding a tarantula on her clothing and removing pieces of clothing, as the tenacious spider darted

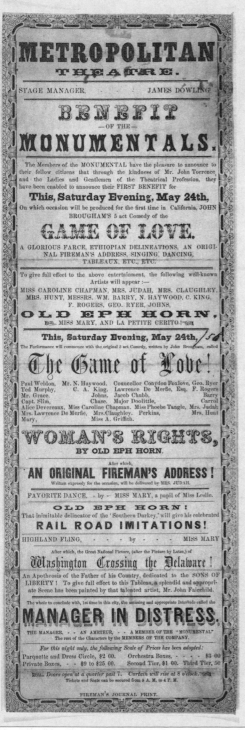

Metropolitan Theatre playbill—1856. —*Author's collection*

from piece to piece, an interpretive performance sometimes deemed "ahead of its time," but usually called scandalous. The city loved celebrity then as much as it does now and Lola received rousing applause from her audience, whom she thanked profusely.

The Metropolitan Theatre joined the American and San Francisco Hall in the fall of 1853. Built by Joseph Trench in a mixed Renaissance style, its furnishings and appointments eclipsed the two other theatres. With the installation of gas lighting in February of 1854, it became the first brilliantly lit theatre. Catherine Sinclair opened the Metropolitan, as both starring actress and manager with *The School for Scandal*, playing in the role of Lady Teazle. Sinclair had recently divorced husband Edwin Forrest, a highly accomplished thespian, escaping to San Francisco to start over and to avoid her ex-husband. Maguire with great instinct (or great malice) hired Forrest in 1866, transporting him to San Francisco to compete with his former spouse.

The great operatic star Madame Anna Bishop made her San Francisco debut at the Metropolitan on that same opening night, appearing as Agatha in *Der Freischutz*. The gaslight moon and stars shone on her as she sang her prayer for the safe return of her lover, the huntsman, and the audience held its collective breath. It was then that the San Francisco Gas Company service failed and the theatre plunged into darkness. She sat down on the stage and sobbed, as the audience poured out of the theatre. During her illustrious career, Anna Bishop returned repeatedly to the San Francisco stage.

In a game of positional leapfrog, July 1854 saw the demolition of the American Theatre and its reincarnation that December for the start of the season. The best reports concerning the new edifice claimed it was innovative, comfortable, and spacious. The worst called it a garish mix of Grecian and Oriental design, lacking harmony. The *Wide West* journal declared everything on the stage, including the new lighting was bad and labeled the drop curtain "a magnificent failure." "A statue of George Washington is in the foreground, with an imaginative view of the bay in the background, bearing a disproportionate clipper ship and an impossible steamship. Having accidentally placed a heavy cannon on the toes of the Father of his Country, the artist was obliged to give him a mournful expression of countenance corresponding to such an event." Not satisfied with denigrating just the facility, the critic then took on the cast and orchestra calling the former moderately good but not capable of entertainment, and it cast the latter as "abominable." The American languished in its mediocrity until a major remodeling in the spring of 1859 earned it acclamation as the finest and largest theatre in the city.

Maguire demolished San Francisco Hall in 1856, since it no longer served his needs. The theatre failed to hold the audience required and wasn't suitable for operatic performances, requiring additional space for the orchestra and a stage that would accommodate a large company and the associated scenery. In its place, he built Maguire's Opera House, the finest theatre in the city and certainly the most modern. Beyond that, Thomas Maguire built the first house in San Francisco dedicated mainly to opera and he did so in grand style. Originally home to Maguire's San Francisco Minstrels, it also hosted grand opera, farce, melodrama, and burlesque.

Ever the showman, Tom Maguire announced that on August 24, 1863, Maguire's Opera House would present the great Menkin in her unprecedented *Mazeppa*, in which "Miss Menkin, stripped by her captors, would ride a fiery steed at furious gallop onto and across the stage and into the distance." Rather than use the traditional stuffed dummy, Adah Menkin rode onto the stage in New York in skin-tights. The audience was shocked and scandalized. Declaring New York too proper to appreciate her art, Menkin said, "I'll go to the one place where the audience demands real art; I'll go to San Francisco."

The newspapers the next day reported that the city's elite thronged Maguire's Opera House. Arriving in handsome carriages, ladies wore diamonds and furs and the men were dressed in capes and silk hats. When "at the sensational climax of the play, the Menkin vaulted to the back of her full-blooded California mustang and, clad in the flesh-colored tights with her hair streaming down her back, galloped her steed at a mad pace across the mountains of Tartary, the enthusiasm of the audience was a mad frenzy never to be forgotten." However, Junius Booth, the leading man promptly forgot his lines or so legend claims. However, the Menkin found herself a home—San Francisco loved her.

Modest in its outside dimensions—fifty-five-feet wide, one-hundred thirty-seven deep, and fifty high, Maguire's new opera house appeared spacious indeed. The stage could accommodate elaborate scenery and a large cast. The enclosure for the orchestra provided enough space for the most elaborate production. Unlike the American Theatre, the curtain appropriately presented a scene of "the sea-born city of Venice with its domes, towers and palaces. One of the great canals is seen in front, with barques and gondolas floating upon it." as stated in the *Bulletin*. The main floor, all parquet, provided seating for seven hundred and the tier seated four hundred more. Improvements made a year and a half later added a second tier, with seating for an additional six hundred, and an additional ten feet increased the depth of the stage.

True to form in San Francisco, the Metropolitan Theatre burned to the ground on a Saturday night in the summer of 1857. Fortunately, the theatre was dark that night, the house empty. The San Francisco Fire Department garnered credit for saving Maguire's opera house next door but the Met proved a total loss. The site remained empty for five years.

CIVIL WAR AND SILVER

San Francisco and California played key roles in the American Civil War, a fact that played only indirectly into the status of the theatre. The state voted for Lincoln and for maintaining the Union, after a hard-fought campaign. Although many Southerners had settled in California, large numbers of volunteers shipped east to fight for the North. Theatres held benefits for volunteers headed east, for widows and orphans, and for regiments that distinguished themselves.

California's gold production was dwindling and now Nevada silver was king, helping to finance the war—nearly all of that silver transported to and through San Francisco. San Franciscans now unable to take up a pick and shovel to dig for silver instead invested in silver mine stocks. Silver required deep mining and heavy equipment to pull it from the mountains. Average people continued to get rich, but this time on paper-based profits. The bubble grew for fifteen years.

The telegraph now spanned coast-to-coast, so theatres could report news of the war prior to performances. Some theatres presented patriotic themes to disappointing crowds. The pubic wanted entertainment, not preaching. The city lost its wide-eyed innocence, taking theatre and its performers for granted. Impressive names drew impressive audiences but competition with the melodeons' skin-shows hurt the door receipts. A form of burlesque called leg shows or sensation dramas gained popularity

Gilbert's Melodeon offered a rougher sort of theatre—more girls and bawdy songs with little attempt at art. —*Photo courtesy of San Francisco History Center, San Francisco Public Library*

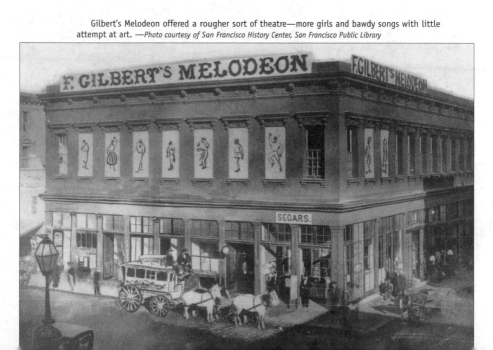

at legitimate theatres, competing with the saloon variety halls, typified by the Bella Union. These drew crowds but also poor reviews. The *Bulletin* wrote of its1862 production of *The Female Forty Thieves*, "It seems principally intended to introduce about two scores of female legs, nearly as good as naked, of all shapes, thicknesses and lengths, which parade for half an hour, or so, backward and forward on the stage." Still, variety shows, the precursor to vaudeville, suffered a decline in theatre attendance, in spite of the police raids and arrests for lewd, scandalous, and indecent exhibitions, that had previously created enhanced interest.

The year 1861 witnessed the rebuilding of the Metropolitan Theatre, built to compete with Maguire's theatres. That year minstrel shows dominated, with no record of operatic performances. The minstrel companies, both black and white, donned blackface and/or white eye circles, and with banjo and tambourines mimicked the slave culture in lingo, music, jokes, and stories in a celebration of racial prejudice. Minstrelsy thrived in San Francisco the 1860s, waned in the 1870s and died thereafter. San Francisco's population had tripled in the last ten years, but melodeon varieties reigned and theatre now struggled.

The Metropolitan Theatre first opened in 1853 and by 1854 had gas lighting. It burned to the ground in 1857 and was rebuilt in 1861. The photo is of the second theatre, taken in 1868. —*Photo courtesy of San Francisco History Center, San Francisco Public Library*

Thomas Maguire continued to expand his significant holdings in California theatre and managed to pull a profit from his ventures. Grasping an opportunity to take advantage of the various avenues of drama and musical theatre, he opened his Academy of Music on Pine Street just off Montgomery in May of 1864.

An early performance at the Academy of Music presented *Norton the First*, an operatic burlesque or burletta of San Francisco's beloved Emperor Joshua Norton, self-

The California Theatre opened in 1869, financed by William C. Ralston of the Bank of California. —*Photo courtesy of San Francisco History Center, San Francisco Public Library*

appointed as Emperor of the United States and Protector of Mexico. Norton went quietly mad after losing his fortune—or did he? A later burletta, *Life in San Francisco*, included Bummer and Lazarus, billed as Emperor Norton's devoted dogs. Comic opera, long the mainstay of the melodeons, had arrived in the theatre.

Though Maguire was said to be illiterate, his instincts were excellent. Recognizing a drop in attendance, Maguire sold the Academy of Music at a fair profit in 1867. The buyers refitted it as a furniture store. The American Theatre burned to the ground in 1868. The owners decided not to rebuild. Gas theatre lighting had proved to be both a blessing and a curse.

Others sought to join the theatre industry. William C. Ralston of the Bank of California bankrolled the building of the California Theatre on Bush Street, beginning construction in the year the American burned down. Ralston had made his fortune investing in the Comstock Lode, and he built a theatre far beyond anything ever seen in San Francisco. The doors opened on January 29, 1869, to a spectacle of marble floors and Corinthian columns, rich hangings of maroon, purple, crimson, and gold held and adorned with cords and tassels. Celebrated local artist G. J. Denny painted spectacular scenes of California in the woodworked facades of the upper circle, gallery circle, and boxes. The drop curtain presented a view of San Francisco's harbor, looking through the Golden Gate from a point northwest of the entrance. It pictured the Marin Coast and the channel through the Gate from Point Lobos and the Cliff House past Fort Point into the distance to the southeast.

The California Theatre's lighting created stunning effects. Using the latest Argand gas lamps, white, green and red stage lights produced varying hues. Eighty-one footlights in three rows and seven twenty-four-foot border lights overhead with twenty-five burners each, fitted with parabolic reflectors, lit up the stage. The theatre boasted being the first to use calcium light aimed at the stage from the auditorium. A single apparatus, compared to a piano, controlled each light.

Per the *San Francisco Chronicle*, "The depth of the stage measured from the footlights to the rear walls is 77 feet, and the width from side wall to side wall is 80 feet. The height of the underside of the rigging floor is 50 feet." The combination of moving flats and movable wings allowed "invisible" set changes, performed quickly. John McCullough and Lawrence Barrett jointly managed the theatre, both actors brought west by Maguire. Barrett recited an opening dedicatory address written by Bret Harte with Harte, Leland Stanford, James G. Fair, James Flood, and Emperor Norton, himself, in the audience. The performance of Bulwer-Lytton's *Money*, starring Marie Gordon and John McCullough, drew rave reviews. The new theatre eclipsed its competition, and McCullough became a new adversary for Maguire.

Lotta Crabtree returned to San Francisco in 1869, and performed at the California Theatre, starring in John Brougham's *Little Nell and the Marchioness*, which had been written for her. It heralded her first return to the city's legitimate theatre after her disappointing single night debut as Le Petite Lotta

Lotta Crabtree started her career singing in the gold camps at eight years old in 1853. She became the protégé of Lola Montez. Lotta was always a favorite on San Francisco's stages and she loved the city. She left Lotta's Fountain in thanks. Her last stage appearance was at the Panama Pacific International Exposition in 1915. —*Author's collection*

at the American in November of 1856. Following that early experience, Lotta trod the boards at the melodeons before taking her show abroad. Now she was back and the city loved her more than ever.

The advent of the transcontinental railroad opened San Francisco to more East Coast talent. It also provided an easy escape for San Francisco's performers to try different markets. The in-and-out movement of performers markedly increased the variety of theatric opportunities for audiences.

The 1870s witnessed a serious decline in classic opera, as light opera and opera bouffe, or comic opera, took its place. When drama and music left empty seats, acrobats, minstrels, and even boxing matches filled the bill. The economy was on a roller coaster and theatre went along for the ride. The theatre market continued to churn. The Congress Hall Melodeon on Bush Street converted to Shiel's Opera House in 1873, and was later called the Standard Theatre. Shiel's represented one of the fine small houses.

Minstrelsy was highly popular in the late 1870s. This playbill was printed in 1878. —*Author's collection*

Maguire managed Shiel's, as well as the Alhambra Theatre, but his luck was failing. According to the *San Francisco Call*, the people cried out for opera, but only about four hundred patrons ever attended an operatic event. Italian fishermen understood opera and wanted to attend, but most couldn't come up with the two dollars for the cheapest seats. When Maguire found he was short of chorus singers, he went to the docks and hired the Italians. They could sing and they knew all the music. Still, it became a losing proposition, with theatres barely making expenses from one season to the next.

Some thought they could succeed where others had struggled. Two new theatres premiered in 1876. Wade's Opera House opened at Mission and Third streets, built by Dr. Thomas Wade, a dentist. Wade's claimed to be the biggest theatre in the country,

Entrance to the Alhambra Theatre on Bush near Montgomery. Built by Tom Maguire in the early 1870s, he sold it in 1877 after the Comstock crash. It was renamed the Bush Street Theatre. —*Author's Collection*

originally seating twenty-five hundred and it certainly was the most elaborate and plush. It exceeded everything California had offered previously and at a cost of three-quarters of a million dollars, it was to be expected. The stage measured eighty-five feet in depth, one hundred and six feet in width and was one hundred feet high. Flats measured twenty-four feet in height and could be lowered down to and stored in the basement. Still more marvelous, the entire facility used the new electric lighting—no gas lights anywhere. It opened on January 17, 1876, with a performance of *Snowflake*, starring Anne Pixley, and based on *Snow White and the Seven Dwarfs*. Wade's Opera House donned the common name of Grand Opera House and the performances pleased its audiences but the returns failed to match the expenses. The size of the house exceeded its audience's ability to fill it.

The other theatre to open that year was the Baldwin Opera House, also called Baldwin's Academy of Music or just Baldwin's Theatre, and it was situated on the six-story Baldwin Hotel. Though smaller than Wade's, it maintained the elegant standards expected. The theatre opened on March 6, 1876, with the great Barry Sullivan in the role of *Richard III*. The theatre was built by Elias Jackson "Lucky" Baldwin on the advice of Tom Maguire and on Tom's lot, and it soon became an issue between Maguire and Baldwin. Maguire managed it, but Baldwin expected profits. Maguire, as always, put the arts first. Neither could have known that Lucky's luck was running out.

Ill winds, already present, picked up their pace in 1877. The Bank of California, owner of the California Theatre, failed in 1875. William Ralston, the bank's treasurer, went for his daily swim off Black Point afterward and drowned. Suicide? No one could say, but the bank reorganized, the city survived the shock, and the California Theatre changed hands. However, the economy, driven by stock speculation, remained unbalanced.

The seasonal California wheat crop planted in the fall of 1876 failed due to a dry winter, as did the production of wool. This, coupled with diminished mineral yields in California and Nevada, caused concern among the speculators. Mining and agricultural workers migrated to San Francisco searching employment. The city's population boomed from one hundred fifty thousand reported in the 1870 census to nearly two hundred twenty-five thousand in 1877, but most of that increase were unemployed. Investment in San Francisco's sound manufacturing businesses had declined in previous years due to speculation in mining stocks. Speculators now retrenched their investments and immediately stopped spending. Merchants and manufacturers recognized a decrease in demand and cut employees and salaries. Many city manufacturers, already impacted by previous investment patterns, simply closed their doors. San Francisco's economy crashed, bringing the theatre to its knees.

Baldwin made his fortune trading on the Comstock Bonanza. Years earlier, he ordered his broker to sell some of his Comstock investments and then set sail for India, with the key to his safe in his pocket. On his return, he'd learned that his stock value had increased to over five million dollars. The 1877 crash reversed that position, and Baldwin found himself property rich but strapped for cash. His wrangling with Maguire resulted in management of the Baldwin Theatre transferring to John McCullough but when McCullough fared even worse, the theater reverted to Maguire again. Maguire closed and sold the Alhambra, which reopened as the Bush Street Theatre.

The late 1870s and early 1880s represented a period of forced innovation. Audiences wanted much for their now hard-earned dollars and the critics turned venomous. It took five years to recover from the depression, but San Francisco emerged a bit wiser and somewhat more discriminating.

Thomas Maguire, with the financial assistance of "Lucky" Baldwin, produced the *Passion Play* at the Grand Opera House in the spring of 1879, which stirred more than passion. The Jewish and Irish Catholic citizenry joined in a furor over the blasphemy committed and the city fathers promptly shut it down. Maguire revived it for Easter week at the request of James O'Neill (father of Eugene O'Neill), who gave the performance of his life, but he also paid a fine of fifty dollars. Cast members pitched in to pay the fine.

Maguire staged *Carmen* at the Grand, but the audience turned their collective back on him and it flopped. His influence and role at the Baldwin continued to dwindle and by the early 1880s, he was no longer bankable and he left for New York. Reports to the *Chronicle* claimed growing success and excellent health, but, in fact, Maguire was destitute, supported only by the Actor's Fund. He died penniless and alone in New York in 1896.

Opportunity smiles even during hard times, though perhaps not so often. Joe Kreling's Tivoli Gardens opened on Sutter Street, between Powell and Stockton. The front of the building was similar in appearance to any other residence on the street but the inside hosted a beer garden and the ten-piece Vienna Ladies' Orchestra, supported between numbers by a chorus of Tyrolean singers. This form of entertainment was new to the city and it prospered. Also, the music of the comic operas proved most popular and Kreling dreamed of a palace for musical comedy.

Fate decided to give Joe his wish. His Tivoli Gardens burned to the ground in 1879, and he replaced it with the Tivoli Opera House, saving the ambience of the gardens by retaining tables in the pit, in the balconies, and the galleries. A beautiful gaslight chandelier hung from the ceiling and lit the stage. Garlands and festoons of flowers draped the stage and statues stood proudly on the sides. Waiters served beer and cheese sandwiches while the actors performed. Gilbert and Sullivan's *HMS Pin-afore* opened at the new house on July 3, 1879, for a successful run of sixty-three nights. The Tivoli Opera House defined its own niche and it prospered.

One innovation of the 1890s stands out—the Tivoli hired a musical comedy stock company composed of singers and comedians, learning a new role every few weeks. This innovation rotated new shows and kept the theatre fresh. However, the city declared the Tivoli Opera House a firetrap in 1903, and manager Doc Leahy ordered it torn down. It was rebuilt at Mason and Eddy streets in 1904.

The Alcazar Theatre rose as the final theatre of note built in nineteenth-century San Francisco. Michael de Young, publisher of the *San Francisco Chronicle*, built the house in 1885 as a multiuse facility for family-oriented theater, concert hall, and lecture hall. Its Moorish

The Tivoli Opera House (shown) replaced the Tivoli Gardens in 1879.

facade, advanced mechanics, and modern lighting, gaslights lit by electricity, created an attractive facility for both performers and audience. The theatre employed a regular company with guests gracing the boards in leading roles. Eddie Foy entertained as a member of that company on two different occasions.

The Baldwin experienced the worst disaster in San Francisco's theatre history to date on the early morning of November 23, 1898. A fire started in the scene lofts and quickly spread through the theatre and hotel, causing great loss of life and the total destruction of the hotel and theatre. The estimated loss of two and a half million dollars, balanced against one-hundred eighty-five thousand dollars in insurance, left Baldwin again cash poor. He sold the land located at the corner of Powell and Market to James L. Flood for just over a million dollars.

The century turned with much fanfare while San Francisco sat poised on its defining event. On April 18, 1906, at 5:12 A.M. San Francisco jolted awake with a pre-shock earthquake. Seconds later the city felt the full force of a devastating earthquake that measured 8.3 on the Richter scale. The city's downtown crumbled and broken gas lines burst into flame. San Francisco burned for three days and when it finally burned itself out, the only theatre remaining was the playhouse at the Chutes.

The previous night found Enrico Caruso performing in *Carmen* at the Grand Opera House. He gave this account of the great earthquake:

> You ask me to say what I saw and what I did during the terrible days which witnessed the destruction of San Francisco? Well, there have been many accounts of my so-called adventures published in the American papers, and most of them have not been quite correct. Some of the papers said that I was terribly frightened, that I went half crazy with fear, that I dragged my valise out of the hotel into the square and sat upon it and wept; but all this is untrue. I was frightened, as many others were, but I did not lose my head. I was stopping at the [Palace] Hotel, where many of my fellow-artists were staying, and very comfortable it was. I had a room on the fifth floor, and on Tuesday evening, the night before the great catastrophe, I went to bed feeling very contented. I had sung in "Carmen" that night, and the opera had one with fine *éclat*. We were all pleased, and, as I said before, I went to bed that night feeling happy and contented.
>
> But what an awakening! You must know that I am not a very heavy sleeper—I always wake early, and when I feel restless I get up and go for a walk. So on the Wednesday morning early I wake up about 5 o'clock, feeling my bed rocking as though I am in a ship on the ocean, and for a moment I think I am dreaming that I am crossing the water on my way to my beautiful country. And so I take no notice for the moment, and then, as the rocking continues, I get up and go to the window, raise the shade and look out. And what I see makes me tremble with fear. I see the buildings toppling over, big

pieces of masonry falling, and from the street below I hear the cries and screams of men and women and children.

I remain speechless, thinking I am in some dreadful nightmare, and for something like forty seconds I stand there, while the buildings fall and my room still rocks like a boat on the sea. And during that forty seconds I think of forty thousand different things. All that I have ever done in my life passes before me, and I remember trivial things and important things. I think of my first appearance in grand opera, and I feel nervous as to my reception, and again I think I am going through last night's "Carmen."

The city and its theatres rose from the ashes once more. The Orpheum leased the Chutes and launched its first production on May 20, 1906. San Francisco built new theatres—its citizens needed diversions from the terror of catastrophe. But an era closed, one of strong characters, innovation, and risk.

Today, San Francisco remains a theatre and opera town, devoted to its stage. To say nothing worthy of note happened in the city since the great earthquake and fire of 1906 would be a gross injustice. The twentieth century was unable to match the zeal of San Francisco theatre in its first ten years, the Golden Era or even its first thirty. Still, San Francisco supports its own world-class opera, a company of the highest regard and dedication housed in the city's own War Memorial Opera House. San Francisco offers everything from the finest local theatre, such as A.C.T., to traveling companies presenting every genre of production, some great, some tripe, but little created locally. Additionally, the city now boasts a few wonderful small theatres capable of surprising and greatly entertaining the audience. After the rebuilding, the city matured enough to build new houses for the theatre and opera, some which would last the next one hundred years, with an occasional refurbishing. Others were converted into movie theatres and most of those later met the wrecker's ball. The city cries out for a Thomas Maguire to revitalize its theatre.

The Grand Court of the California Midwinter International Exposition. *—Collection of Christopher Charles*

Chapter 6

California Midwinter International Exposition—1894

Before San Francisco became self-focused, the city loved to show itself off to the world. Celebrating its wonderful winter weather, the city's 1894 Midwinter Fair displayed the latest technology available, including newly harnessed electricity. The opening of the Panama Canal and the expected increased ship trade was the reason for the 1915 Panama-Pacific International Exhibition. The 1939 World's Fair required the creation of the new Treasure Island in San Francisco Bay and focused on the city's two new bridges, the Golden Gate Bridge and the San Francisco-Oakland Bay Bridge.

The true reasons for the three fairs differed from the published purposes. San Francisco and California fought the throes of a devastating depression in the early 1890s after the crash of the silver stocks. The 1894 Midwinter Fair provided an opportunity to draw the world to the Port of San Francisco in an open invitation to trade and investment. The 1915 Panama-Pacific International Exposition presented a rebuilt San Francisco to the world—the city was back and better than ever after the great quake and subsequent fire of 1906. The 1939 Golden Gate International Exposition and World's Fair introduced two new bridges, the Golden Gate Bridge and the San Francisco-Oakland Bay Bridge, each the largest in its class, both reducing the isolation of the peninsular city. The 1939 fair also placed a bid for increased trade between San Francisco and the world with a focus on the Pacific Rim countries. Each of these expositions promised great entertainment for locals and for tourists drawn from around the world but their goals remained adding an influx of cash to the local economy and trade expansion for the city of San Francisco and the state of California and its neighbors.

CALIFORNIA MIDWINTER INTERNATIONAL EXPOSITION—1894

The 1892 Chicago Columbian Exposition known commonly as the Chicago World Fair drew thousands of exhibitors from the United States and around the world. Near the close of the fair, many exhibitors bemoaned the mixed quality of the exhibits as well as the expense of tearing down and shipping their exhibits home. Edward Everett Hale said of the Vienna Exposition, "If this be a specimen of the world, then one wants a museum which shall be a specimen of the Exposition." The desire to consolidate into a smaller, more select follow-up event caught the attention of Michael Harry de Young, vice-president of the Columbian Commission and California commissioner to the 1889

California International Exposition Grounds. —*Author's collection*

Opening Day of the California Midwinter International Exposition, San Francisco, January 27, 1894. —*Courtesy of The Bancroft Library, University of California, Berkeley*

Paris fair. Co-founder and publisher of the *San Francisco Chronicle*, de Young recognized an opportunity for his city. San Francisco provided an ideal environment for the envisioned scaled-down fair. In midwinter, with most of the country locked in cold and snow, San Francisco and California wore robes of emerald, its hills and valleys an iridescent green. The 1892 Chicago fair was proving a disappointment to California, unable to display her resources, achievements, and potential adequately.

On June 1, 1893, de Young announced his plans to open a midwinter fair in San Francisco by January of 1894, less than eight months hence. Wealthy San Franciscans visiting the Chicago fair scoffed at the idea. It couldn't be done in so short a time. Taking it to the people through local politicians and his newspaper, de Young held a second Chicago meeting on June 11, and declared $41,500 already subscribed to begin the project. Within days forty-four hundred exhibitors promised to move to San Francisco at the close of the Columbian Exhibition in Chicago. However, only those of superior quality were accepted. By August, with sufficient funds raised and approval by congress confirmed, midwinter fair transitioned from concept to reality. The fair committee, with de Young as its president, selected Golden Gate Park as the site, dedicating the land on August 24 with sixty thousand in attendance. The committee raised more than three hundred and fifty thousand dollars in subscriptions to fund the fair, none from the federal, state, or local governments. The awarding of contracts for the structures took place in late September and, after four short months, on January 27, 1894, the California Midwinter International Exhibition formally opened. The grounds actually opened early in December allowing visitors to preview the fair as it was assembled.

Throughout the country, large numbers of the well-to-do took the opportunity to escape the snow and cold via train in order to see the fair and the state of California. Many wealthy farmers envisioned a chance to decide for themselves if California agriculture measured up to the stories. "Investment Opportunity" touted the Eastern newspapers. Invest before the Nicaragua (Panama) Canal opens and with it, unlimited trade with the East. The canal took nearly another twenty years and a revolution to complete, but the investments remained sound.

Descriptions of the fair varied, some calling it barely worthy of notice, but the vast majority using the words "magnificent" and "dazzling" in their descriptions. The grounds encompassed two hundred acres, centered on what is now the sycamore-shaded Music Concourse in Golden Gate Park. The city's landscape gardeners, managed by the stubborn Scotsman John McLaren, planted thousands of trees. McLaren detested the concept of midwinter fair yet did his utmost to blend it in subtropical greenery. His vision for the park was a serene place without signs, statues, or undue ornamentation.

The fair centered on a large quadrangle of land consisting of a series of courts, including the central Grand Court and the Court of Honor, all surrounded by a roadway. These sunken gardens made up the main concourse, today called the Music Concourse. Erected in the center of the Grand Court, Bonet's Tower rose to a height of two hundred and sixty-six feet. Designed to display the power of municipal electricity, it

View of Lake Alvord. —*Collection of Christopher Charles*

presented a beacon drawing people to the fair. Constructed similar to the Eiffel Tower, the top supported an electric spotlight capable of two and a half million candlepower. Promoters claimed it threw a light so intense one could read a newspaper under its rays ten miles away and distinguish a ship at a distance of fifteen miles. Thousands of lights decorated the tower, outlining its structure in a breathtaking electric light show. The Belvista Café huddled beneath the center of Bonet's Tower.

The Palace of Fine Arts, constructed in brick and stone and designed in a tasteful Egyptian revival style, stood in the same position as the current M. H. de Young Museum. Palm and lotus leaves adorned the exterior, as well as Egyptian deities, all carved in low relief. A pair of stone sphinxes guarded the entryway and the vestibule floor dazzled visitors with its mosaic of ancient Egyptian figures. The interior blazed with Egyptian adornments, heads of birds and

Allegorical Fountain. —*Collection of Christopher Charles*

beasts, emblems, and friezes. The main ceiling rose to form a pyramid and the walls emulated the yellow sands of the Nile.

Electric Tower at night, with the searchlight on Strawberry Hill. —*Courtesy of The Bancroft Library, University of California, Berkeley*

The central hall housed most of the statuary, the adjoining chambers contained the watercolors, and the annex displayed the oils. Representative artwork arrived from the Chicago Fair presented by France, England, Russia, Poland, Italy, Canada, Spain, and Germany. They included pieces from Jules Dupré, Charles-Francois Daubigny, Jean-Baptiste Corot, Claude Monet, Jean-Jacques Henner, and Konstantin Egorovich Makovsky. The display also included American artwork, featuring the finest collection of California art ever assembled, and displayed the works of twenty-eight women. Local artists such as Alice B. Chittenden, known for her outstanding floral paintings, Helen Hyde for her paintings of non-Caucasian children, and Dora Williams, whose watercolors captured the imagination and helped prove the open mindedness of San Francisco were represented.

The Agriculture and Horticulture Building erected next to and just west of the Palace of Fine Arts on the north side of the main concourse highlighted California's abundance in agriculture, viticulture, dairy, fisheries, and forestry products. Agriculture had far surpassed the state's production of mineral wealth in value to the economy and the fair provided an opportunity to promote it. In 1893, California's wheat production alone brought in over eighteen million dollars, while mining of her precious metals only accounted for thirteen million dollars. The state had reinvented itself and the Horticulture Building reflected that new bounty, enticing fair goers to invest in this new economy.

Horticulture and Agriculture Building. —*Collection of Christopher Charles*

The Viticultural Palace, California State Wine Exhibit. —*Courtesy of The Bancroft Library, University of California, Berkeley*

The mission-style, adobe-colored building enclosed a massive single room consisting of a rotunda and two wings. A glass-covered dome one hundred feet in diameter towered over the rotunda, with two smaller domes flanking the main entrance in the center. The wooden interior of the wings reflected the rustic look of a giant barn providing an ideal display background.

Surrounded by the agricultural groupings from other counties, a striking architectural fruit display from Fresno County rose up in the center of the rotunda. A rotating Ferris wheel of oranges occupied an adjacent court. Richly designed pavilions and rows of display booths, interspersed with trees, ferns and flowering plants, displayed the best that both California and its neighbors had to offer. The latest in farm implements caught the attention of the state's farmers, and a model fish hatchery from Mendocino County presented the latest innovations in aquaculture. Manufactured food products and dressed meats abounded. The galleries of the second floor overflowed with endless displays of various harvested grains, fine wines, malted brews, and distilled spirits as well as seasonal fruit, flowers of every description, native or not, and forest specimens and products including the displays of the state board of horticulture. The color, fragrance and visual displays rivaled those of the most spacious and richly stocked conservatories.

In addition to the main Agriculture and Horticulture Building, the Southern and Northern California buildings, located off the concourse, offered horticultural displays specific to those regions. Each highlighted the resources of the region, with very little overlap. Rather than choose a region, potential farmers could determine what they wanted to grow and then learn where it grew best. California put its best foot forward in promoting her natural wealth, and the displays impressed the world.

Southern California Exhibition Building. —*Author's collection*

The Administration Building sat at the far western end of the concourse. Decked out in a Moorish architecture, its great, gold center dome and four corresponding corner domes, atop a castle-like structure, gave it a commanding presence over the fair. The streaming sunlight shining through the tall cathedral windows augmented the electric interior lighting. Supporting a major enterprise, the building was a beehive of activity. The building housed the fair managers, the foreign department, and served as headquarters for the press.

Continuing counter-clockwise, the Mechanical Arts Building stood on the south side of the concourse near the Steinhart Aquarium and Museum of Natural Sciences. The Oriental theme again prevailed, featuring a design reminiscent of an Indian temple with its lofty pinnacles and gilded kiosks. Prayer towers stood guard at the corners and stately minarets graced the

Alameda County Building. —*Collection of Christopher Charles*

San Joaquin County Building. —*Collection of Christopher Charles*

entrance pavilion and the recessed third floor structure. A giant arched opening marked the entrance, mimicked by secondary entrances on the sides and by the first and third story windows. Ivory, accented in turquoise and gold, dominated with roofs of orange tile. The rear of the building hid the furnace smokestacks and the boiler house required for its operation.

The types of machinery displayed dictated the three interior divisions—mines, including mining and metallurgy; transportation, covering railways, vessels, and vehicles; and electricity, highlighting generation and electrical appliances. The rear of the building housed the thirty-one hundred horsepower steam engines and the dynamos that provided electricity for light and power to the fairgrounds and buildings. The mining exhibits of California occupied a major portion of the main floor and displayed the mineral wealth of the state. In the center, a large gilded globe rested on a granite pedestal supported by granite columns. The globe illustrated California's total reported yield of gold to date. If made of that metal, the globe would weigh two thousand, seventy-one tons and would represent a value of one point three billion 1894-valued dollars or just over twenty-seven billion dollars converted to inflated 2003 values.

The Mechanical Arts Building housed models of railroads and steamboats, electrical appliances by General Electric Company, as well as electrical devices from coun-

Mechanical Arts Building. —*Collection of Christopher Charles*

tries as far away as Germany. Running engines of every sort reverberated throughout the facility. Displays of mining techniques and machinery plus specimens from around the state, touted the state's mineral wealth.

The Manufactures and Liberal Arts Hall, located on the east end of the concourse, contained three divisions—manufactures, liberal arts and ethnology/archeology. The largest of all the buildings, it mirrored the Moorish style of the Administration Building on the opposite end of the concourse. The porticoed facade sheltered a deeply recessed arcade that extended from each side of the central domed court. Secondary domes, minarets, and spires bore flags of different states and countries. The Quonset-style roof of glass and dark red Spanish tiles opened onto a lower roof garden planted in fuchsias, palms, chrysanthemums, and other plants that thrived in the mild California winter.

The division of liberal arts filled the upper galleries. The University of California exhibit occupied the entire north gallery, overlooking the full interior of the building. Decorated in Greek style, using blue and gold, the school's colors, its displays richly illustrated the achievements of the university. The Lick astronomical department exhibited photographs and photographic transparencies taken at the Lick Observatory located on Mount Hamilton in San Jose. The display highlighted its great success achieved in the merging of astronomy and photography and proved a major attraction to those who could peer through a telescope. Each department, whether academic or technical, displayed its best works. The mathematical department presented a beautiful collection of mathematical models, decipherable to only a few.

The east gallery presented an extensive photographic display of life and education at Yale University, the only Eastern school represented. Other California schools joined Yale on the east gallery, including Cogswell Technical School, Mills College, and the California School for the Deaf and Dumb and its associated School for the Blind, which presented practical explanations of its methods of instruction. The largest scholastic representation after the University of California was that of the Brothers of Chris-

Manufactures and Liberal Arts Hall—manufactured goods and anthropological displays, exhibited by countries worldwide. —*Courtesy of The Bancroft Library, University of California, Berkeley*

tian Schools, promoting the work of Saint Joseph's Academy and the colleges of Saint Mary and Sacred Heart. The remaining scholastic exhibits were from private schools and they varied greatly in content and excellence.

The division of manufacturers presented displays devoted to manufacturing equipment, processes, and products. Most of the displays came directly from the 1892 Columbian Exhibition in Chicago. The division of ethnology and archaeology presented "models and views of ancient monuments, cities and habitations; the furniture, clothing, implements and weapons of aboriginal races; inventions and statues and portraits of inventors; objects which illustrate progress in the conditions of life and labor." The displays represented collections from thirty-eight nationalities, gathered from all corners of the world, both modern and primitive.

In all, contractors had erected over one hundred buildings for the fair within four months. Counties, regions, and adjacent states contracted buildings to house their collections and displays. Concessions, eateries, and attractions popped up almost overnight. Twenty-five cents gained general admission prior to the grand opening, and the entrance cost was fifty cents thereafter.

The Midwinter Fair promised more than just a celebration of commerce, education, and the arts. Indeed, the fair had its delights. Cultural exhibits offered a view of life far different from those of the visitors. Moor's South Sea Island village presented the islanders in their native dress. Cannibal dances, club drills, and sword drills all performed by men with expressive gestures and poses to the beat of a drum chilled the viewers. Bare-breasted women demonstrated women's work, including food preparation, basket making, and the stringing of flowers into leis. Some were shocked by the nudity but it was all done for the sake of scientific curiosity.

A Japanese village, located west of the Horticulture Building, took the form of a Japanese garden with pavilions and a traditional teahouse. Makoto Hagiwara, a wealthy local Japanese landscape designer and member of Japan's aristocracy, funded, built, and managed the project, depleting the family fortune for his labor of love. Japan remained a great unknown to most Americans at this time, maintaining a closed society. The few Japanese who immigrated to San Francisco proved very different from the local Chinese population. The village offered an opportunity for Mr. Hagiwara to share his unique culture.

Japanese Village—replaced by the
Japanese Tea Garden, Golden Gate Park.
—*Courtesy of The Bancroft Library, University of California, Berkeley*

The first fortune cookies served in the United States were to patrons of the Japanese village at the Midwinter Fair. Mr. Hagiwara asked his baker, Ben-Kyo-Do, to produce the Japanese "Tsuji ura sembei," or sembei cookies, served at Shinto shrines during the New Year celebration. They were sweetened to appeal to Western tastes, and kimono-garbed hostesses served them with tea as welcome refreshment to visitors, often gratis. Modern fortune cookies are not Chinese in origin and, yes, they did originate in San Francisco in 1894.

Other cultural exhibits included an Esquimaux (Eskimo) village, a Hawaiian cyclorama with the volcano Kilauea erupting, Cairo Street, a Chinese joss (gambling)

Above: Chinese Pavilion. —*Collection of Christopher Charles*

Right: Cairo Street Theatre—a touch of the exotic. —*Courtesy of The Bancroft Library, University of California, Berkeley*

house and theatre, an Arizona village featuring American Indians, a Colorado gold mine and a forty-niner camp, theatre and dance house, called Gold Gulch. Amazed by the lack of a school or church represented in the camp, visitors learned that there were very few women and no children in the early camps. The demonstrations of early mining techniques and the display of appliances for modern mining drew considerable interest. More than a few visitors were enticed by the exhibits to try their hand in the gold fields following the fair. This author's great-grandfather William Smith quit his position as an accountant for Brown Brothers Men's Clothing and by 1895 bought a gold claim in the Tehachapi Mountains in Kern County, down south.

The Midway abounded with attractions guaranteed to please. Colonel Boone's Arena featured trained wild animals, a show previously offered by Woodward's Gar-

Gambling house in '49 Camp at California Midwinter International Exposition. —*Courtesy of The Bancroft Library, University of California, Berkeley*

dens. Boone's show featured a lion standing in a chariot with the reins between his teeth while being drawn around the ring by a pair of tigers. A trained wolf jumped through a fiery ring and other animals went through their routines. The Ceylon Pavilion served Asian delicacies and a fragrant tea much loved by the fair goers. Mrs. Carolina S. Brooks, the Centennial Butter Sculptress, produced statues carved in butter, a medium that allowed for quick results. She was, in fact, an artist famous in San Francisco, and she later converted her butter to successes in fine marble.

Thrill rides drew the crowd. These included the Firth Wheel, designed to compete with the Ferris Wheel, Dante's Inferno, a journey through the burning lakes and bottomless pits of Hell. The Moorish Mirror Maze, a scenic railroad around the park, and a merry-go-round offered fun for all ages. The Haunted Swing proved a favorite. A large swing hung suspended from a beam inside a large furnished parlor. Two or three dozen people entered one of six compartments on the swing, the electric lights were switched on, and the doors closed. The swing rocked lightly as the young operator warned the folks not to be nervous. Each oscillation of the swing rotated it higher until the youth shouted, "Now, over she goes!" The swing quickly rotated until the riders felt themselves hanging from the ceiling looking down on the chairs, table, and piano each wondering how they could remain suspended without falling out of the swing. People crawled under the seats and others called out to whatever saint appealed to them. In fact, the swing did not go over—the room did. The swing only provided the gentle motion needed to create the illusion that the rotating room remained stationary.

The Midwinter Fair finally closed on July 9, 1894, a ten-day extension to allow for a rousing Independence Day celebration. The attendance of the fair totaled 2,255,551 although that number likely included free passes. Subscriptions totaled $361,000, while the improvements cost $730,000. Income from gate and others receipts surpassed the costs and the difference, said to be $129,000, funded the creation of the Midway Fair Memorial Museum. However, the unspoken goal of the fair was to generate a recovery from the depression that gripped the state. While no instant cure appeared, the recovery had begun, thanks to the fair and the trade it inspired. By 1898 and the start of the Spanish-American War, California had already rebounded.

Following the closing of the fair, all structures fell to the wrecker's ball with the exception of the Japanese village and the Palace of Fine Arts. Makoto Hagiwara and his family, who built the village, maintained it under a handshake agreement with John McLaren, and it operated it as the Japanese Tea Garden. The family maintained the garden, living there until 1942 when the federal government sent the Hagiwaras an eviction notice and transported them to a concentration camp in the interior. Renamed the Oriental Tea Garden, it fell into disrepair, lacking the intricate care necessary to maintain it. After the war, the city refused the Hagiwaras' request to resume management of the garden per McLaren's promise and also failed to reimburse them for the cost of creating and maintaining it. In March of 1974, the City of San Francisco placed a bronze plaque in the garden honoring the family for their accomplishments and service. Unfortunately, the garden bears little resemblance in look and aesthetic feel to the Japanese Tea Garden of the Hagiwara family.

The Palace of Fine Arts remained a museum, the collections primarily funded and managed by Michael Harry de Young. Originally named the Memorial Museum, the city later renamed it the M. H. de Young Museum after his death. Expanded in

Firth Wheel, competitor to Chicago's new 1893 Ferris Wheel. The Firth Wheel was designed for the MidWinter Fair. It was moved just east of the Sutro Baths after the fair closed. —*Courtesy of The Bancroft Library, University of California, Berkeley*

1917, the original structure survived the quake of 1906 but not the inspectors of 1926. Declared unsafe, it was dismantled and rebuilt. It closed again after the year 2000 due to structural damage caused by the Loma Prieta earthquake of 1989. Demolished shortly after its closing, the new museum opened October 15, 2005.

Interior of the Fine Arts Building—this became the first de Young Museum. —*Courtesy of The Bancroft Library, University of California, Berkeley*

Avenue of the Palms—the most popular thoroughfare after The Zone. *—Author's collection*

Chapter 7

Panama-Pacific International Exposition - 1915

In 1904, ten years after San Francisco staged its epic California Midwinter International Exposition, Reuben B. Hale proposed another international exposition in San Francisco to celebrate the opening of the Panama Canal. Hale, a respected member of the San Francisco Merchant's Exchange, recognized a great commercial advantage to the city. His proposal drew an immediate and enthusiastic response. Planning the campaign and gathering the necessary funding began at once. Representative Julius Kahn of San Francisco introduced a bill in the House asking for the appointment of a federal commission and an appropriation of five million dollars contingent on a matching sum raised in San Francisco.

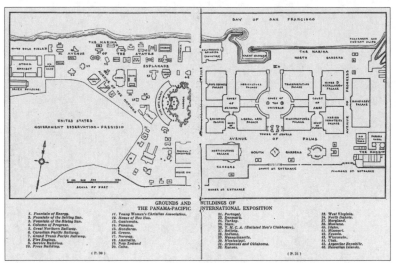

Grounds and buildings of the Panama-Pacific International Exposition. —*Author's collection*

As with many city activities, the great earthquake and fire of April 18, 1906 put the plans on hold. By December of that same year, with the rebuilding well underway, the proponents resurrected the concept and created the Pacific Ocean Exposition Company to promote the fair. Planning crawled due to reconstruction priorities until October 1909 when President William Taft announced January 1, 1915, as the date for the opening of the canal. A meeting of the Merchant's Exchange held on December 7, 1909, created a ways and means committee that resulted in a resolution to create a company to fund and operate the exposition. The Panama-Pacific International Exposition Company incorporated March 22, 1910.

Local support for the exposition rallied and, at a meeting on April 29, 1910, the membership subscribed over four million dollars in two hours. Within two months an additional two million dollars bolstered the fund. Charles C. Moore, a leading San Francisco businessman known for his success with San Francisco's 1909 Portola Festival, earned the position as president of the exposition.

Contesting San Francisco's claim as site for the fair, New Orleans mounted its own campaign citing its centralized location. California governor Gilette pushed the state legislature to raise five million dollars to be paid for by a general state tax, permitting San Francisco to issue bonds for that same amount. Given that sum plus the subscribed funds, San Francisco proposed to use no federal funds, an offer New Orleans failed to match. New Orleans and the South continued to press their claim. The

The Exposition site before the start of construction—pre-1913. —*Library of Congress*

California delegation, joined by Charles Moore, R. B. Hale, M. H. de Young, James McNab, W. C. Ralston, William Crocker, William R. Hearst, Julius Kahn, and Governor Gilette, among others, waged a brilliant strategic campaign. On January 31, 1911, Congress passed a hotly contested resolution by a vote of 188 to 159 authorizing the president to invite the world to the Panama-Pacific International Exposition at San Francisco in 1915. The fair honored the discovery of the Pacific Ocean by Vasco Nuñez de Balboa in 1513 and the planned completion of the Panama Canal in 1915.

THE PLANNING BEGINS

Choosing a site for the exposition proved problematic. Advocates promoted Lincoln Park, Lake Merced, and Golden Gate Park, hoping to gain structures and landscaping of lasting value. Others proposed the Presidio and Harbor View (the heart of today's Marina District), citing the opportunity to expand the city by filling in the unimproved tideland without causing a delay in the opening. The directors chose portions of four sites, excluding Lake Merced. On October 13, 1911, President Taft broke ground in Golden Gate Park before one hundred thousand people. Shortly thereafter, the architects countered that the exposition should consist of a grouping of the grounds and structures for esthetic and attendance reasons. The site quickly reverted to Harbor View with a portion of the Presidio included.

The architectural commission represented a national Who's Who of that field led by San Francisco's Willis Polk. Polk introduced the California mission and brown shingle styles of architecture to California and designed San Francisco's Hallidie Building at 130 Sutter Street, notably the first in North America built with glass curtain-wall construction creating an all-glass facade. He also designed the two San Francisco Water Temples at Sunol and Crystal Springs but gained fame for what he gave away. Polk set aside the Palace of Fine Arts project for himself, but later gave the project to his friend Bernard Maybeck after reviewing Maybeck's conceptual design. Maybeck later wrote to Polk, "You have put up a monument to your ideals (through me) and made a sacrifice for them—there is in you a yearning for the highest ideals." Maybeck, a humble man, used that comment to give the credit back to Polk for the trust Polk had placed in him. The Palace of Fine Arts remains today as a monument to Polk, Maybeck, and the artistry of the fair.

The architects completed their plans by the end of 1912 on schedule, a first for any international exposition. The resultant plans created an exposition city of such artistic unity that it stands today as the finest example of world's fair architecture and aesthetics.

BUILDING THE EXPOSITION

The work of preparing the site proceeded concurrently with the design. The team built a seawall parallel to the shore, used hydraulic dredgers to fill the tidelands, pumping sand from the bottom of the bay and removed the existing buildings from the site. Three feet of topsoil overlaid the fill. The entire process took eighteen months to complete. John McLaren held the responsibility for the fair's landscape engineering and once again, his genius played out in shades of green. Walter D'Arcy Ryan, director of

South Gardens (west)—the landscaping was done under the direction of John McLaren. —*Author's collection*

General Electric's Illuminating Engineering Laboratory took the responsibility for lighting the fair, a role critical to the planned ambience. His innovative glories took thirty-five years to find common usage. Jules Guerin and K. T. F. Bitter led the departments of color and sculpture respectively. The groundbreaking for Machinery Palace in January 1913 marked the start of the final phase of development.

The corps of architects, particularly Polk, selected a beauxarts style for the exposition as interpreted free-style per the arts and crafts movement. In lay terms, the architecture displayed a classical symmetry characterized by formal planning and rich decoration. Most of the design reflected classic but eclectic European design with Spanish, Moorish, Greek, Roman and Italian Renaissance influences. Columns, statuary, floral cornices, domes and ornate entries and windows carried the theme. Reproducing these ornate objects presented a challenge solved centuries earlier by Rome in the creation of the Coliseum and Saint Peter's Cathedral. The Romans used travertine, cement made from carbonate of lime. Polk selected imitation travertine made with concrete and plastic travertine made with gypsum, hemp fiber and color pigments for the most intricate work. The latter, never designed to last, partly explains why the Palace of Fine Arts suffered so severely from lack of maintenance by the end of the 1950s. Vandalism destroyed what time did not. The Palace of Fine Arts cost seven million dollars to replicate in reinforced concrete in 1962.

Eleven great palaces took shape under an army of skilled craftsmen. Eight of those made up the Central Palace Group also called the Walled City, a design so cohesive they seemed to encompass one magnificent building intersected with walkways and courts and topped with the magnificent Tower of Jewels. A uniform color theme

Column of Progress—rising 265 feet, it's one of four colossal sculptures on the Exposition; the other three are Nations of the East, Nations of the West and the Fountain of Energy. —*Author's collection*

Panoramic photographs of the completed exposition and the people who made it possible. —*Library of Congress*

under the guidance of Guerin created a study of natural tints, enforcing the sense of a grand design, the tints providing a soft, glare-free facade.

Avoiding the glare of the bare bulb incandescent lighting of the time, Ryan's new indirect lighting lit up the grounds at night. Multicolored spotlights and flood lamps hidden from view cast a magical glow on the exposition, especially on the tower. A bank of colored spotlights with 2.6 billion candlepower made up the scintillator that lit up the fog in a light show of epic proportions. When fog failed to materialize, a locomotive engine placed on the bay shore produced billows of steam that rose into the air to create the effect. The Panama-Pacific International Exposition became a wonderland at night.

THE EXPOSITION CITY AND ITS EXHIBITS

The forty-three-story Tower of Jewels encircled by fifty-four hidden search lamps shimmered from the reflected light cast back by more than one hundred thousand multicolored glass jewels. The builders strung colored Austrian cut-glass beads called Novagems by wires in outlining the tower structures. Sensitive to the lightest breeze, a

Illumination of the Tower of Jewels and Italian Towers—this was the first effective use of flood lighting to indirectly light a building rather than outlining it with small bulbs. —*Author's collection*

Court of the Universe—its symbolism represents the meeting place of the Eastern and Western hemispheres. —*Author's collection*

tiny mirror backed each jewel enhancing the effect. Four hundred thirty-three feet from ground level, the tower stood as the dominating feature of the fair and at night its illuminated beauty drew the breath out of onlookers.

Eight buildings comprised the Walled City: the Palace of Education and Social Economy; the Palace of Liberal Arts; the Palace of Manufactures; the Palace of Varied Industries; the Palace of Transportation; the Palace of Agriculture; the Palace of Agriculture (Food Products); and the Palace of Mines and Metallurgy.

The Palace of Education and Social Economy offered the educational exhibits for the exposition, providing a virtual university of education. The exhibits by states, cities and other countries presented developments in the fields of education and socio-economics. The exposition assigned specific problems only to exhibitors with noteworthy solutions or methods, avoiding duplication and ensuring the

Palace of Education—Moorish in design, the half-dome represents Philosophy. —*Author's collection*

proper address of critical issues. This particular fair, unlike its predecessors, also focused on future developments, looking forward into the twentieth century. Education exhibits concentrated on prominent movements and reforms in the United States and abroad seeking to forecast the future of education from kindergarten through university. The exhibition placed an emphasis on the special educational needs for "abnormal children" as well as industrial and vocational training, public health, and playgrounds. The Department of Social Economy looked toward the improvement of the human condition. Child welfare came to the forefront, as did working conditions, distribution of goods and finance in relation to public welfare. Considerable attention on women's vocations and urban problems including everything from welfare, corrections and criminology to park systems, public buildings and public sewerage stretched the tolerance of some visitors. The exhibit showed how private social organizations working in concert with government could meet the needs of a changing society.

The National Child Labor Committee Exhibit—some bad old times still persisted, but twentieth-century America looked forward to better times for all. —*Library of Congress*

Court of the Palms—though a minor court, it's also one of the most beautiful. —*Author's collection*

The Palace of Liberal Arts seems a misnomer today. Dedicated to applied science, the technology of the day consumed the entire six acres of floor space. It lauded the means to express one's artistic nature, not the art itself. The exhibits demonstrated "electrical means of communication including wireless telegraphy and telephony, musical instruments, chemistry, photography, instruments of precision and of surgery, theatrical appliances, engineering, architecture, mapmaking, typography, printing, bookbinding, paper manufacture, scientific apparatus, typewriters, coins and medals and innumerable other articles." Talking machines demonstrated in musical theaters occupied considerable space. The American Telephone and Telegraph Company maintained the first transcontinental telephone connection allowing participants to make calls from the theater at the exposition to New York City. Germany's exhibit on radium and its allied radioactive metals earned special note.

The Palace of Varied Industries provided demonstrations of the processes for goods manufacture. Displayed in operation, cotton and woolen mills, linen looms, knitting machines, machines for weaving fire hose, a shoe-making factory, a broom factory and others attracted interest because they manufactured everyday goods. Each country represented exhibited its own latest refinements in manufacturing and modern processes. Germany presented the largest exhibit including the manufacture of cutlery and pottery.

The Palace of Manufactures differed from the Palace of Varied Industries by exhibiting finished goods and fine wares rather than manufacturing and processes. Presenting goods for sale opened markets for emerging nations as well as those with innovative or well-placed products. Fine goods such a lacquer-ware, ceramics and silks from Japan as well as commercial art from Italy received special attention. A few manufacturing processes demonstrated the creation of the trade items, but those were rare.

The Palace of Transportation previewed the latest innovations in automobiles and roads, electric locomotives and streetcars, motorboats, water transportation and the massive modern steam locomotives. Diesel engines represented a new technology just gaining credibility. The exposition canceled

Court of Abundance—The court is dedicated to music, dancing, acting and pageantry. —*Author's collection*

Palace of Manufactures—one of the eight great buildings that give the sense of a walled city. —*Author's collection*

planned aerial displays due to the war but one plane did make the first indoor flight through the Palace of Machinery just before its completion.

Ford Motor Company set up an assembly line and produced a new car every ten minutes. Accurately colored topographical road maps lured potential car buyers to tour California. Clean electric vehicles including locomotives and streetcars climbed on the electric mania bandwagon with eager acceptance.

The Palace of Agriculture dealt

Arch and Fountain of the Setting Sun—Triumphal Arch of the Nations of the West, it represents the march across country to the Pacific. —*Author's collection*

with every phase of the agriculture industry including forestry but excluding the fruits and vegetables, classified then as horticulture. Farm equipment, techniques, seed varieties and modern irrigation from around the world found an eager audience. Agricultural colleges throughout California and the United States touted the great advances made in agriculture and agricultural education. Application of the gasoline engine to an array of farm machinery pointed toward changes in the size and operation of farms. The Philippines, New Zealand and Argentina put forward a display of the finest natural resources in the world.

The Palace of Food Products, called the "temple of the tin can and the food package," covered processed food ready for the kitchen or table along with machinery for preservation and production. Production lines expelled foods as advertised in magazines

Above: Court of the Four Seasons—the centerpiece is the fountain of Ceres, the two columns represent Sunshine and Rain. —*Author's collection*

Right: Court of the Four Seasons—the following representations are made: Harvest, Sunshine and Rain; Spring, Summer, Autumn and Winter. —*Author's collection*

and a flour company installed a complete mill with grain going in one end and a row of bakers at the other creating cakes, pastries and bread, 400 loaves at a baking. Cooperative group like the wine industry and Pacific Coast Fisheries joined to create industry-wide displays. Edible samples from an endless line of booths inspired another local humorist to dub the building "the Palace of Nibbling Arts."

The Palace of Mines and Metallurgy avoided the Midwinter Fair's praise of the Gold Rush, focusing instead on twentieth-century industrial needs. The steel and petroleum industries dominated this building. United States Steel set up model iron and coal mining plants, coke ovens, furnaces, rolling mills and docks with ships and barges. The companies emphasized employee welfare and safety and insurance companies put on safety demonstrations stressing accident prevention. The United States government simulated a mine explosion daily with a demonstration of rescue work.

Palace of Horticulture—the design follows the theme of a bounteous harvest. —*Author's collection*

The Palace of Horticulture was the first of the three exposition buildings outside the Walled City. Horticulture meant fruits and vegetables as opposed to anything else agricultural. Countries displayed photographs or examples of their finest produce, orchards and gardens. Preparation and preservation processes under factory conditions allowed visitors to view the handling of California's fruits and vegetables. Cuba and Hawaii's tropical plants attracted worldwide produce buyers and Luther Burbank showed off his creations.

The Great Palace of Machinery, constructed almost entirely of glass, covered five acres, as mentioned, big enough to fly a small plane through end to end. The most modern structure in the exposition, it measured 968 feet by 368 feet. The theme of the building centered on transitions: steam to diesel and gasoline, coal to hydroelectric power generation. Groups of exhibits covered the generation, distribution and control of electrical energy used for mechanical and motor power, lighting and heating. Tools used for shaping metal and wood fostered industrial automation. The United States government presented the largest exhibit with models of docks and dams, lighthouses and aids to navigation. Road-making machinery pointed the way to a network of highways crossing the nation, promising a coast-to-coast highway soon. They rattled the saber with models of warships, submarine mines, torpedoes, artillery, shells, armor plate and army equipment. Operating ammunition-making equipment demonstrated an ability to produce high quality munitions in quantity. The world was at war and the United States wanted them to know it was prepared.

The Palace of Fine Arts that stands today measured eleven hundred feet in an arc that ran from north to south. The Palace contained what the International Jury declared the best and most important collection of modern art ever assembled in America.

The war in Europe had limited the art sent to the exposition because of fear of damage from hostilities. The collier *USS Jason* was to sail from New York with eighty-five carloads of food supplies and Christmas presents for refugees and their children in the war zone. The fair directors gained permission from the United States government to gather exhibits for its return trip. Austria, Belgium, England, France, Greece, Italy and Spain willingly lent their treasures to the safekeeping of the exhibition. The *Jason* arrived in San Francisco on April 11, 1915, with the greatest collection of treasures ever shipped overseas. The only limitation to acceptance for exhibition was the amount of insurance the exposition carried. An annex opened to take the overflow arriving by ship from Europe.

The exposition presented contemporary work consisting largely of statues and paintings, although one also found lesser displays of miniatures, etchings, prints, drawings and tapestries. The Historical Section displayed classical art; works by Whistler, Sargent, Keith and others, as well as a highly praised exhibit of ancient Chinese paintings on silk.

Arranged in fifteen sections, the Palace of Fine Arts segregated exhibits by national, sectional, and personal collections. American art took center stage; finally accepted in league with the European offerings. American paintings of that decade stressed boldness and illumination over detail, while not falling into the radical Impressionism. German and English art only appeared in privately loaned collections. The German collection had been on exhibit at the Carnegie Institute in 1914. A British cruiser captured the ship that was returning the collection to Germany. The British captain, recognizing the value of the art, turned it over to the neutral United States.

France, Italy, Holland, Sweden, Portugal, Japan, China and several South American countries placed representative collections in the Palace. The annex held a large Hungarian collection, a Norwegian display that filled seven rooms, a small Spanish display and a large private British collection.

STATE AND INTERNATIONAL BUILDINGS AND FACILITIES

Each state and participating country added a building to the 636-acre campus in a well laid-out plan. Forty-six of the fifty-two U. S. states and territories participated,

Starting from top:

The California Building—an example of the Mission style of architecture, the court inside is a reproduction of the Forbidden Garden at the Mission Santa Barbara. —*Author's collection*

The Avenue of the States—the New York State Building is in the foreground. A detachment of the United States Marine Corps prepares for the daily drill and dress parade. —*Author's collection*

China Pavilion—A bit of China in The Zone. Each country took the opportunity to increase both understanding and trade. —*Author's collection*

Japan's groundbreaking ceremony for the Japanese Pavilion. —*Library of Congress*

each setting up an impressive display, putting their good dollars to work in San Francisco. Twenty-nine foreign nations joined the exposition in spite of the war in Europe. Some, such as Great Britain, dropped out due to hostilities at home. England suffered air bombardment by Germany during the run of the fair and dedicated all available resources to defense.

Other exposition structures included the Musical Concourse, the Festival Hall, a livestock exhibit, a dairy building, a polo field, an airfield and a stadium. A modern, sheltered yacht harbor took shape on the marina, as did a series of large slips for passenger ships and freighters, enabling easy safe access from the ocean and bay, significant since the theme centered on ocean access and trade via the Panama Canal.

Festival Hall—French theatre style of architecture, it seats 3,000 persons. —*Author's collection*

THE JOY ZONE

"The Zone" extended from just south of the Machinery Palace nearly a mile eastward to Van Ness Avenue. A five-acre working model of the Panama Canal set the tone for the quality of exhibits. The reproduction faithfully recreated the landscape of the Canal Zone with real water in the models of two oceans, the Gatun Lake, the Chagres River and the canal. Visitors rode in rail cars, listening on telephone connections to a phonograph that explained the features of the

On The Zone—a view looking west along The Zone or amusement street. The entire Zone required $10,000,000 to build. —*Author's collection*

canal as the car passed each appropriate point. Model ships entered the locks, the water raised or lowed as appropriate, and the ships moved on. The canal model offered a clear reminder of the theme of the Panama-Pacific International Exposition.

Reproductions of the Grand Canyon and Yellowstone Park also drew large crowds. The Grand Canyon exhibit included Navajo and Hopi families living in reconstructions of their desert homes. They demonstrated their customs and skills in rug and pottery making and in the performance of tribal songs and dances. The Yellowstone exhibit offered a copy of the Yellowstone Lodge as well as emulations of the park's natural wonders.

In keeping with past expositions, cultural exhibits of indigenous peoples included a Samoan village from American Samoa in the South Pacific, a New Zealand Maori Village and a Tehuantepec village from the south of Mexico. (Suggested as a possible site for the canal, the Isthmus of Tehuantepec proved more forbidding than the Isthmus of Panama.) The Zone also included a Japanese village displaying a giant sitting gold Buddha and a Chinese village centered on a large pagoda.

The Hawaiian Pavilion featured George E. K. Awai and his Royal Hawaiian Quartette who introduced Hawaiian music, the hula and the ukulele to San Francisco, all an instant hit. The popular Hawaiian music and ukulele craze burst from that show with songwriters from San Francisco to New York cranking out hundreds of Hawaiian tunes including ukulele chords above the notes.

Avenue of Progress—The view down the avenue is toward San Francisco Bay. This avenue was the main artery between the palaces and The Zone. —*University of California, Berkeley*

THE PANAMA-PACIFIC INTERNATIONAL EXPOSITION EXPERIENCE

San Franciscans bought 100,000 opening day badges, good for entry to the exposition, for fifty cents each. At six o'clock on the morning of February 20, 1915, those San Franciscans turned out to march down Van Ness Avenue to Fort Mason and the main gate, accompanied by bands and fluttering flags, intentionally making as great a noise as possible—no vehicles were allowed. When the head of the procession entered the gates, the end reached back two and a half miles. Newspapers claimed 150,000 marched that day.

At the end of the opening ceremony, President Woodrow Wilson keyed a signal from the White House to the wireless station in Arlington, Virginia, triggering the switches in San Francisco to light up the fair and start all of the machinery. He declared the Panama-Pacific International Exposition officially open.

Having sailed through the Panama Canal, a great fleet of warships from many nations, including the United States and Japan, entered the un-bridged Golden Gate in tribute to the canal and the exposition. The city had never seen so many warships, not even when the Great White Fleet sailed into the bay in 1908. People arrived at the fair from the East Coast, sailing in comfort on giant cruise liners through the "Big Ditch." No more dangerous runs around the stormy horn; the canal cut eight thousand treacherous miles off the trip. The bay brimmed with ships, all paying tribute to Balboa, the canal and San Francisco.

The Golden Gate from the Tower of Jewels—a reminder of difficulties of trade before and the relative ease of trade after the building of the Panama Canal. —*Author's collection*

MEMORIES OF THE PANAMA-PACIFIC INTERNATIONAL EXPOSITION

R. L. Duffus, reporter for the *San Francisco Bulletin* wrote in his book *The Tower of Jewels: Memories of San Francisco*:

It astounds me now to recall how permanent it [the Panama-Pacific International Exposition] looked, and how, in spite of my assiduous cynicism, I couldn't help loving it. I didn't want to love it. I thought it was a spurious bit of publicity.

But I did love it. I wish I could tell it, now, how much I loved it; that is one of the many affectionate messages to the dead I would like to send.

The hokum, the baloney, the applesauce, and the eye for a quick dollar were all there, just as I suspected, they were the normal by-products of a commercial civilization, and they were a lot prettier than some of the by-products of another civilization that was soon to appear.

But in 1912–1917 we did not anticipate the Russian Revolution, Italian Fascism, and Hitlerism. We believed the world would get better and more kindly, as soon as the first World War ended.

And meanwhile, in this world's fair, conceived by worldly people for worldly purposes, there was a degree of beauty, which we could not openly deny. It was sometimes hard to agree with the chamber of commerce, but we did, and they with us. This was San Francisco and the great pulse of life, and we shared a civic patriotism that never took up lethal weapons.

Or almost never.

Upon reaching the main entrance at the foot of Scott Street, the fair assaulted the five senses in a most glorious way. The Tower of Jewels loomed ahead, the Novagems catching the sun, throwing back a fiery display. A three hundred-voice chorus sang *Hail, California* supported by an orchestra, John Philip Sousa's band, and a massive pipe organ, the sound and percussion carrying throughout the exposition. Cooling breezes and the almost ever-present fog kept the temperatures comfortable, never hot— typically light jacket weather. Carefully tended gardens of green contrasted with the great ornate buildings in soft coordinated pastels. Water sprayed, splashed and danced in fountains everywhere, the sound blending

Outdoor pipe organ—the music from this massive instrument carried throughout the grounds. —*Author's collection*

with the excited conversations and exclamations of the fair patrons. Aromas wafted on the light swirling breezes carrying the enticing scents of cakes and bread baking, mysterious dishes from the Orient, popping popcorn, fresh roasting peanuts and hot buttered jelly scones, all mingled with the fresh smell of the sea from the marina. Almost every nation represented offered tastes of traditional foods. The Food Products Palace encouraged bites of this and that. Concessionaires tempted fair-goers with delicacies guaranteed to spoil dinner.

South Gardens (east)—French and Italian formal gardens and reflecting pool create a serene setting for the Tower of Jewels to the right. The Tower was covered in Novagems strung on wires that sparkled in the sunlight but dazzled at night. —*Author's collection*

Children tugged parents toward The Joy Zone and its roller coaster, miniature riding train, Boone's Animal Show and the Aeroscope, a double-decked cabin lifted

Fountain of Energy—the symbolism represents man's energy triumphant over all difficulties. —*Author's collection*

This stretch limo picked up folks at their hotels and other places to deposit them at the Exposition. Rain? Not in San Francisco.
—*Author's collection*

two hundred fifty feet above the ground by a huge steel arm, swinging around in a great circle over The Zone.

Parents tugged unwilling children toward the great halls and the Panama Canal, Yellowstone Park and Grand Canyon exhibits.

A day wasn't long enough to see the entire exposition. In comparison, Disneyland opened with fifty-five acres of entertainment area, and now encompasses eighty-five acres, excluding Disney's California Adventure. The Panama-Pacific International Exposition covered over seven times that area at 636 acres.

Lincoln Beachey amazed the crowds with his aerobatic antics in a German monoplane until he lost control at the top of a loop, crashed into the bay and drowned. Art Smith immediately replaced him and lived to see the end of the fair. Night flights with flares drew patterns in the sky accented by the spar-

Art Smith (pictured) flew his acrobatic bi-plane in shows over the grounds and marina of the Panama-Pacific International Exposition. Smith replaced Lincoln Beachey, who died when his monoplane crashed into the bay. —*Author's collection*

kling Tower of Jewels, fireworks, colored spotlights and the scintillator in a breathtaking light show.

Lucky attendees stayed at the Inside Inn, a 610-room hotel built right on the grounds at the Baker Street entrance. Providing all the modern conveniences, the hotel allowed patrons to spend their entire visit at the exposition.

THE END OF A GREAT FAIR

The fair closed on the night of December 4, 1915, after a ten-month magical run. Nearly nineteen million people attended the exposition in spite of the war in Europe. Even after covering the costs of building the Civic Center's Exposition Auditorium, the backers realized over one million dollars in profits. It was a counterpoint to the World War in Europe though the war outlasted the fair by three years. Immediately after its close, the exposition returned its treasures and bulldozers began demolishing the buildings, exhibits, and gardens, finishing the task in 1917. The land, recently valueless, now had power, city water, sewers, streets and public transportation right up to its edge as well as three feet of fertile topsoil. Developers and land speculators grabbed it up, creating the Marina District, a seismic disaster waiting for 1989's Loma Prieta Earthquake. Only the Palace of Fine Arts, which they couldn't bear to destroy, and the marina remained when the bulldozers finally left.

The Panama-Pacific International Exposition stands as one of the finest world's fairs ever in terms of the exhibitions, the aesthetics of the complex and the fair's financial success. The exposition marks a transition for San Francisco and the world. The world entered an unprecedented global war, leaving few countries untouched, changing its political makeup and America's position in it. San Francisco changed too; recognized for the first time as a true international city, not just a Gold Rush town. The fair included a look back to less complicated times and a view forward into the twentieth century. At the time, the city and the world failed to recognize the exposition's significance as a historical pivot point, in spite of all the platitudes about the future. The world never returned to what it was when the architects of the fair laid their plans.

An automobile entrance to Treasure Island and the Golden Gate International Exposition—about 12:30 P.M., July 4, 1939. —*Courtesy of The Bancroft Library, University of California, Berkeley*

Chapter 8

Golden Gate International Exposition—1939

As early as 1933, San Franciscans urged their politicians to host another world's fair, and the suggestion was made at the city's Chamber of Commerce meeting by a number of Bay Area civic groups. The city's first two fairs had succeeded gloriously and the city had something personal to celebrate this time—the opening of two new bridges. The local population anticipated the opening of the San Francisco-Oakland Bay Bridge and the Golden Gate Bridge, both engineering marvels. The concept for the Golden Gate International Exposition grew quickly. The Great Depression or what they called "hard times" had the country mired in despair and the San Francisco

Bay Area suffered with the rest. The city looked for relief and hope-
fully the increased trade that had resulted from the Midwinter
International Exposition of 1894 and the Panama-Pacific Interna-
tional Exposition of 1915.

THE PLANNING BEGINS

An exposition company formed and site selection began. The sites of the first two fairs, Golden Gate Park and the Marina, were no longer options. Highlighting both new bridges demanded a site with a clear view of each. The San Francisco Bay Exposition, incorporated in 1934, selected Yerba Buena Shoal from among seven sites, including China Basin. The shoal, always a navigational hazard, lay just north of Yerba Buena Island. Construction of Treasure Island began in February 1936, as presented in Chapter 1. The federal Works Progress Administration (WPA) earned credit for the three marvels of the fair: the San Francisco-Oakland Bay Bridge, the Golden Gate Bridge and the creation of Treasure Island.

The Golden Gate International Exposition Architectural Committee accepted the responsibility to create a new style of architecture for the fair. Called "Pacifica," it drew its motifs from the shores around the Pacific Ocean, both East and West. George W. Kelham headed the commission, followed by Arthur Brown, Jr., after Kelham's death. The remainder of the commission included Lewis P. Hobart, William G. Merchant, Timothy L. Pflueger, and Ernest E. Weihe. The massive style paid homage to the heavens, the seas, and the earth, with Mayan and Oriental influences. The windowless exhibit palaces stood one hundred feet tall, creating the effect of an ancient walled city. The main gate, flanked by two Mayan pyramids each topped by huge stylized elephants enhanced the effect in a merging of Eastern and Western symbolism. While claiming a new trend in architectural style for California, many of the architects had earned their creden-

The Court of Pacifica—celebrating the Pacific Rim countries. —*Stan Daniloski Collectio*

148

tials at San Francisco's 1915 fair and borrowed much from that highly praised event. Pacifica never caught on and the elephant pillars in particular and the architecture in general garnered more criticism than praise.

BUILDING THE EXPOSITION

Treasure Island offered four hundred acres, connected to Yerba Buena Island by a short causeway. Construction began before the fill had dried. Federal aid paid for the construction of the administration building at a cost of nine hundred thousand dollars. Two concrete and steel hangars, each three hundred and thirty-five feet long and seventy-eight feet high, cost four hundred thousand dollars each. These buildings would serve the planned San Francisco International Airport on Treasure Island

Construction of the Golden Gate International Exposition on Treasure Island, March 9, 1938. —*Photo courtesy of San Francisco History Center, San Francisco Public Library*

after the fair closed. A control tower topped the four-story Administration Building, built as an open semi-circle. It offered five underground passageways that fanned out from the single underground level to become future gateways providing direct access for aircraft boarding.

The layout of the exposition grounds divided the island into six theme areas: the Exposition Buildings, the Pacific Area, the Latin American Court, the Foreign Pavilions, La Plaza Area and Homeland. Constructed to last only for the duration of the fair, the structures offered an opportunity to express the fair's theme in quickly erected frames, comprised of stucco, plaster, and spray paint. Most of the buildings maintained a muted cast of earth tones, natural colors, and related shades. Primary colors appeared only in approved advertising displays for companies such as Coca-Cola. Chromotherapy dictated the colors and lighting—a new scientific treatment designed to create healing moods.

Inspired by the successful color scheme of San Francisco's Panama-Pacific International Exposition of 1915, the Golden Gate International Exposition took advantage of indirect neon "black lighting," ultra-violet floods, and luminescent tints to create nighttime illusions of a "magic city of light floating on San Francisco Bay." The luminescent paints and reflective vermiculite washed the fair in dazzling colors at night, some in shades that constantly varied.

The massive Elephant Towers, bathed in rose red by distant spotlights, glowed against the night sky. Fountains sprayed showers of liquid gold. The Tower of the Sun glowed in yellows and orange, topped by a red illuminated phoenix. The eighty-foot statue of Pacifica glowed stark white against a backdrop of vivid oranges and blues. The pools in the Court of Reflections returned casts of calming pink and coral. The lighting alone represented one million dollars in cost, but the effect proved stunning.

By early 1938, the major exhibition buildings and the Tower of the Sun neared

One of the Elephant Towers at night. —*Courtesy of The Bancroft Library, University of California, Berkeley*

The Tower of the Sun, illuminated at night. —*Stan Daniloski Collection*

The Court of Reflections—looking toward the Tower of the Sun. —*Stan Daniloski Collection*

completion and Lloyds of London offered guarantees for an on-schedule opening at nine to one odds. The exhibit palaces occupied the southwest side of the island and were situated next to the Administration Building and the two hangars housing the Air Transportation exhibit and the Fine and Decorative Arts exhibit. The four main exhibition buildings, each "L" shaped, came together at the corners of each "L" at the landmark Tower of the Sun, an edifice visible from both the San Francisco and Oakland shores. The Portals of the Pacific, with its Elephant Towers, the Court of the Sun, the Court of the Moon, the Court of Reflections, the Court of Flowers, the Court of the Seven Seas, and the Court of

The Court of the Moon—looking toward Yerba Buena Island. —*Courtesy of The Bancroft Library, University of California, Berkeley*

Pacifica, separated each of the buildings. The southwest building, smallest of the four, housed the Mines, Metals and Machinery exhibits. North of it, the next building housed the Hall of Science and the Electricity and Communication exhibit. Directly east stood the largest building, offering the Vacationland exhibits and the Foods and Beverages exhibits. The fourth building, on the southeast side, contained the Agriculture Hall, the International Hall and the Homes and Gardens exhibits.

Limited only by a loose set of guidelines, other structures quickly popped up, financed and developed by various individual entities, governments, and concessions. Companies like Ford Motor Company, National Cash Register (designed with a giant cash register on top), Ghirardelli Chocolate, and PG&E erected their own exhibition buildings. Pacific Area countries built

The Court of the Moon—looking toward the Tower of the Sun. —*Stan Danilc Collection*

structures reflecting their own cultures and architectures. A subdivided portion of the Pacific Area named the Latin Court held the countries of the Americas. Other major areas included the Foreign Pavilions, housing non-Pacific countries; the Homeland area, dedicated to housing and landscaping; a large federal building; a California area; and

The Court of Flowers—located between the Festival Hall and the Agriculture Hall. —*Stan Daniloski Collection*

an area dedicated to Western states, including Canada's British Columbia. The La Plaza area promoted local commerce and organizations. Entertainment took shape in the form of the California Coliseum for athletic events; the Livestock Pavilion; the *Cavalcade of the Golden West*, a pageant of the West's history; and the Gayway, providing arcade entertainment that included the Cyclone roller coaster and two Ferris Wheels. It also included Sally Rand's Nude Ranch.

Luxuriant gardens were designed and planted, exhibiting thousands of tree and plant varieties from the Pacific Basin countries, each set off by engineered lighting, abundant statuary, and magnificent fountains and reflecting pools. Walkway designs directed foot traffic from one point of interest to the next in a plan that diminished congestion points. Ferry docks provided access for public transportation, and slips for ocean liners and yachts catered to the wealthy. The parking area provided space for twelve thousand cars.

The most prominent feature of the fair was the Tower of the Sun, rising four hundred feet over the island. A twenty-two-foot tall wrought iron phoenix topped the tower, symbolic of San Francisco's ascendance from the ashes three decades earlier and multiple times prior. A carillon of forty-four bells hung within the tower. The bells were cast and tuned in Croydon, England, in 1938 for San Francisco's Grace Cathedral, a gift of Dr. Nathaniel T. Coulson, who lived for years in poverty to accumulate the required funds. The church loaned the carillon to the fair for its duration since the church's bell tower was not yet complete.

Sally Rand's Nude Ranch on the Gay Way. The cowgirls wore hats and boots and not much else. Be careful while doing those chores. ...and yes, it looked like a working dude ranch. —*Author's collection*

The largest bell in a carillon is called the Bourdon bell and is typically the bell used to strike the hour. The Tower's Bourdon bell weighed six tons and it resounded with the note of low G. It was and remains the largest bell in the West, large enough to allow a six-foot man to stand fully upright inside it. The other bells ranged in weight from thirteen pounds to five thousand one hundred and twenty-six pounds, all arranged in five tiers fitted into a massive steel frame mounted above the Bourdon bell. These bells spanned three and a half octaves starting at low C. Frames included, the carillon weighed thirty-four tons.

Electro-pneumatic-driven hammers rang the carillon bells, actuated by a piano-like keyboard, or via a punched paper role such as that used by the contemporary player pianos of the time. Alec Templeton, the innovative blind piano virtuoso, played the carillon and sometimes performed Bach fugues. The composer of "Bach Goes To Town" and "Mozart Matriculates," Templeton delighted in using the carillon to demonstrate his latest arrangements and interpretations of classical music.

THE EXPOSITION CITY AND ITS EXHIBITS

When the Golden Gate International Exposition at Treasure Island opened, it offered the most enchanting locale for any world's fair then or now. The views both of the fair and from the fair proved stunning. The island provided breathtaking views of the new bridges, the bay, and the San Francisco and Oakland skylines. The fair offered more pavilions and exhibits from Pacific Basin countries than any previous fair, all celebrating the sweeping theme "Pageant of the Pacific." Meanwhile, threats of war in the Pacific clouded the fantasy atmosphere.

Access to the island was via private automobile, taxi, or Key System ferryboat. The Key System trains didn't stop at Yerba Buena Island and there was no bus service to the fair. San Francisco and the country still suffered from the Great Depression. The cost of the fair proved moderate to a bit expensive for the times. A dollar in 1939 equated to thirteen dollars and thirty-two cents in 2004, and fair entrance cost fifty cents for adults and twenty-five cents for children under age twelve. The fare for ferry from either the San Francisco or Oakland ferry terminals was a dime for adults and a nickel for children, each direction. Drivers paid a parking cost of fifty cents per car and fifty cents for bridge fare one-way. The return trip was free since there was no San Francisco-to-Oakland transit, but a fair parking receipt was required.

Visitors found the island to be a garden interspersed with structures, fountains and statues. Julius L. Girod, a San Francisco parks superintendent, designed and managed Treasure Island's spectacular gardens. Girod learned his craft under the watchful eye of Golden Gate Park's John McLaren. The WPA funded the gardens with a grant of $1,800,000, which was intended to create jobs, and Girod accomplished that goal with labor-intensive designs that included seasonal annuals and plants requiring continual tending and pruning. At one point before opening, Girod employed 1,200 workers who carefully tended his gardens.

The Mines, Metals and Machinery Building presented exhibits that highlighted the story of metal, beginning in prehistory and presupposing the future as far as 1999. Treasure Mountain, a fifty-foot high, one hundred and seventy-foot diameter structure located within the building, offered working models of the types of mining done in the West, including hydraulic mining in Nevada, open pit mining in Utah, and of course a gold mine and processing plant in California. The models were viewed during a fifteen-minute, five hundred-foot guided tour inside the mountain. United States Steel demonstrated the strength and uses of steel, creating a massive diorama of San Francisco as it might appear in 1999, due to the increased use of steel in urban construction.

The Hall of Science touted "Science in the Service of Man" in the fields of physics, chemistry, biology, and the medical sciences and was hosted by the University of California in cooperation with a dozen other universities from across the United States and Europe. The University of California at Berkeley created the premier exhibit—a miniature of its new two hundred and twenty-five-ton Cyclotron. The model demonstrated the principle of atom smashing using spheres like ping-pong balls to represent particles. The particles whirled after being injected and then accelerated until shot toward an imaginary target. Demonstrators and placards explained the atom smashing process.

Various state of the art X-ray images were displayed including a set of yet-to-be born triplets. The Mayo foundation offered a display of the fundamentals of human anatomy and Saint Francis Hospital modeled modern plastic surgery techniques. World respected authorities in various fields gave scientific lectures daily in a 170-seat auditorium.

The Electricity and Communication Building drew the masses with demonstrations in the latest electronic technology. Magnetic sound recording technology, a new innovation that promised to overshadow phonograph records, caught the interest of many. Television promised a new medium of entertainment and fair goers relished the opportunity to be televised. Westinghouse introduced "Willie Vocalite," a voice-activated robot that could sit, stand, smoke a cigarette, and talk, all actions commanded by voice. One wonders if Willie was susceptible to robotic cancer as well.

A General Electric show entitled "House of Magic" allowed the audience to "see" music, "hear" light and watch metal float in the air. A talking Magic Kitchen introduced new electrical appliances. A "Woman's Workshop of Wonders" demonstrated new innovations that included the effect of various types of lighting on makeup and advances in home lighting. International Business Machines (IBM) synchronized all the clocks located around the fair.

The Ford Building shamelessly promoted the materials and the quality of the parts that went into Ford automobiles. It included displays by Champion, maker of Ford's spark plugs, Firestone Tire and Rubber Company, and Johansson's Gage Company, maker of the precision measuring equipment used in manufacturing. Assembly of actual production cars offered an opportunity to see Ford's assembly line in action, as had been done for the 1915 fair. Ford displayed the latest line of automobile accessories and presented its latest models, including the Lincoln Zephyr.

Not to be outdone, General Motors sponsored "Progress on Parade" in the Vacationland Building. Its glass "see-through" Pontiac drew crowds who were awed by seeing through its skin into the inner workings of this fine automobile. GM presented its full line of cars and accessories but also presented its newest innovations like cloth spun from glass (fiberglass). Cutaways of the latest easy shift transmissions and differentials let the consumers see them in operation. Chrysler chose to display its vast array of models in miniature, a real hit with the kids. A collection of old-time cars indicated just how far automotive transportation had evolved.

But Vacationland encompassed far more than just cars. It encouraged the concept of the traveling vacation. Four acres of displays included Pullman train cars with the latest appointments in luxury, streamlined cross-country buses with reclining sleepers and restrooms, displays of the latest in traveling the world by ship and dioramas of the far reaches of the earth. Southern Pacific's "S.P. Roundhouse" told the story of railroading. The biggest display, "Story of Petroleum," told the history of petroleum from its discovery to its modern uses and described the many uses for petroleum and its byproducts. An educational puppet show entertained children so their parents could focus on the scientific aspects of petroleum.

The Foods and Beverages exhibitors aimed their pitch at the buying public rather than commercial consumers. Home products, from frozen and canned foods to wines and liquors, packed this building. Exotic foods from the far reaches of the world, like China and Brazil, were offered in hopes of increasing consumption and, with it, trade. A one thousand-pound Exposition cake was baked and slices offered to attendees. Demonstrations and old-time kitchen displays created points of interest throughout the building. Enticed by the smells and samples, no one left without tasting something.

The Agriculture Hall educated a largely urban audience in modern farm techniques and its goal to help supply the world with the best quality food for the least money. Again, the fair used three-dimensional dioramas to show the history of agriculture in California. The University of California College of Agriculture described its research and education in the areas of agricultural engineering and economics, animal science, control of disease and pests, and irrigation, a key factor in California's agricultural success. The Agriculture Council of California highlighted the efforts of twelve different cooperatives that helped the farmer to harvest and market his crops.

The International Hall housed those participating countries that didn't have their own pavilions. Czechoslovakia, Denmark, the Netherlands, Portugal, and Sweden each displayed cultural artifacts, travel information, products, and facts intended to increase trade and tourism. Unfortunately, America was in the Great Depression and Europe was at war, so the most that was accomplished, perhaps, was the planting of seeds and knowledge. Other organizations, such as the Boy Scouts of America, the Amateur Radio Operators, and two private displays shared the hall. One display, by Jules Charbneau, contained a collection of 28,000 hand carved miniatures. The other displayed the history of costume on miniature dolls, presented by Audrey Kargere.

The Homes and Gardens Building exhibited the very latest in inventions, ideas, materials, and techniques that made modern living better living. The "Wonder World of Chemistry" described advances, such as Lucite, a glass-like substance that could direct and even pipe light, and displayed the new synthetic rubber made from petroleum by-products. This critical advance was necessitated by the lack of natural rubber caused by a world at war. The many uses of glass included glass wool for insulation, fiberglass for strength and flexibility, glass blocks for building, and tempered glass for safety.

Home building and furnishing focused on local building, garden and furnishing products and materials. These included wood products like douglas fir, redwood, wood paneling, cedar shingles and of course, asbestos shingles for fire safety. If it went into, on, or around the American home, you could find it in the Homes and Gardens Building.

Homeland, held outdoors adjacent to the Homes and Gardens Building, offered displays of five homes and the exhibit of the California Nursery Company, the largest and oldest nursery in the state. The homes included a partially pre-fabricated steel frame and concrete home, a Cape Cod colonial made from Western pine, a steel "Uni-built" house made of steel frame and stucco, two conventional homes built for home tours and the San Francisco Chamber of Commerce and one concrete home built in the Monterey style.

The Hall of Air Transportation, located in the first of two permanent hangars, housed the operations and maintenance base for Pan American's transoceanic fleet, including the China Clipper. Visitors watched the operation from an isolated spectators balcony above the floor that included a Link trainer, a cutaway of the B-314 transoce-

South Tower—entrance to the Homes and Gardens Building. — *Daniloski Collection*

anic seaplane, the repair shops in actual operation, and the actual customs areas for travelers to and from the Far East. A waiting room for travelers led to the Port of the Trade Winds where the China Clipper docked.

The hall exhibited a number of historic planes like Douglas "Wrong Way" Corrigan's famous nine hundred dollar "crate" used to fly non-stop from New York to Ireland in 1938. The San Francisco Gas Model Airplane Club displayed a collection of model planes of all types that were one-ninety-sixth actual size (from two to twenty-six-inches in length).

The Palace of Fine and Decorative Arts took up the second hangar and was declared the finest collection of paintings, sculptures, and decorative arts ever assembled in the United States. Separated into four divisions, the exhibit claimed a worth of thirty-five million dollars. The European division displayed paintings, sculpture, and tapestries that included some of the finest examples from Italy, Belgium, France, Holland, and England. The Italian art included Botticelli's *Birth of Venus*, Raphael's *Madonna of the Chair*, Titian's *Portrait of Paul III* and Michelangelo's *Madonna and Child*.

One of the big clippers in the Port of the Trade Winds at Treasure Island. —*Courtesy of The Bancroft Library, University of California, Berkeley*

The Decorative Arts division provided thirty miniature period rooms representing four centuries, all decorated in a perfect study of the interior decoration and architectures of England, France, and the Netherlands. The scale of one inch to one foot applied to all furnishings, including pictures, ornamentation, chandeliers, and furniture. The division also presented fifteen full-sized rooms and areas assembled by noted architects, decorators and designers from the United States and Europe.

The Decorative Arts division also hosted workshops where artists and craftsmen demonstrated their skills and wares. Showcased international galleries of glass, silver, ceramics, jewelry, textiles, rugs, lace, and bookbindings surrounded the workshops.

The Pacific Cultures division presented arts and craftwork from the fifty countries of the Pacific Rim represented at the fair. Everything from intricate Maori wood and shell carving from New Zealand to artifacts from seventh-century China left the visitor in awe. The greatest such collection ever, many priceless treasures such as goblets of gold encrusted in turquoise from Peru, a gold encrusted howdah or sedan chair from Siam and a stone lintel with rich lace carving from Cambodia offered a viewing opportunity never repeated. It took eight galleries to display this massive collection of works.

The Contemporary Art division provided the best modern artists had to offer. The United States, Mexico, Canada, Australia, and twelve European nations participated with 831 artists represented. A gallery was also set aside for historical American paintings.

STATE AND FEDERAL BUILDINGS AND FACILITIES

The State of California appropriated $5,000,000 toward representation at the fair. The funds built the California State Building, the Coliseum, the Livestock Pavilion, and California Auditorium and sponsored various exhibits, such as Treasure Mountain, and funded the landscaping in the California area. The California State Building promoted state industry and tourism, and also provided offices for the governor and his staff, with reception rooms for visiting dignitaries. Each wing presented a diorama of California, the west wing recounting the Portola expedition to California in 1769 and the southeast wing offering a twelve hundred-mile trek through California's natural resources, complete with redwoods, a startlingly realistic Sierra stream and waterfall, traversing from north to south, ocean-side to the high Sierra. The Highway Department presented a series of scenes depicting the growth of California's highway system.

The San Francisco Building provided offices and reception rooms for Mayor Rossi and his staff to receive guests. Ten dioramas presented snapshots of San Francisco's history, including the burning of the city in 1906 as seen from Nob Hill and scenes from the Gold Rush days of 1849. It seems dioramas were in vogue in 1939. Artifacts on display included an original Wells Fargo stagecoach and the gold railroad spike that connected the East to the West with the completion of the first transcontinental railroad.

Regional buildings completed the California area. Alameda and Contra Costa counties joined in their own facility, complete with educational displays describing the

A diorama of the famous Portola expedition, located in the California building. —*Author's collection*

counties as well as their own detailed diorama depicting the counties' major cities and the short trek from Treasure Island to reach them.

Los Angeles and San Diego counties jointly promoted the vacation opportunities of the Southland. Movie making, deep-sea fishing, luscious fruit, and references to balmy weather along with rich oil resources and a nod to the Tournament of Roses Parade made this building a must-see. If that wasn't enough, Fred and Ginger's dancing shoes were also on display.

The Mother Lode counties of the Sierra told the history of gold in California in the Alta California Building. Visitors followed the Emigrant Trail, viewed Grass Valley in the days of Lola Montez, and gaped at the Calaveras Big Trees, all via a series of large and small dioramas. Movies with sound and color completed the story of these counties and gold specimens demonstrated the attraction first-hand.

The Mission Trails Building, inspired by the California missions, represented the coast counties between San Francisco and Los Angeles. The building housed a replica of an early California Spanish street scene and a padre's secret garden. It displayed the world's largest photo-transparency murals and also a moving panorama one hundred and sixty-five feet long that reflected the beauty of the Pacific Coast.

The San Joaquin Valley Building covered the central counties, offering the Yosemite Valley in miniature for those not fortunate enough to have seen it. Half-scale sequoia redwood trees offered a glimpse of just how big these giants grow. Fresh cake promoted the fruits of the Valley, and a model with murals described the Central Valley Water Project, destined to provide the water needed for Valley farmers to feed the nation. Transoramas (panoramic dioramas) demonstrated the natural wealth of the Valley counties.

The Sacramento-Tahoe Region Building, the Redwood Empire Building, and the

Shasta Cascade Building each typified the areas with representations of their attractions and offerings. All were described in the form of the ubiquitous dioramas. Agriculture, California's greatest industry, prevailed as the theme in the state and county buildings. No one doubted that the state and local economies hinged on growing, processing, and shipping agricultural and forest products throughout the world.

The California Commission's Hall of Flowers proved one of the most popular exhibits. The state, known for year-round flowers, showcased the best it had to offer, plus imports from as far away as Australia. Maintained and tended by volunteers, the hall presented an ever-changing kaleidoscope of color and fragrance. Due to its popularity, this building and its exhibits moved to the California State Fairgrounds at Sacramento after the close of the fair.

Recreational activities found a prominent place at the fair for the first time in history. The Recreational Building stressed public recreation in California, including a little theatre for stage plays, puppet shows, and motion pictures, a music room for instrumental and vocal performances, and a children's museum featuring arts, crafts, and hobbies. Outside the building, picnic areas, a well-equipped playground, and a sports stadium with seating for eleven thousand promoted California's enthusiasm for living out-of-doors.

The Coliseum seated ninety-two hundred visitors for events as diverse as livestock shows, symphony concerts, rodeos, sporting events, and horse shows. The California Auditorium staged bands and singers, as well as the Follies Bergere. It also housed the most complex radio station built to-date, capable of managing up to twelve simultaneous broadcasts from within its studios or from twenty-six remote locations on the island.

The Federal Building and wings, built at an expense of one and a half million dollars, encompassed seven acres located near the southeast end of the island. George Creel, head of the U.S. Commission, said they needed to portray what the government did for the people. Rather than departmental displays, the Federal Building functionally explained what it was doing and why, or as he put it, "America in action!" Personification helped narrow the gap between the people and their government, making it clear who owned the government. Dynamic exhibits furthered the goal.

Ten separate exhibit areas divided the building consisting of the American Indian Exhibit, Conservation, Social Affairs, Economic Affairs, the March of Science, the Federal Theatre, WPA Art, WPA Recreation, Housing, National Defense, and the Coast Guard. The American Indians exhibit divided the tribes into six broad, overly simplistic groups—the fishermen of the Northwest Coast, the corn planters of the Southwest, the buffalo hunters of the Great Plains, the woodsmen of the East Coast, and the seed and root gatherers of California. Given that, a genuine attempt to showcase their cultures and art produced admirable results.

The WPA set up scores of booths and activities. Created by the federal government to create jobs, this agency took great pains to demonstrate the myriad benefits it offered to individuals and to the communities. A model portrayed WPA projects ranging from creating public facilities like golf courses and tennis courts to public buildings, public landscaping, water mains, and dams. One small building carried a placard that claimed the WPA had built nearly four thousand school buildings in the United States. Other activities demonstrated included the Writer's Project and Arts Project, termite research, and the perpetuation of American handicrafts.

The south wing touted "The Helping Hand of Uncle Sam," explaining the government's role in protecting the financial well-being of the individual and rebuilding areas devastated by the depression. New agencies, such as the Reconstruction Finance Corporation, the Federal Deposit Insurance Corporation, Rural Electrification, and the Veterans Administration, demonstrated their roadmap to climb out of the morass of the depression. Murals demonstrated communities made possible through federal funding, comparing instant slums to model housing with the slogans, "Today's Jerry Building, Tomorrow's Slums" and "Beauty and Originality Cost No More than Ugly Uniformity." A sharecropper's shack was moved intact to the East Court. Photographs showed the generations raised in that building with adjacent photographs of new homes provided by the Rural Resettlement Agency.

The southeast wing provided a view into the scientific and technological advances made by public servants working in government. Contributions in military science, meteorology, and aeronautics drew considerable interest. The Army offered an escorted tour through a new, fully equipped "Flying Fortress" B-17 bomber, parked just outside the building. Agricultural and forest science displayed the advances made in pest control, production, harvest, and uses of products and by-products of each industry.

INTERNATIONAL PARTICIPATION

President Roosevelt issued an invitation to the world to participate in the Golden Gate International Exposition and many countries accepted enthusiastically. *A Pageant of the Pacific* focused on the Pacific Rim countries, though others accepted as well, with thirty-one countries participating. Isolated by locale, the fair grouped international guests into the Pacific Basin Area, the Latin-American Court and the Foreign Pavilions. Ten countries without their own pavilion, Denmark, Holland, Belgium, Bulgaria, Greece, Sweden, Czechoslovakia, Turkey, Portugal, and Hungary, joined together in the International Palace.

Pacific House formed the hub of the Pacific Basin Area, offering a ten thousand-volume library on Pacific lands, as well as a hospitality center for the area. All four of its cruciform sides were identical, depicting equality. One arm jutted into the Lake of All Nations. Exhibits provided insight into the culture, history, social lives, arts, music, dancing, handicrafts, and commerce of the peoples living in countries adjoining the Pacific Ocean.

The Japan Pavilion, a reproduction of an old feudal castle, featured Mikimoto Company's pearl cultivators working in the adjacent lagoon. The oysters were tended and harvested by the famous female pearl divers. Half a million oysters imported from Japan and planted in the lagoon produced the pearls that awed the exhibit's visitors. Japanese women performed all the work in this exclusive industry. A second exhibit, a reproduction of a Japanese silk factory, demonstrated the conversion of the cocoons into the finest fabrics.

Opening day at the Japan Pavilion. —*Author's collection*

The Japan Pavilion at night. —*Author's collection*

Japanese ladies in their traditional kimonos.
—*Author's collection*

The Japanese samurai House—part of the Japan Pavilion. —*Stan Daniloski Collection*

American ladies enjoying tea and tempura in the restaurant at the Japan Pavilion. *—Author's collection*

The Japan Pavilion offered the first of many international pageants at the fair. Hina-Matsuri, the Festival of the Dolls, celebrated the day of worship at each family's doll shrine, festooned with the peach blossoms of marriage. Japan offered peace, beauty, and serenity on Treasure Island while it waged a brutal war in Asia. The Golden Gate International Exposition ended just over a year before Pearl Harbor. Meanwhile, America's advances in military ground equipment, naval power, and aircraft were open for public inspection, just a short walk from the Japan Pavilion.

The Netherlands East Indies (now Indonesia) Pavilion appeared in the form of a Hindu-Javanese temple. The contemporary Javanese architecture, decorated with traditional Javanese and Balinese art, created one of the most striking and comprehensive presentations on the island. Lush gardens offset the fine, stone Balinese sculptures, and a large aquarium showcased rare and beautiful fishes from the Pacific archipelago. Batik artists demonstrated an art form that caught the imagination of fair goers from across the nation.

The Dutch and their protectorate saw trouble coming in the form of war in both

Europe and Asia. Germany threatened the Netherlands, later invading in May of 1940. Japan invaded China and threatened French Indo-China. Concerned for both the homeland and the Netherlands East Indies, they decided not to return for the 1940 fair. That pavilion became the Treasure House, exhibiting art from around the world. Countries represented included Egypt, Arabia, Nepal, Tibet, Turkey, Greece, the Malay States, China, Japan, and

Left to right: Latin-American Court, North Lake, the Johore Temple, and Pacific House—Johore is now the State of Johor in Malaysia. —*Courtesy of The Bancroft Library, University of California, Berke-*

others. Artifacts of gold and silver complemented ancient weavings, including the"Wishing Rug" woven in 1793 by Suzanne of Tiflis, sold to the Shah of Persia to ransom Prince Jean from Sharaf Ali Ogloo of Arabia.

French Indo-China (Vietnam) produced a revival of the arts and culture of prior regimes. Big game trophies including boar, elephants, leopards, wild bulls, and crocodiles created a sense of the wilds, offset by the civilized fourteenth century statuary and stone bas-relief sculptures of the Mon-Khmer people of Angkor.

The Commonwealth of the Philippines, then an American possession, demonstrated the richness of that island land and hailed its partnership with the United States. A complete panorama of the Philippines presented aspects of everyday life and the beauty of the country. Commerce, industry, and natural resources were central to the pavilion's exhibition. The Philippines chose not to participate in the 1940 fair. The pa-

A diorama in the French Indo-China Pavilion, now Vietnam. —*Courtesy of The Bancroft Library, University of California, Berkeley*

vilion became the International Market, displaying goods for sale from more than two dozen countries.

Other Pacific pavilions included those of Hawaii, Australia, New Zealand, and independent Johore, now the Malaysian state of Johor. The New Zealand pavilion took the form of a Maori meetinghouse and highlighted their customs and lands. Australia brought some of their strange animals such as kangaroos, wombats, and kookaburras for visitors to view in the gardens outside the pavilion as well as mounted animals like lyrebirds, koalas, and platypus in their natural settings. Aboriginal handicrafts were displayed alongside dioramas, photographs, and slides of the great southern island. The Malaysian States took over the Johore pavilion for the 1940 fair.

The Latin-American Court, surrounded by eight pavilions, offered one of the most colorful vistas on the island. The Mexican pavilion presented an authentic cantina and restaurant from the days of old Mexico, with a floorshow of the Folklorico, the traditional dances of Mexico. Silversmiths and leather workers demonstrated their intricate skills with examples of these and other Mexican crafts available for sale.

El Salvador's pavilion focused on its excellent coffee and the country's scenic beauty. Housed in a single cavernous room, a large-scale model of a coffee plantation followed the process of coffee production from growing the beans through harvesting, washing, drying, and shipment of product. After viewing the coffee display, visitors entered a reproduction of a section of an El Salvadorian city complete with a coffee shop, brightly decorated patio, handcraft shops, and a bandstand featuring the "Sonora" Marimba Band.

Chile encouraged tourism at its pavilion with photographs and murals of its famous beach resorts and the town of Pucon, a beautiful mountain lake resort noted for its sport fishing. The town is located at three thousand feet above sea level in the Andes. German immigrant families settled Pucon in 1904 with the first international resort built in 1923, attracting artists and intellectuals. Murals, scale models, and photographs presented a sense of what Chile offered. A second room promoted Chile's industry and natural resources, including its nitrite mining and refineries.

Colombia's Spanish Colonial pavilion also promoted its coffee, much in the manner of El Salvador, but samples were offered: whole beans in miniature shipping sacks and ground coffee in cans. Brewed coffee was served at the Colombia Café. The main attraction to visitors however was the emeralds. Colombian emeralds displayed in various stages from uncut and still encased within quartz to finished jewels held viewers agog. Craftsmen demonstrated ancient and contemporary jewelry making as well as other local crafts. Colombia presented a large archeological display as well.

The Peruvian pavilion made much of its Inca ancestry. Displays of pre-Columbian Inca jewelry gleamed in guarded display cases. It was said the collection surpassed a value of $1,500,000, in 1939 dollars. These archeological treasures stretched the imagination of archeologist and layman alike. Ancient and modern cultural artifacts traced Peru's history and in another room, murals and displays touted Peru's industrial future.

The Guatemalan pavilion promoted the country's natural resources, including coffee and other agricultural products, mineral products, and hardwoods. It also included a replica of the front portion of the one thousand-year-old Piedras Negras Mayan jungle

The Colombia Pavilion—free coffee was a major attraction.
—*Courtesy of The Bancroft Library, University of California, Berkeley*

ruin hidden amidst tropical trees. Would-be explorers climbed the worn steps in the same manner as the original discoverers.

Other Pacific-facing Latin-American countries hosting full pavilions included Ecuador, Panama, and Costa Rica. Ecuador featured contemporary artists portraying life in that country. The Panama exhibit focused on its ancient pottery, the colorful handmade native dresses, and paintings by the San Blas Indians. Costa Rica displayed colorful dioramas and murals, which combined with ore, wood and produce samples, told the story of the republic's natural resources and history.

Other non-Pacific Rim countries petitioned to participate. Brazil's pavilion included lush gardens with live Brazilian coffee plants. Indoors, Café Brazil served brewed coffee of varying strengths and "Maté," a South American tea. An orchestra played both American and Brazilian music. A giant topographical map of South America identified attractions and the source areas of Brazil's natural resources. Sensing an upcoming opportunity, Brazil stressed its role as a major source of resources during the First World War.

The Argentine pavilion, built in only forty-nine days, dedicated itself to the literature of Argentina. Foremost was the epic poem of the gaucho by Martin Fierro, translated to English by Walter Owen. A two-story cocktail lounge, the Martin Fierro Room, displayed enlarged illustrations from the *Book of Poems* by Jose Fernandez. An orchestra played Argentine tangos and melodies as waiters served native dishes and drinks. A theatre seating 160 patrons showed films of picturesque Argentina.

France laid claim to the largest of the international exhibit buildings. Actually two buildings, one promoted fine arts, fashion, and tourism. The other, the Café Lafayette, emulated a Parisian restaurant. It included a large, circular dining room in blue and cream with curved mirrored walls. A cocktail bar and two champagne lounges offered drinks and both domestic and imported champagne. Outside, umbrella-covered "sidewalk" tables overlooked a shallow pool and formal garden. The Café Lafayette was a major hit.

The main French exhibit hall boasted some of the country's finest art works. Rodin's *The Shadow* greeted guests who stared in awe at the works of master painters and sculptors, including Bourdelle, Marie Laurencin, Utrillo, Dufy, Vlaminck, Derain, Renoir, and Marque. Musee Carnavalet of Paris displayed eighteenth-century gowns on sculptured mannequins, in contrast to the displays by modern French couturiers. A third area encouraged travel and tourism in France, using maps, photographs, murals, dioramas, and moving picture shows.

Italy put on one of the better exhibits, demonstrating that fascism hadn't changed the country's nature. The Italian pavilion, patterned after a Roman coliseum, promoted tourism and goodwill. Imported to Treasure Island, Italian marble faced the portico and much of the interior in shades of white, blue, red, and green. A tower rising one hundred and fifteen feet from the floor listed the names of major Italian cities, embossed in the stone. At the base, a fascist axe declared the new form of Italian government. Flower girls wore the costumes representing the eight important regions and three-dimensional niches placed within the inner rooms displayed the features of Italy's regions in a series of dioramas.

The Norwegian pavilion took the form of old Viking buildings built of rough-hewn logs constructed without nails in the style then in vogue for ski lodges. The roof supported growing turf to keep water out and heat in. Norway dropped out of the fair due to the war; however, the Norwegian Shipowner's Association and the Norwegian shipping firms assumed responsibility for the exhibit. The pavilion promoted the Norwegian lifestyle, including a steam bath large enough for a family. Modern Norwegian furnishings filled the replica ski lodge.

One additional exhibit, the Peace Project pavilion, promoted a negotiated approach to the worsening international situation. In an address signaling the opening of the Peace Project exhibit, Dr. Henry F. Grady, chairman of the United States Tariff Commission, stated, "The threat of world war is gradually being lessened today as Germany, Italy and Japan are beginning to suffer economically to the point where they will be forced to accept international trade for mutual benefit, rather than to risk war and subsequent chaos." The project did not reopen in 1940 due to the downward spiral of the world situation and the group's no-longer feasible position.

The Norwegian Pavilion—not the big stone building, but the little rustic cabin, intended to look like a rustic ski and sports lodge. —*Stan Daniloski Collection*

THE JOY ZONE

Every fair needs a midway and the Golden Gate International Exposition had its Gayway. The Gayway included the Fun Zone, Joy Zone, or Street of the Barkers. It was an attraction that drew people to the fair, and at the same time provided a distraction for people who attended the fair for its scientific, educational, or cultural aspects. With something for everyone, man, woman, and child, the Gayway offered the tinge of sin, the thrill of risk, and the sweet smell and rich taste of foods not overly healthy, but oh, so good.

Sally Rand's Nude Ranch covered one end of the spectrum with attractive young ladies cavorting around a simulated dude ranch in no more than boots, a G-string, and a hat. A gentleman had to be twenty-one to get in, but many a nineteen-year-old boy tried to gain admittance and many succeeded, bragging later to peers about the sights they had beheld. Robert Ripley offered a somewhat tamer show with his collection of oddities and freaks in the *Ripley's Believe It or Not!* exhibit. Barkers called to the masses, luring them in to liberate them from their money—"A spin of the wheel to win a ham just by placing one thin dime on the winning number" or "Place your bet on

The Gay Way—all was not G-rated here. Hang onto your kiddies (your husband). —*Photo courtesy of San Francisco History Center, San Fran Public Library*

the Monkey Speedway" or "Take a gander at the thirty-foot live pregnant python for the miniscule sum of a nickel. Look as long as you like." A visitor could ride the Flying Scooter, the Roll-O-Plane, the Roller Coaster, the Octopus or the Diving Bell for a dime

One of Sally's cowgirls—watch it with that rope. —*Courtesy of The Bancroft Library, University of California, Berkeley*

and ride twice on nickel day. Hungry fair goers might buy a Coke and a foot-long hot dog, enjoying the snap of the casing and the bite of the mustard, washed down by the sweet, icy drink. The Gayway drew the crowds and the fair management quickly learned that any open space meant lost revenue and diminished attendance. Many fair goers came only for the midway attractions—each new attraction increasing the interest.

Money was tight and the term "free" had an allure not to be ignored. The New York Fair proved that high prices guaranteed disaster. San Francisco did better with its lower costs but attendance was the key to revenue. The management realized that the *Cavalcade of the Golden West*, a free stage show offered in 1939, drew patrons.

The pageant, played out on a giant stage 450 feet long and 150 feet deep, called for five hundred actors presenting the 400-year history of the West from Balboa through Portola, Drake and Father Serra, on to the Gold Rush, and climaxing with San Francisco's "Gay 90s." Voice actors in a booth read the script written by Art Linkletter *(Kids Say the Darndest*

A stage coach from the Cavalcade of the Golden West. —*Courtesy of The Bancroft Library, University of California, Berkeley*

Things) and broadcast it out to the audience. The actors lip-synced the words since there was no way for them to be heard. The show claimed the record for attendance in 1939. Updated for 1940, *America! Cavalcade of a Nation* offered a new show for returning patrons.

THE GOLDEN GATE INTERNATIONAL EXPOSITION EXPERIENCE

The people made up the real story of the Golden Gate International Exposition at Treasure Island. The Great Depression weighed heavily on San Francisco, which suffered from unemployment and tight money. War raged across much of the world, as it had in 1915 during the city's Panama-Pacific International Exposition. Unlike 1915 when the city thought the Great War wouldn't involve us, the people knew it was only a matter of time before the United States joined the fray. Yet San Franciscans aren't a crowd to cry in their beer. Then and now, if a good time is to be had, they will be there and yes, the people came…and they had fun!

Bud Clark, a San Francisco native, recently recounted his experiences at the Golden

Gate International Exposition, which he attended when he was about fifteen years old. He scraped together enough money for a day at the fair as often as possible. Catching the ferry to the island, he marched straight for the amusement zone where he joined the line for "The Ride." He couldn't recall the name, maybe the Flying Scooter or the Roll-O-Plane. The ride simulated the motions of flying a real plane. Each "pilot" climbed into one of a number of cockpits, each held by a pair of cables. The planes hung from a large wheel mounted horizontally at the top of a tower, flying outward by centrifugal force when the wheel rotated. Clark recalled climbing into the cockpit and grabbing the stick. The stick controlled the altitude of the plane, allowing it to rise and dip at the rider's whim. From there, he could see across the bay to the city, inspect the new bridges, and scan the fairgrounds. Young Clark flew until his money ran out—it was the only ride that really mattered.

The Golden Gate International Exposition's early music program proved dated. The management had engaged Dr. Edwin Goldman and his musicians, who had performed twenty-four years earlier at the 1915 Panama-Pacific International Exposition. Twice daily, they played operatic and classical selections. Midway through 1939, the fair management in charge of music changed and the music program switched to popular music performed by the San Francisco Symphony Orchestra. The offering proved popular enough to consistently pack the California Coliseum. Low prices for these concerts allowed thousands to enjoy the best in music.

Realizing the advantage of catering to the public's desires in music, Dr. Charles H. Strub, newly appointed managing director, ordered "more and better free entertainment" as the keynote of the new programs. Name bands featured on the programs in June of 1939. Benny Goodman, the "King of Swing," agreed to take a major risk by playing "for free." Swing, the hottest musical craze at the time, packed the Treasure Island Music Hall and then the outdoor Temple Compound when the performances demanded more space. After twenty days, the fair awarded Goodman a scroll declaring his unprecedented achievement of playing to a million people in that short time.

Benny Goodman and his Orchestra—they played for free and broke records for crowds. —*Author's collection*

Based on Goodman's success, the fair hired Kay Kaiser and his "College of Musical Knowledge" to perform at forty cents a head in the Treasure Island Music Hall. He consistently packed the house, with no loss of attendance to Goodman's shows. Other name entertainment followed, including Jack Benny and his wife Mary Livingstone with Phil Harris' Orchestra, Edgar Bergen with his wooden Charley McCarthy, and the biggest draw ever, Bing Crosby. Fair attendance soared, especially on discount days like "Dime Days" for kids. The management recognized a winning formula and continued to present the best they could find in musical and entertainment attractions. By the end of the 1939 fair, management and the crowds declared that it couldn't end just yet. A revamped fair was planned for 1940.

The 1940 Golden Gate International Exposition lost some of its international participants but gained key attractions. Among those, Billy Rose's Aquacade moved intact from the less-than-satisfactory New York World's Fair. Rose excavated International Hall, constructing a special pool and designing his own seating arrangements. Featuring Johnny Weissmuller (the most famous Tarzan), Esther Williams, the beautiful Aquabelles, a diving troupe and singer Morton Downey with an all-male chorus, the Aquacade packed the house. Close to two million people paid to see the show, many claiming it as the hit of the 1940 fair. Out of the pool, the attractive nineteen-year-old Williams had her hands full fending off an overly amorous, but married Tarzan.

The Clifford C. Fisher Follies Bergere, which enjoyed two successful runs in 1939, became a permanent attraction in 1940. The formula employed beautiful scantily clad girls, performing various dance routines to light-hearted music accompanied by uproarious comedy acts. The sets and costumes proved elaborate and colorful and the prices remained reasonable. Each of the three runs differed, with different casts and acts, and patrons argued the merits of each, many attending multiple times to ensure a fair comparison. Mr. Fisher took it all to the bank.

Salici's Puppets occupied the Hall of Western States Auditorium in 1940, giving kids and adults alike the best in family entertainment. Managed and performed for over two hundred years by the Italian Salici family, the show demonstrated the pinnacle of the art. In one act, a large maestro puppet walked onto stage and sat at a small piano, then proceeded to play Paderewski's minuet. A pianist in the pit synchronized his playing to the puppet's amazing fingering of the keys. A puppet vocalist then accompanied the pianist with his voice synchronized to that of a singer offstage. Often playing to a capacity house, the puppets took fourth in attendance that year, surpassed only by Aquacade, Cavalcade and the Follies.

A fire broke out at the rear of the ballroom stage of the California Building on Saturday morning, August 24, 1940. Twenty-seven engine companies, five water wagons, and two fireboats responded with fifty-two officers and 252 men. Realizing the building couldn't be saved, the firemen contained the blaze for a long as possible while state and local police and two hundred soldiers encamped at Treasure Island from Camp Hunter Liggett began removing the contents of the building. Two Navy minelayers, the USS Montgomery and the USS Ramsey, quickly deployed 160 sailors to assist in the effort to retrieve the art, historical artifacts, and displays as well as a large amount of equipment files and furnishings. The fire destroyed the entire building with the exception of the detached wing housing the Natural Resources displays, yet little of the contents were damaged, thanks to the valiant efforts of many. Three hours after the fire died out, the state established new headquarters with full communications, determined to maintain operations during the final month of the fair.

THE END OF A GREAT FAIR

By the end of the summer of 1940, the fair's management declared September 29, 1940, as the final day of the Golden Gate International Exposition. The people of the San Francisco Bay Area didn't buy it, expecting a continuation, as before. In order to drive the fact home, a publicity campaign stated emphatically, "Treasure Island closes forever September 29." Fair attendance one again jumped as the message struck home. Everyone wanted one last look, a final visit. On the final day, the Golden Gate International Exposition hosted a nationally broadcast radio show recounting the story of the Golden Gate International Exposition. A crowd of 85,000 attended the broadcast, which was also heard by a radio audience of millions. A narration featuring music and sounds closed San Francisco's final world's fair.

The Golden Gate International Exposition is burdened with a reputation as the worst of San Francisco's three world's fairs, but perhaps that's a bit unfair. Admittedly, the architecture proved less than inspiring. Pacifica, as a style of architecture, quickly fell out of favor. The only San Francisco fair to lose money, it lost $1,203,582.20 in 1939 but earned $644,158.94 in 1940, for a total loss just over a half-million dollars. Yet it brought jobs and non-fair revenue to a depressed area. Beyond that, it provided a bright light in dire times. Ask any depression-era resident who saw the Golden Gate International Exposition about the fair and the stories start tumbling out. It was a great fair held at a time when it was sorely needed.

San Francisco's airport never made it to Treasure Island. World War II interceded and the navy laid claim to the island to use as a much-needed naval base. Although the non-permanent fair buildings were bulldozed, a few of the mementos were placed in storage. The Navy opened the Treasure Island Museum in 1976, displaying the fair's artifacts in the lobby of the fair's Administration Center, built in 1938 and previously destined to become the San Francisco Airport Terminal. The Navy closed that museum in 1997 when it began the process to return the island to the City of San Francisco. At this writing, the museum and all the articles saved from the Golden Gate International Exposition remain in limbo, their fate in the hands of the Navy and a number of redevelopment agencies. The Treasure Island Museum Association, volunteers who first supported and later managed the museum, are negotiating and lobbying to reopen the museum on Treasure Island.

A YOUNG VIEW OF THE GOLDEN GATE INTERNATIONAL EXPOSITION

My Dad was the foreman of the Pacific Telephone and Telegraph Company crew at Treasure Island at the time of the Golden Gate International Exposition, enabling him to get passes for my sister Betty and me. What a great summer that was! There was so much to see and do.

To add to the atmosphere of the fair and the celebration of the opening of the Golden Gate and the San Francisco Oakland Bay Bridges, San Francisco took on a Western theme. The citizens had to dress in some type of cowboy gear. It was great fun for us Catholic grammar school kids because we could wear cowboy stuff to school instead of our uniforms, cap pistols and all. By the way, that's how Levis jeans got so popular. Everybody bought some and really liked them after finding out how rugged and comfortable they were. The original Levi factory was on Valencia Street between 15th and 16th streets. My dad thought the whole thing was silly and didn't join in until he was caught by the Keystone Cops on Market Street and put in *Kangaroo Court*, a wooden play jail on a trailer with a judge. What a burn up for him! He was fined and ordered to wear something Western. He finally broke down and bought a neckerchief that he kept taking off and on.

Almost every major company had an exhibit at the fair. I saw television for the first time. They transmitted from the GE exhibit to the other end of the Island. There also were free outdoor shows with name performers. I remember my sister and several of her high school pals catching the first ferry in the morning to get good seats for Bing Crosby's show. It also featured most of the big bands like Jimmy and Tommy Dorsey, Glenn Miller, Benny Goodman, Harry James and Count Basie.

I saw it all, even *Elsie the Cow*, who was the trademark of the Borden Milk Company. Elsie was in a streamlined trailer, one side made of glass. Bing Crosby, Bob Hope, and the Andrew Sisters also gave a free show but you couldn't get near that one. There was a show with a cast of hundreds called the Cavalcade of the Golden West. It was a history of the United States, telling about driving the final stake for the trans-continental railroad with actual locomotives moving on the stage. It reenacted Custer's "Last Stand" with the cavalry and Indians on horseback, shooting their rifles. There also was Billy Rose's Aquacade featuring Esther Williams and Johnny Weissmuller, the Folies Bergere and a great amusement park at the north end of the Island. The movie *Alexander Graham Bell*, starring Don Ameche and Henry Fonda as Mr. Watson had its West Coast premier in 1939 on Treasure Island. My mom and dad had a photo, now missing, of Ameche, Fonda, the president, and other officers of PT&T with my dad in front of the theater before the premier. The telephone company had an exhibit in the Trade Building. One of our very close friends Beverly Grubb, the future Mrs. Jim Hagarty, was one of the hostesses there in 1940. She recently showed us a picture of her and the crew in front of the "Tower of the Sun." What a beauty she was and still is.

The fair was originally built to become the San Francisco-Oakland International Airport. The three permanent buildings on the south side of the island were to serve as the administration building and two hangars. Pan American Airlines' "China Clipper" was housed and took off from there. The inlet between Yerba Buena and Treasure Island was known as "Clipper Cove." The war came along and changed all that. "TI" (Treasure Island) became a naval base, the operations base for the Western Sea Frontier.

—Matt O'Neil, Sacramento, CA

Coppa's Restaurant in the Monkey Block attracted the Bohemians. —*Photo courtesy of San Francisco History Center, San Francisco Public Library*

Chapter 9
San Francisco's Restaurants of the Past

San Franciscans love to eat. San Francisco's restaurants vie for customers with a highly varied fare. Some restaurants are gathering places for the famous and infamous. Others, feeding a loyal local following, reach icon status. Coupled with a port that brought in foods and spices from the world over, as well as one of the most culturally diverse populations in the world, any culinary desire finds its match in the city. The loss of a restaurant triggers an emotional incident, burning up newspaper columnists' space, and causing the passage of meaningless city hall resolutions.

Three American cities, New York, New Orleans, and San Francisco, are recognized for their restaurants and the high quality of their food. Admittedly, locales exist that are noted for specialty foods, like Chicago's beef and great Polish food, Kansas City's barbecue, and Los Angeles with its pretenses. (Yes, I just made an enemy or two, but don't be fooled, L.A's food is all for show, not the palate.) San Francisco boasts first class local ingredients such as Dungeness crab, sand dabs (local flounders—sweet and tender), artichokes from Castroville, Italian dry salami with a local mold growing on the casing, and crusty bread the locals call French bread and everyone else calls sourdough. The list goes on, although some delicacies, like the San Francisco Bay shrimp (*Crangon franciscorum*), are lost to history. They died out after World War II. They were small but sweet and succulent beyond words according to those who still recall.

San Francisco's restaurant craze began with the Gold Rush and the influx of money and foreigners. As described previously, the men of the Gold Rush arrived unencumbered. No wives, no mothers, no one to cook dinner. The men heading for the gold fields didn't have time to cook and likely didn't know how. Those remaining in the city used every hour extracting gold from those coming or going to the gold fields. They lived in a room or shared a room. Few had a house of their own and if they did, they rented out rooms. The high demand for skilled cooks and chefs attracted men and a few women from across the world. San Franciscans paid well for a good meal and paid exorbitantly for a sumptuous meal. By the 1860s, no other city in the United States had more restaurants per capita, with the possible exception of New York.

France offered San Francisco some of her best. The restaurant industry there brutalized aspiring chefs with too many top chefs competing for a stagnant number of restaurants, given France's stable population. New York grew slowly, attracting primarily poor immigrants. Bustling New Orleans offered better opportunities as the stepping off and return port for Panama and California but that also made it easy to get from there to San Francisco where the real money lay. The French chefs quickly found themselves a home that appreciated and lauded their skills. Alexandre Dumas, author of *The Three Musketeers*, wrote, "After Paris, the city with the most restaurants is San Francisco. It has restaurants from every country, even China." Dumas died in 1870, but his comment was finally published in his *Le Grand Dictionaire de Cuisine* in 1873. By 1912, San Francisco listed 438 restaurants in operation.

THE POODLE DOG

The Poodle Dog restaurant opened in 1849—one of San Francisco's first and certainly its most famous French restaurant. The origin of the name remains obscure. One legend claims the restaurant gained its name from the owner's long-haired pet poodle because the locals just wouldn't attempt the

The Poodle Dog Restaurant as it appeared in 1849 on Dupont Street. —*Image courtesy of Claudine Chalmers*

French name. An old Frenchwoman ran the rotisserie-style restaurant. She offered the comforts of a civilized meal, and returning miners quickly opened their pouches of gold dust to sit at her table. Diners would suggest, "Let's go to the Poodle Dog," and the name fell into popular use. Another story suggested the poodle was a stray that hung around the establishment and was soon adopted as the restaurant's mascot. A third story claimed that a Frenchman who arrived from New Orleans in 1849 managed the restaurant of this tale, *Le Poulet d'Or*. Since many of the miners were only semi-literate, sounding out the name produced Poodle Dog.

At the turn of the century, the owners published a brochure in celebration of the Poodle Dog's fiftieth anniversary. They stated that a couple of Frenchmen, Messrs. Peguillan and Langsman, opened the restaurant. The dog, a small, white poodle owned by the wife of Francois Peguillan was a rarity, drawing almost as much attention to the restaurant as its cuisine. Named Ami, the poodle assumed the position of host, greeting all with friendship and hospitality. Indeed, some considered Ami the proprietor, thus exclaiming, "Let's eat at the Poodle Dog!"

The famous Poodle Dog logo as it appeared in an 1898 fiftieth anniversary celebration menu. —*Image courtesy of Claudine Chalmers*

Located in what would later become Chinatown at Washington and Dupont streets (now Grant Avenue), the Poodle Dog was housed in a wooden shanty with sanded floors, rough wooden tables covered in oilcloth, a rudimentary bar at one end. It offered a menu and price list that belied its fine cuisine—a fine dinner cost just fifteen cents. The meal began with a rich peasant soup, followed by a fish course of local catch, freshest sole, rock cod, flounder, or smelt, served with a tasty French sauce. The meat course, served *en bloc*, allowed each guest to slice his own portion from a large roast or boiled joint and was served with a pot of mustard and two large dishes of vegetables. The chef followed that course with a big bowl of his own mixed salad, served with ceremony. The final course was "fruit in season," all each guest could eat. A pint of the owner's new, watered claret accompanied the meal, the wine pressed and fermented from local mission grapes. The restaurant offered a large beer stein full of coffee for an additional five cents.

By the middle of the 1850s, food prices had dipped dramatically, providing an enviable level of quality. Californians pressed the finest olive oil, grew luscious fruit

A sketch of dinner at the Old Poodle Dog, 1898—very Victorian. —*Image courtesy of Claudine Chalmers*

just below the city's borders, and raised healthy sheep and cattle on the grassy hills. They raised fat, healthy pigs and chickens within the city limits. Many gold miners soon found they could make a better living tapping the state's other natural resources. In less than a decade, the state economy hinged more on agriculture and trade than it did on gold.

The restaurant moved to its Bush Street location in 1868, now officially taking the Old Poodle Dog name. The dog, Ami, died two days after moving from the original location. Whether caused by old age or a broken heart, the Poodle Dog lost its namesake. The new restaurant, made of fireproof pressed brick, towered six stories with a basement below.

The lavish first floor dining room of the new facility offered public accommodations where a man could safely take his wife and daughter to dine in elegance—a décor in a style torn between the Rococo and Louis XIV styles. With a meal priced at around a dollar, it offered the highest quality cuisine in the city. The second floor hosted private dining rooms suitable for a meeting and dinner with a member or two of the opposite sex, which was considered to be risqué, but not particularly terrible. Accessed via a side door leading to an elevator, the third, fourth and fifth floors offered cozy rooms for private assignations often only whispered about. Each suite included an elegant bed, rich Axminster carpets from Europe, and an attached bathroom. The elevator operator became a very

The Poodle Dog Restaurant, 1868—1898

wealthy man on the tips provided "for service." Propriety, and later bribes, kept the upstairs activities from developing into public scandals touching many of the city's elite. The sixth floor main banquet room hosted opulent parties of up to two hundred and fifty guests with a hidden alcove for the orchestra. A smaller banquet room was available for "presentations, college fraternities, lodges, anniversary dinners, etc."

By the 1890s, the Poodle Dog acquired Chef Calixte Lalanne as its *chef de quisine*. Lalanne's artistry elevated the restaurant to the height of French haute cuisine. Throughout the nineteenth century, and due to changes in ownership and management plus multiple incarnations, the Poodle Dog maintained its position as the foremost French restaurant in town.

French restaurants, and most likely the Poodle Dog, participated in the graft of Mayor Schmitz and Boss Abe Reef, as mentioned previously. Bribes formed the basis for the businesses' ability to keep their upper rooms in operation and scandal-free. It was all part of doing business in San Francisco; people knew but people looked away.

The principals of the Old Poodle Dog in 1898. —*Image courtesy of Claudine Chalmers*

A lady might dine with her husband downstairs on Sunday knowing full well he may have been upstairs on Saturday night. Private dining rooms have remained a San Francisco fixture through its history.

The earthquake and fire of 1906 destroyed the original Poodle Dog and the Old Poodle Dog. The Old Poodle Dog reopened on Eddy Street in mid-1906 under J. B. Pon and Calixte Lalanne. As the city's reconstruction continued, the demand for upscale restaurants grew with it.

In 1908, the owners of the Poodle Dog, the Old Poodle Dog, John Bergez's Restaurant and Frank's Rotisserie merged their businesses, opening Bush Street and Claude Lane under Lalanne, with partners Jean B. Pon, Jean Bergez, Louis Coutard, and Camille Mailhebeau. The restaurant now boasted five floors; the top floor offered a ballroom. A side door mimicked the earlier establishment, and a birdcage elevator took the men and their "companions" upstairs. They brought the elegance of the Nineties back to San Francisco, as the Bergez-Franks Old Poodle Dog. The cuisine reflected the skills of some of the finest French chefs in the city but also included innovations unique to San Francisco. The original Louis salad dressing originated in the Bergez-Franks Old Poodle Dog, circa 1908, a product of the skills of Louis Coutard.

It should be noted that Mr. Lalanne, Mr. Coutard, and Mr. Pon were brothers-in-law. They married three sisters who were born in France, and whose maiden name was also Lalanne, a common name in France.

The Old Poodle Dog unfortunately failed to hold up under prohibition. The restaurant closed it doors the night of April 15, 1922. Lalanne stated that "great cuisine cannot be served without wine." He did, however, open a new establishment opposite the Palace Hotel on New Montgomery, though little is written of it. The menu included sparkling apple and grape juices from Motts and the old Cresta Blanca Winery (now Wente) in Livermore, among others.

Lalanne opened the Ritz French Restaurant at 65 Post Street in San Francisco in 1933. Prohibition had ended and the wine flowed anew. Calixte Lalanne died in 1942 and his son Louis promptly renamed his restaurant the Ritz Old Poodle Dog to honor his father's first love. Eight years later, the San Francisco *News* recognized the senior Lalanne as a "chef without peer."

The restaurant continued the traditions of old San Francisco, a lively business not without its conflicts. Lalanne's son Cal related an incident his father Louis had told him about a time when the second cook picked up the fry cook, who was small, and sat him on the stove. Another time his mother got between them (one of them had a cleaver in his hand). She said, "If you're going to hit anyone, hit me." The two just couldn't get along. Louis died in 1968 and his wife took over management of the restaurant. It quietly closed following her death in 1980. For the couple, the Old Poodle Dog was a labor of love.

Cal Lalanne fondly related, "My favorite remembrance was that on every Sunday night, after the guests were gone and the restaurant closed, they would have a perfect Manhattan and the two of them would sit down and have dinner and the closing waiter and the maitre d' would wait on them. The staff loved them."

In June 1984, Cal Lalanne and his wife Wendy reopened the Old Poodle Dog in the glass-roofed Crocker Galleria at 1 Montgomery Street at Post. It rated the maximum number of stars by the food writers of the *Chronicle* and was written up in *Gourmet* magazine. While maintaining a successful CPA practice, and admittedly not being familiar with the restaurant business, Lalanne hired a successful chef, recommended by Robert Mondavi. His new chef decided to also assume the role of manager.

They remained open for a year and a half. The lunch business was fine, but the night business began falling off. The overhead created by the chef proved overwhelming. The type of food served was labor intensive, strictly nouvelle cuisine, right out of the Chefs of France at the Mondavi Winery where the chef previously taught. Lalanne recommended changes but the chef/manager couldn't agree on implementation. Determining he couldn't go on with the overwhelming overhead, Lalanne decided to close. San Francisco's finest restaurant tradition ended.

The heritage of the Poodle Dog restaurants offers a reflection of San Francisco's changing traditions, from the need for good food, then to world-class food, rising to opulence and excess, then settling back again to great food in lavish surroundings. Per Ron Filion, a San Francisco historical researcher, the Poodle Dogs went through the following changes.

- 1849 Poodle Dog Restaurant, Stork & Peguilhan, Proprietors, Dupont & Washington St.
- 1868 Poodle Dog Restaurant, Stork & Peguilhan, Proprietors, 445 Bush St. at Grant Ave.
- 1880 Poodle Dog Rotisserie, Jacob Stork & Co., Proprietor, 445 Bush St. at Grant Ave.
- 1885 Poodle Dog Restaurant, Leopold Ligon, Proprietor, 445 Bush St. at Grant Ave.
- 1890 Poodle Dog Rotisserie, Andre Potentini, Proprietor, SE corner Grant & Bush St.
- 1891 Poodle Dog Restaurant, G. Mariscotti & Co., Proprietor, SE corner Grant & Bush St.
- 1895 Poodle Dog Restaurant, Allarme & Blanco, Proprietors, SE corner Grant & Bush St.
- 1899 Poodle Dog Restaurant, Blanco & Brun, Proprietors, NE corner Mason & Eddy St.
- 1890s Old Poodle Dog, SE corner Grant Ave. & Sacramento St.
- Mid-1906 Old Poodle Dog, Proprietors J.B. Pon and C. Lalanne, 824–826 Eddy St.
- 1908 Old Poodle Dog Co. Hotel and Restaurant, Bergez, Franks, Pon & Lalanne, Proprietors, 415–431 Bush St. at Claude Lane.
- 1910 Poodle Dog Restaurant and Hotel (European plan), A. Blanco, Proprietor, 111 Mason St.
- 1913 New Poodle Dog, Proprietors unknown, 1115 Polk St.
- 1920s Old Poodle Dog, Lalanne & Barrere, Proprietors, 35 New

Montgomery, opposite the Palace Hotel.

- 1933 Ritz French Restaurant, Calixte Lalanne, Proprietor, 65 Post St.
- 1940 Ritz Poodle Dog, Louis Lalanne, Proprietor, 65 Post St.
- 1983 Old Poodle Dog, Cal & Wendy Lalanne, Proprietors, Crocker Galleria, 1 Montgomery Street at Post.

THE FRENCH ROOM

Most recently, the French Room at the Clift Hotel closed its doors. It had opened in the theatre district next door to the Curran Theatre in 1934, quickly taking the stage as San Francisco's premier dining room. The French Room was famed for its award-winning cuisine as well as its original crystal chandeliers, tall, arched, curtained windows, antique mirrored walls, floral carpeting, potted palms, and Louise XV décor. It lightened its cuisine in the 1990s, serving California French cuisine with influences from around the world, and continuing to garner awards. The extensive menu offered a wide range of choices and eating styles, from pre-theatre to Chef's Prix Fix seven-course meal. The wait staff exuded confidence and cordiality, treating each patron, young or old, with dignity and the utmost in service, an art that is quickly fading. The French Room arguably offered San Francisco's last vestige of genteel dining.

Replaced by the trendy restaurant Asia de Cuba, its elegance and fine cuisine is sorely missed. In place of fine French or French-inspired cuisine, the food is a mélange of spices and ingredients that assault the palate as well as the pocketbook. In place of polite patrons attired in fine dresses or coat and tie, loud hipsters sport t-shirts, jeans or shorts, sneakers, and baseballs caps worn backwards. The adjoining Redwood Room still displays its rich redwood paneling and bar, said by all have come from one tree, but it has lost its ambiance in an uncomfortably revised Art Deco frenzy.

Frommer's online review of the Clift Hotel stated, "The Redwood Room underwent renovation and is noticeably different, with its original sexy redwood walls and light fixtures accompanying Philippe Starck's whimsically luxurious and rather uncomfortable interior. The French Room is gone (replaced by hip restaurant Asia de Cuba).... But in my mind, the only reason to pay the high prices here is if you're interested in being surrounded by the young and hip and want instant access to the bar and restaurant." Herb Caen, the city's famed columnist, would burn more than a few column inches over the remodeling of the Redwood Room, his favored old haunt. One expects Asia de Cuba and the newly remodeled and hip Clift Hotel to shortly follow in the French Room's demise.

THE FRENCH ROOM—CLIFT HOTEL
SEPTEMBER 1996
MENU

~APPETIZERS~

Escargot
*Sauteed with Sweetbreads and Lobster,
Cognac Cream Sauce*
twelve dollars

Osetra Caviar
*Corn Blinis, Quail Egg Salad, Lemon-
Pepper Cured Salmon*
twelve dollars

Sonoma Foie Gras
Baked Apple and Onion Marmalade
fourteen dollars

Steak Tartare
*Fresh Ground Tenderloin with Toast
Points, Black Pepper Pappadams &
Traditional Condiments*
Requires advance notice
fifteen dollars

Iced Seasonal Seafood
*Jumbo Prawns, Oysters, Clams,
Marinated Mussels, Fresh Ceviche and
Hawaiian Seaweed Salad*
fifteen dollars

Griddle Lobster Cake
Buttered Leeks and Beet Jus
sixteen dollars

Truffled Risotto
*Roasted Portabello Mushrooms,
Asparagus, Prosciutto and
Goat Cheese*
ten dollars

Charcuterie
*Ask your server about the Chef's selection
of Fresh Pate on Terrine of Sausage served
with Toast Points & Tradional
Condiments*
eleven dollars

Hearts of Romaine
*Caesar-style Dressing and
Parmesan Crisps*
eight dollars

Normandy Brie Soup
*Black Truffles and
Rosemary Croutons*
eight dollars

The Gorgonzola Salad
*Baby Lettuce tossed with Fresh Pear,
Bacon, Red Onion, Spiced Pecans with
Beet Chips and Gorgonzola*
ten dollars

The Vegetarian Prix Fixe Menu
*Ask your server about our
Alternative Menu*
twenty four-dollars

Executive Chef
Mercer A. Mohr
The Clift Hotel, San Francisco

~Entrees~

Pressed Skillet Chicken
*Herb Marinated Petit Poussin with
Artichoke, Mushroom and
Tomato Hash*
nineteen dollars

Grilled New York Steak
*The only USDA Certified Prime Beef in
Town, Dry Aged in our own Cellar,
Grilled on the Bone*
thirty dollars

Niman Schell Tenderloin of Beef
*Asparagus, Morel Mushrooms
and Foie Gras Potatoes*
twenty-eight dollars

Veal T-Bone Steak
*Marinated in Guinness and Honey
Smoked Ham Sweet Potatoes*
twenty-eight dollars

Cedar Plank Salmon
*Broiled on a Seasoned Wood Plank
Sauteed Spinach and White
Bean Cassoulet*
twenty-four dollars

Seasonal Wild Game
thirty-one dollars

Roast Rack of Lamb
*Dry Aged Colorado Lamb, Toasted Pine
Nut Crust Arborio Rice*
thirty-six dollars

Hawaiian Fresh Fish
twenty-six dollars

**San Francisco
"Lobster" Ciappino**
*Live Whole Main Lobster
and so much more*
thirty-four dollars

Prime "Certified Angus" Rib
*Traditional Clift Prime Rib
Carved Table-Side
Spinach Souffle and Yorkshire Pudding*
twenty-seven dollars

Theatre Menu
Suggested Selections for those on the go!
thirty-nine dollars

Chef's Prix Fix Menu
Seven Course Custom Menu
fifty-five dollars

~Vegetarian Selections~

Starters

Choice of:

Tomato Consomme en Croute
Straw Mushrooms Julienne
Vegetables
Spinach & Brie Soup
Truffles & Rosemary Crouton
Asparagus & Portabello Salad
Oven-dried tomatoes & Feta
Crispy Potato Terrine
Lentils, French Beans & Feta
Greens & Gorgonzola
Pears, Pecans & Beet Chips
Sorbet Intermezzo

Entrees

Choice of:
Grilled Vegetable Tart
White Beans & Fresh Mozzarella

Truffled Risotto
Portabello, Asparagus & Goat
Cheese
Vegetable Stir Fry
Noodles and tofu
Quiche
Mushroom, Spinach and Tomato
Pasta Pasta Pasta

Choices daily
The Vegetarian Sampler
Spring Rolls
Spanakopita
Vegetables
Legumes
Tomato Consomme
Pasta
Asparagus and Portabello
Dessert & Mignardise
twenty-four dollars

~Theatre Menu~

STARTERS
choice of:

Charcuterie
Ask your server about the chef's
selection of Fresh Pate Een Terrine
or Sausage served with Toast points
and Traditional Condiments

or

Normandy Brie Soup
Black Truffle & Rosemary Croutons

or

Truffled Risotto

or

Hearts of Romaine
Caesar-style Dressing

or

The Gorgonzola Salad

ENTREES
choice of:
All Natural Bradley Ranch Beef
Tradional Clift Prime Rib
Carved Table-Side

or

Hawaiian Fresh Fish
Received daily, the freshest and highest
quality seafood available from Royal
Hawaiian Seafood Importers

or

Cedar Plank Salmon
Broiled on a seasoned wood plank,
Sauteed Spinach
and White Bean Cassoulet

Traditional French Room
Dessert Cart Served Table-Side
choice of:
Imported or Domestic Cheese with
Fresh Fruit or Berries
D'anjou Pear Tart
Raspberry Linzer Torte
Seasonal Fresh Fruit Tart
Berries and Creme Fraiche
Mignardise
thirty-nine dollars

CHEF'S PRIX FIXE DINNER
First Course
Osetra Caviar

or

Sonoma Foie Gras
Try a California Late Harvest Wine

Second Course
Truffled Risotto

or

Escargot
Lobster & Sweetbreads
Sorbet Intermezzo
Dry Aged Colorado Lamb Rack

or

Lobster Cioppino

Third Course
Dry Aged Colorado
Lamb Rack

or

Lobster Cioppino

Fourth Course
Organic Baby Lettuces
White Truffle Vinaigrette

or

Gorgonzola Salad
Pancetta, Spiced Nuts, Onions
and Pears

Fifth Course
Choice of Dessert

or

Fruit and Cheese Mignardise
fifty-five dollars

The French set the mark for cuisine in San Francisco. They brought culture, a love of good food and wine, and no little appreciation for life. They also imported fashion and their standards for the building arts. Frenchtown, centered on Dupont (Grant) and Sacramento and down Commercial Street to Long Wharf, provided a glimpse of France. Other restaurants and other cultural fare had to stand at the top of their class to compete.

Of course, not all San Franciscans ate at fine restaurants. Meals came in all price ranges and most were hearty, if not refined. The "Three for Two" restaurants such as the waterfront Clipper of the 1870s offered three dishes for two bits, or twenty-five cents. These restaurants depended on volume, serving five or six thousand meals daily. The diner usually ordered a soup or vegetable, a portion of meat, usually beef or mutton served with potatoes, and a dessert dish. Generous serving sizes and a long list of choices made up for the plainness of the food served. Bread and butter came with the meal but a beverage, coffee, tea, chocolate, beer or wine cost a dime unless substituted for the soup or dessert. The table settings met reasonable standards, with a clean tablecloth for each sitting, plus sparkling but heavy glasses and heavy white dishes designed to take the knocks of continuous use.

A substantial number of mid-range restaurants filled the gap between the "Three for Two's" and the expensive restaurants. Usually French or Italian inspired, they offered a fine meal in a nice setting with a pint of wine. By the early 1870s, San Franciscan's tastes included wine with their meals, a habit that shocked most newcomers. To fill this need, French Claret arrived in oak barrels, but by the early 1880s, California's wines outclassed the ordinary French wine. San Francisco had developed the ability to distinguish the qualities of a fine wine.

At the bottom of the scale, there was indeed a "free lunch." Bars offered a lunch counter to entice patrons to remain and drink. Unlike the rest of the country where stale crackers and hard sausage offered a bit of a nibble, San Francisco's bars provided a broad range of the city's finest food that sometimes rivaled the restaurants. Those lacking the wherewithal to frequent a "three for two" could stop by a local tavern and enjoy a free lunch. The purchase of a drink was truly optional. The proprietors knew that when funds were available, loyalty ruled.

THE ITALIANS

Today, most folks considering San Francisco restaurants around Fisherman's Wharf picture Italian. North Beach and Fisherman's Wharf took their heritage from Italian fishermen, most arriving in the late 1800s, largely from the region around Genoa, but also from the north and south of Italy. A few came at the time of the Gold Rush and quickly learned that gold swam in the bay. San Francisco's Italian fishery tradition began early. The Genovese fished but they also cooked, offering pasta, scallopini and a great fish and shellfish stew they created called cioppino, a dish unique to San Francisco. They cooked the cioppino right on the boats, freshly caught. The smell was said to be overwhelming to those who came down to the wharf to buy fish fresh off the boats. Given a serving, San Francisco learned how heaven must taste.

Initially, the fine cuisine remained in their homes and on the boats at wharf-side but it wasn't long before wharf-side pots and small sidewalk cafés caught the attention of the non-Italians. Giuseppe Bazzuro's Italian restaurant located at 105 Pacific Street proved most notable. Bazzuro took over a stranded sailing boat at Davis and Pacific and turned it into a restaurant. Some historians credit him with the creation of cioppino but regardless, he made it, sold it, and the non-Italians ate it by the bucket. When the city filled in the bay around his ship, Bazzuro build a house and restaurant on that spot. It burned to the ground in the '06 quake and fire but he quickly rebuilt. Still, Bazzuro's couldn't survive prohibition and the depression that followed.

By 1890, over five thousand Italians lived in San Francisco. North Beach at the foot of Telegraph Hill soon became the Latin Quarter, also called Little Italy. It offered the checkered tablecloth restaurants and Italian delicatessens that quickly stole the city's hearts. The aroma of fresh pasta sauces, spices, garlic, sausages and of course, freshly cooked fish filled the air and piqued appetites. Most Italian eateries equated with family food: inexpensive, satisfying, and tasty. Landmark Italian restaurants like the Fior d'Italia began life serving a rough crowd, becoming working-family oriented at the turn of the twentieth century, and going "up town" in the 1950s after the war. A few earned a reputation in the early days of the twentieth century.

Coppa's restaurant began with a pedigree. Joe Coppa came to San Francisco from Turin, Italy, but not before honing his skills as a chef in Paris. In San Francisco, he worked as a chef at the Occidental Hotel, Martinelli's, and at the Poodle Dog. Coppa opened his own restaurant in the Montgomery block, which quickly gained a reputation as Bohemian, based on its clientele. The excellent but reasonably priced food drew the literary crowd. High ceilings with large thought-provoking, literary-inspired murals created a "Bohemian Hall of Fame," offsetting a small dining room set with twenty tables. The restaurant often saw the likes of Jack London, George Sterling, Will Irwin, and others of note. Art-conscious patrons crowded the small restaurants in the hopes of gazing on these literary greats. Coppa's closed after the big quake, though the building survived.

Coppa opened other venues in other places, the Neptune Palace on Sutter and Coppa's Pompeian Garden, located just beyond the city limits. Unfortunately, Coppa never managed to recapture the magic of his first restaurant in the "Monkey Block." He finally retired in the late 1930s.

Sanguinetti's, an old-time Embarcadero spaghetti house dating back to the 1890s, gave up the ghost after the ferry traffic dwindled in the early 1950s. You could get all the fish you could eat for a nickel during the depression. Sawdust on the floors soaked up spilled steam beer but the cooking was superb and the Italian bread was fresh and hot. However, the new Bay Bridge bypassed the Embarcadero, taking away the restaurant's customers.

Name restaurants like DiMaggio's on Fisherman's Wharf suffered from changing times—folks didn't patronize them because they seemed too "touristy." The restaurant wasn't named for Joe or his brother, Tom. They were born into it. The DiMaggio family began, as did many, in the fishing industry then transitioning into the restaurant business. Joe's brother Tom operated it in the later days, offering grilled rock cod,

broiled salmon with drawn butter, and veal scallopini a'la DiMaggio, as well as a great New York steak. True to their heritage, they also served spaghetti, lasagne, rigatoni, mostaccioli, ravioli and other pastas. DiMaggio's, a first rate fish grotto, closed in the 1980s. Joe's Crab Shack, a Texas Gulf Coast chain eatery, replaced DiMaggio's.

Vanessi's, a true San Francisco institution, closed its doors on June 28, 1997. Opening in 1936, Vanessi's led the way in upscale Italian restaurants, promoting its staff and skills to star status and creating a multitude of spin-offs. Joe Vanessi and Silvio Zorzi opened the house at 438 Broadway on North Beach, featuring their now famed osso buco and creamy zabaglione. When Vanessi later sold his interest, new co-owners Bart Shea, managing the restaurant and the dinning room manager, and Giovani Leoni, kitchen director, carried on the tradition of fine Venetian-style fare. A customer could watch the pasta chefs toss their creations or sit in the Venetian Room and enjoy a truly fine dining experience.

By the 1980s, Vanessi's moved up to Nob Hill on California Street and Leoni set off to open his own restaurant. The dinner crowd suffered long waits at the bar and the house specialties lost a bit of their luster—too few clams in the linguine, a rare steak cooked medium, or perhaps a sauce that lacked gusto. It lost the North Beach feel and the crowd found other places to eat. Vanessi's became the dowager queen you took friends to in order to remember when. Homage had to be paid, but eventually, no one came.

Vanessi's Italian Restaurant at 438 Broadway. —*Photo courtesy of San Francisco History Center, San Francisco Public Library*

EATING CHINESE

Did you know chop suey was created in San Francisco by a Chinese chef who ran out of food? Presented at the end of his day with hungry, inebriated patrons and no food left, he chopped up leftovers, vegetables and meat scraps, and served it to

Grand dining room of the Chinese restaurant on Dupont.—*Courtesy of The Bancroft Library, University of California, Berkeley*

his guests, calling it chop suey. The concoction proved popular and chop suey houses sprung up on the fringes of Chinatown. At least, so legend claims.

For most of the nineteenth century, San Francisco's Chinese restaurants catered primarily to the Chinese, although some caught on with the Caucasians who visited Chinatown for its many vices. The odd venturesome soul strolled Chinatown looking for unique culinary experiences. Few were disappointed. Until the quake and a bit of Westernization of the menu including chop suey and Westernized chow mein, most Chinese restaurants with names like "Balcony of Joy and Delight," "Fragrant Almond Chamber," and "Chamber of Odors of Different Lands" remained primarily the domain of the "Celestials."

The best Chinese restaurant of early San Francisco may have been Hang Far Low. It's difficult to tell since most early guide books overlooked or warned tourists away from Chinese restaurants, claiming the cuisine made no attempt to accommodate the Western style or customs and some ingredients would offend Western tastes.

John S. Hittell in his 1888 *Guide Book to San Francisco* singled out Hang "Fer" Low (Hang Far Low) as his recommended restaurant in Chinatown. It was located on Dupont (now Grant Avenue) between Clay and Sacramento, and Hittell stated it was the Delmonico's of Chinese restaurants. Multi-storied, the business reserved the second floor for regular boarders, paying by the week or month. The upper floor, reserved for wealthy guests, offered private accommodations achieved by movable parti-

Above: Restaurants in Chinatown in the early '30s—the sign on the building halfway down the block on the left says, "Noodles - Hang far Low." —*Author's collection*

Left: Interior of a San Francisco Chinese restaurant in 1890s. — *Author's collection*

tions or screens. Dinner for six guests could cost between twenty and one hundred dollars and were frequently hosted by wealthy Chinese. Dinner often lasted past 2 A.M. including intervals for taking the air or for private business transactions. Delicacies served during such occasions included bird's-nest soup, shark's fins, taranaki fungus (from a New Zealand tree), Chinese terrapin, Chinese goose, Chinese quail, fish brains, tender shoots of bamboo, various vegetables "strange to American eyes," arrack (a rice wine), champagne and sherry, as well as a few Westernized dishes.

Hang Far Low was destroyed in the 1906 quake and rebuilt quickly in the reborn Chinatown. Clarence Edwords in his 1914 *Bohemian San Francisco* claimed "Chinese restaurant life never appealed to Bohemians" though he did state that he enjoyed some excellent dishes there. He identified Hang Far Low, about whose name many jokes were told, as the best Chinese restaurant in San Francisco at that time. Edwords asked the restaurant's manager what he should order if he wanted to taste their best dish. The manager "protested that there were so many good things it was impossible to name just one as being the best. 'You see, we have fish fins, they are very good. Snails, China style. Very good, too. Then we have turtle brought from China, different from the turtle they have here, and we cook it China style. Eels come from China and they are cooked China style, too. What is China style? That I cannot tell you for the cook knows and nobody else. When we cook China style everything is more better. We have here the very best tea.'"

Hang Far Low continued successfully into the fifties, always offering the finest in Cantonese cuisine. Another Chinese restaurant, Shanghai Low, a dinner club, gained fame through the film *The Lady from Shanghai,* starring Rita Hayworth and Orson Welles. Located at 532 Grant Avenue, it was a favorite dinner spot during the forties and fifties, but it also failed to survive the sixties.

THEME RESTAURANTS

San Francisco's patrons encouraged restaurants that had more than just good food. Some places were noted as much for their character and atmosphere as they

The Dungeon—a great way to celebrate Prohibition, September 1920. —*Courtesy of The Bancroft Library, University of California, Berkeley*

Coffee Dan's—the hammers sound approval for good performances and also get the waiter's attention. One of the liveliest little holes in the city. —*Author's collection*

COFFEE DAN'S

No one should forget the riotous Coffee Dan's at Powell and O'Farrell streets, later relocated to 430 Mason Street, just off Geary. It opened for breakfast, serving customers long past dinner. The quickest access to the Powell and O'Farrell street location was via a slide which deposited customers to the cafe's basement level. Ladies with skirts and dresses soon learned of the slide's pitfalls requiring a special "Coffee Dan's grip." Some used the stairs made available for the less adventuresome. Nighttime entertainment was great jazz—Artie Shaw performed at Coffee Dan's. Small wooden mallets were provided for applause and the tables took a beating. The dishware was cheap and breaking dishes signaled the highest level of appreciation. Calling for service also required rapping on the table with a mallet or dish.

The original club opened in the early 1920s as a cabaret and speakeasy. It gained international fame when featured in the 1927 early talkie, *The Jazz Singer* with Al Jolson. It became a café after the repeal of prohibition, but retained the entertainment at night. Regardless, it claimed the title as the noisiest joint in the city throughout its existence. Coffee Dan's remained open through the 1950s, and then slipped away with minimal clatter.

were for their cooking style and menu offerings. Anywhere else they'd be gimmicks, but in San Francisco, they were just a part of the city.

The Domino Club is a fine example. Tucked away at 25 Trinity Place in a small alley off Sutter in the Financial District, the Domino Club was indeed unique—entertainment included jazz, bands, and small groups like the Bell Sisters during the fifties. The Ronnie Klemper Orchestra (known for the song *Cecelia*) was featured there in the sixties, drawing large crowds for the dinner show. Regardless, the main attraction was the art.

Owner Charlie Anderson collected paintings and shared them with his patrons. The club had one of the finest collections of nudes in the city. Uniquely, the collection continuously grew due to the fact that most were created in the restaurant. The club often displayed a live nude female modeling for the house artist, painting his latest creation. The artist was Roberto Lupetti, a well-respected Italian-born painter. Patrons could eat or drink and watch Lupetti create another masterpiece.

The club opened sometime after the 1939 World's Fair at Treasure Island and immediately exhibited a painting from that event called *Gloria*, painted by Irving Sinclair. Anderson placed *Gloria* prominently above the bar, to the admiration of all. Sinclair, a set designer for Fox Studios, painted many pin-ups and magazine cov-

Paul Arens and Margaret O'Connell at a fashion show at the Domino Club, 1947—*Gloria* is in the background. —*Photo courtesy of San Francisco History Center, San Francisco Public Library*

The Domino Club was just off Sutter Street in the heart of the Financial District. —*Author's collection*

A postal reminder.... —*Author's collection*

ers as well at the program cover for the Follies Bergere at Treasure Island. *Gloria* graced that program cover. Anderson's office featured a photo of Follies Bergere stripper Sally Rand, fully clothed.

"Meet me at Gloria's" became the phase that meant going to the Domino Club. Lupetti's artwork and *Gloria* remained on display at the Domino Club until its closure in the late 1970s.

"Trader Vic" Bergeron once remarked, "San Francisco, the City that knows chow!" That's a fact and he took full advantage of it. However, he didn't start his empire in San Francisco. Bergeron opened a restaurant and bar on San Pablo Avenue in Oakland in 1932 or 1934 (Vic wasn't too good with facts). He called it Hinky Dink's, a crusty hunting-shack affair with a potbellied stove. Bergeron had a penchant for fun and lively stories as well as exquisite skills mixing exotic drinks and preparing French-American dishes. His easy banter, outgoing nature and great offerings turned Hinky Dink's into a hit. This fact gained recognition with local writers like Herb Caen and Lucius Beebe, both columnists for the *San Francisco Chronicle*.

Born in San Francisco in 1902, Victor Bergeron's father waited tables at the Ritz Old Poodle Dog and at the Saint Francis Hotel. The senior Bergeron later opened a small grocery on San Pablo in Oakland, across the street from the site where Victor would eventually open his club. Six-year-old Victor injured his left leg, which eventually required amputation due to a knee infection. The loss never slowed him down.

By 1936, Oakland's Hinky Dink's had become "Trader Vic's" and Bergeron was "The Trader," a name earned by trading food and drink for services and goods. A trip to Cuba introduced him to rum-based drinks like the daiquiri, but repeating the recipes

The interior of Trader Vic's Restaurant—that one is missed! Great food and drinks. —*Photo courtesy of San Francisco History Center, San Francisco Public Library*

required skill and experimentation. Tiring of his rustic cabin theme, Bergeron looked at Don the Beachcomber in Los Angeles and decided on a South Pacific theme, one that hadn't been created up north. Switching to a Polynesian theme, Trader Vic's took on a new persona, requiring new food and drinks. He based his drinks on rum, favored by sailors the world over, and his food changed to a Chinese-Polynesian style. His ingredients went tropical and his drinks could peel the paint off walls.

The South Seas theme propelled his patrons to another time and another place, the best sort of escapist fun. Trader Vic's customer base increased dramatically with the building of the Bay Bridge in 1936 and the opening of the 1939–1940 Golden Gate International Exposition on Treasure Island. Later, the war in the Pacific drew servicemen on leave, eager to "re-experience" the South Pacific. Bergeron's business continued to grow. In 1944, Trader Vic invented the "Mai Tai," which in Tahitian means "the very best." The sweet rum cocktail became the Trader Vic's slogan as well as its signature drink. Bergeron introduced the Mai Tai to the Hawaiian Islands in the fifties.

Trader Vic's opened in San Francisco's Cosmo Alley in 1951 and immediately carved out a new niche in the city. The restaurant, built from an old corrugated iron parking garage, offered an escape from the mundane. Passing along the narrow walkway through a tropical garden, customers entered the rustic shed and were transported into a world of Tiki dolls, dried puffer fish, woven mats, Maori war clubs, and even a shrunken head or two, if memory serves. The restaurant maintained three dining rooms—the Tiki Room, the Garden Room, and the Captain's Cabin, an opulent room reserved for local royalty. Trader Vic's had arrived and the whole town sat up and took notice. Herb Caen wrote rave reviews. In *Herb Caen's Guide to San Francisco,* 1957, he wrote about Bergeron:

> Unlike some of his successful contemporaries, he refuses to rest on his considerable laurels. Instead he experiments continually with new and exciting dishes and likes nothing better than a challenge (make him a bet that he or his big crew of French and Chinese cooks can't prepare your favorite dish, whatever it may be, and you'll likely lose. Vic built his reputation originally on Chinese and Polynesian dishes, but don't let that limit your thinking. His French cookery is in a class with New York's Le Pavilion and France's Les Pyramides, and I defy any restaurant in the world to touch the steaks, chops, spare ribs, and fowl that emerge in crusty splendor from his great Chinese barbecue ovens.

San Francisco's Trader Vic's holds the distinction of being the first restaurant to serve Queen Elizabeth II. Until that visit with the Reagans in 1983, she had never eaten in a restaurant. Per MisterSF.com, "… the queen, Prince Philip, the Reagans, and their party were served Indonesian lamb roast with peanut sauce, Chinese pork, smoked salmon, and three California wines. In addition to the wines—Chardonnay and a Cabernet—the queen had a daiquiri on the rocks and a Tanqueray martini. Dessert was rum ice cream with praline sauce and fortune cookies."

Victor Bergeron retired in 1972, owning an empire of many restaurants worldwide and a burgeoning specialty food trade. He died in 1984, leaving that empire to his descendants. By the nineties, San Francisco lost interest in Trader Vic's, rushing off to gaze at the works of the latest stars of the culinary world. Trader Vic's closed in 1994 and San Francisco lost a bit of its heart and a bit more of its ability to take itself with a grain of salt. Still, don't write them off yet. Rumors say that like the phoenix, Trader Vic's may rise again in the City by the Bay.

Trader Vic's wasn't the first theme restaurant in the city, just as fish grottos weren't just Italian. Bernstein's Fish Grotto opened at 123 Powell Street in 1912. Maurice Bernstein operated a successful fish stall in Oakland and wanted to expand in a big way. He designed Bernstein's to look like a ship, a full scale, accurate reproduction of Christopher Columbus' *Nina*. The restaurant operated seven nautical-theme dining rooms: the Fisherman's Cave, the Pilot Room, the Sun Deck, the Main Salon, the Cabin Nooks, the Upper Deck, and the Porthole Counter. Mottoes posted in the dining rooms and on their advertising postcards included "Colorful in every respect," "A Fact! Fish caught at 5 A.M. served here the same day!", and "The Ship That Never Goes to Sea."

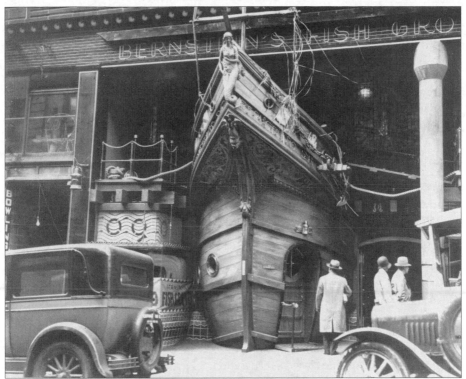

Bernstein's Fish Grotto—the ship was modeled after Columbus' *Nina*. April 5, 1934. —*Photo courtesy of San Francisco History Center, San Francisco Public Library*

Inside Bernstein's, the nautical theme prevails. —*Photo courtesy of San Francisco History Center, San Francisco Public Library*

Bernstein's Fish Grotto served three dishes unique at that time to San Francisco: abalone steaks, mussels bordelaise, and coo-coo clams. The nearby States Restaurant's chef, "Pop" Ernst, rescued abalone from its reputation for being impossible to chew. He trimmed the muscle, sliced it crossways half an inch thick and pounded it like veal. The resultant steak, dredged in egg wash and flour, proved delectable. The States, a German restaurant, went out of business with the start of prohibition. Bernstein's carried on the tradition and abalone caught on.

Bernstein's signature dish, cioppino, remained on the menu from the first day it opened in 1912 until it sadly closed in the early 1980s. The city lost an entertaining restaurant with a unique character.

The Roundhouse, located at the foot of the Golden Gate Bridge, offered something unique, an unobstructed view of the bridge, and the ships that passed through. Built in 1938, the restaurant offered basic American food and featured its "Farmhouse Breakfast," which was served all day. The owners, Ila and Ben Stacy were restaurant veterans from the Oakland Airport Restaurant, and they prepared the famous "Buttermilk Pancakes" at Treasure Island's 1939–1940 Golden Gate International Exposition. Ila Stacey portrayed the original Betty Crocker for NBC. The restaurant offered eighty-five seats and twenty-five windows. Today, the Roundhouse still stands, but only as the gift center and snack bar for the Golden Gate Bridge.

Other historical restaurants, such as Victor's atop the Saint Francis Hotel, George Maradikian's renowned Omar Khayyam's on O'Farrell, the Black Cat on Montgomery, or Kan's on Grant Avenue, deserve recognition. So many great restaurants have come and gone, only to be replaced by more great restaurants. San Francisco remains "the city that knows chow!"

However, a restaurant still exists that seems to elude most histories of the city's heritage. In 1849, Croatian immigrants Nikola Budrovich, Frano Kosta, and Antonio Gasparich opened a small coffee stand on Long Wharf. It's not known what they served, other than coffee, but it was likely local fish grilled over wood coals, the Croatian method of cooking. The New World Coffee Stand, later called the Cold Day, went through successive partnership changes, moves, and growth, as did most others, due to both fires and changing opportunities. John Tadich, a Croatian American, joined the business in 1876 as an employee and bought into it in 1887. The quake and fire of 1906 destroyed the restaurant, but Tadich, like many business owners, immediately rebuilt.

When his partnership broke up in 1912, Tadich moved again, this time naming his restaurant the Tadich Grill. The next year he hired Tom Buich and his brother Mitch Buich the year after, both Croatian immigrants as well. A third brother joined Tadich's employ in 1922. In ill health, Tadich sold the grill to Mitch and Louie Buich. That family still runs the restaurant, famous for its fine food as well as its longevity. Hats off to John Briscoe, author of *Tadich Grill*, for taking the time to share a great story. It's recommended reading and the Tadich Grill is required eating. May it never grace the pages of a "Lost Landmarks" book.

THE DOMINO CLUB

September 1968, the Domino Club—my first visit of many to come. I was on my second date with a lady who had lived in San Francisco and was familiar with the Domino Club. Upon entering, I was struck by the provocative, striking, and impressive collection of nude females on the walls. There were what appeared to be paintings from the masters as well as some more modern. There were Rubenesque nymphs and svelte sinewy beauties that were more to my taste. My date, being familiar with the decor, was interested in my reaction to the environment. I enjoyed it immensely.

We enjoyed a cocktail before going to the second level to be seated for dinner. The bar, as I remember, was impressive. Several mirrors on the tall back bar with dark, rich wood gave one the ability to observe the activities at other tête-à-têtes. The red velvet accents were, in my opinion, appropriate for the atmosphere. There was a sense of naughtiness that heightened the enjoyment of a young couple on a second date. This had the feel of an upscale Barbary Coast venue. Broadway might have Carol Doda, but I enjoyed the tasteful ambiance of this so much more. It was sophisticated San Francisco as I had imagined it having come from the Midwest.

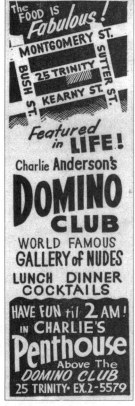

I had requested a private, secluded table, I was surprised to find several private dining rooms with tables accommodating two to six people. While going to our room, we passed an alcove where an artist was in the process of painting a nude model. We watched for a few moments and then proceeded to our room. We enjoyed a sumptuous dinner and a great bottle of wine (I hadn't discovered California wine at that point) from the expansive wine list. We spent some time after dinner at the piano where the cognac was the best and the company was convivial. I returned many times with this date and others, but that first time was truly memorable, which makes writing this today seem like the experience was only yesterday.

—E. Don Werner, San Jose, California

The Domino Club—*Gloria* was a painting of a nude, done for the Golden Gate International Exposition in 1939. —*Author's collection*

An Exile's Toast

Frank Norris, noted author of *The Octopus* and *McTeague*, wrote a toast for his brothers from the Delta Xi chapter of Phi Gamma Delta, a fraternity at the University of California at Berkeley. Intended for reading at the Pig Dinner held at the Old Poodle Dog in 1900, it was written as a parody of poor German-inflected English. The style is said to be a takeoff of Hans and Fritz of the comic strip *The Katzenjammer Kids*, printed in the Hearst newspapers at that time and still running. Those kids never could resist a mischievous prank.

The Pig Dinner evolved from a prank pulled on "Class Day," May 18, 1893, by Norris and his fraternity brothers. Class Day included senior orations and entertainment, the latter provided by the Glee Club. The prank protested the Delta Kappa Epsilon (Dekes) and Beta Theta Pi (Betas) fraternities' monopolization of campus activities, particularly the Glee Club. A barrel tied by a cord was placed on the platform and was labeled, "U. of C. Glee Club." The knotted rope indicated the stranglehold imposed by these two rival societies. When tipped, a squealing pig tumbled out, "honoring" their singing abilities.

The first Pig Dinner, held at Fiji House in Berkeley that night, opened with an elaborate mock ceremony written by Norris. "All hail the Pig!" rang through the hall, and a kiss on the pig's snout sealed each vow. The Fijis (Phi Gams) vowed to repeat the dinner annually, always on the eve of the big game against Stanford. It was held thereafter at the Old Poodle Dog Restaurant in San Francisco until 1906 when the fires of the great earthquake turned the building to ash.

The Palace Hotel, 1890—San Francisco's grandest of all. Its sister hotel, the Grand Hotel, is on the left. —*Author's collection*

Chapter 10
San Francisco's Early Grand Hotels

James Lick arrived in San Francisco just before the Gold Rush with thirty-five thousand dollars in gold and a belief in the potential of the West. He bought up large blocks of land and invested in the local economy. With the advent of the massive creation of wealth that was breaking all the world's rules, Lick built one of the first grand hotels in the city. The Lick House, which opened in August 1862, set a high standard of quality and excellence that encouraged the building of more grand hotels.

The city, destined to be a gateway from its earliest days, needed hotels. Miners headed for the gold fields needed a place to sleep while they collected their gear. Miners returning with gold wanted to luxuriate a bit after months of deprivation. Traders, capitalists, merchants, tourists, and government representatives required temporary accommodations. The disproportionately large number of unmarried men and the married couples without children all needed a semi-permanent place to live. The unsettled nature of the population encouraged a young hotel industry to compete and excel in its trade.

SAN FRANCISCO'S EARLY HOTELS

Early histories claim the first hotel in San Francisco, the City Hotel, opened in November 1846 at the corner of Clay and Kearny streets. It had previously been the home of the Mexican government's American vice-counsel, William Alexander Leidesdorff. An adobe and clay tile structure, its Spartan room accommodations lacked any amenities beyond a bed, likely shared by a number of unacquainted guests. James Lick arrived at the City Hotel on January 7, 1848, and promptly took a room, which included meals. Lick quickly sized up the town and began investing—unbelievable foresight given the fact that gold was yet to be discovered in California.

After the discovery of gold in 1848, the City Hotel became the center for gambling and entertainment, being the city's only public house. After the discovery of gold and before the great rush of '49 began, early miners and gamblers regularly staked thousands on a single hand at the hotel. Speculation hadn't begun in earnest and the gold seemed to come so easy. In the spring of 1849, the owners subdivided the building into small stores and rooms, earning an annual $16,000, with some of the leases then subleased at enormous profits.

Soon after the opening of City Hotel, Captain John Vioget transformed his Vioget House on Portsmouth Square at the southwest corner of Clay and Kearny into the Portsmouth Hotel. The Vioget House had been a rooming house for newcomers from the ship *Portsmouth,* who requested the name change. Vioget is noted as San Francisco's first surveyor and his original map hung in the bar and billiard saloon of the Portsmouth Hotel. Other hotels soon followed including the Parker House (which later became City Hall), the St. Francis, the Union, the Oriental, the Tehama House, the American Hotel, Wilson's Exchange and the five-story wooden-framed Rassette House. The Rassette boarded 416 guests at the time, most of whom were lodgers as well. A fire that started in a room above the hotel's kitchen on May 2, 1853, completely destroyed the hotel causing $100,000 damage, not including the losses of the lodgers and a few

The City Hotel, which claimed to be the first in San Francisco, opened in November 1846 at the corner of Clay and Kearny streets. —Author's collection

surrounding homes. Fortunately, brick hotels prevailed in the area, so the fire didn't become another citywide conflagration. A new Rassette hotel soon replaced the former.

THE NIANTIC HOTEL

Interestingly, the early shortage of building materials and builders turned the abandoned fleet of more than seven hundred abandoned harbor vessels into a source for hostelry. No city ever grew as quickly as San Francisco.

The ship *Niantic* arrived in San Francisco from Panama "with a cargo of tropical produce and 248 passengers, arriving in this harbor on the fifth of July, 1849, after a voyage of sixty-eight days. Within a week after her arrival, the crew deserted, in accordance with established usage, and the old ship was left anchored idly in the stream—a useless 'elephant' on the hands of her consignees, Cook, Baker & Co. A few months later she was sold to parties here." The *Niantic* was hauled ashore at high tide and anchored at the corner of what is now Clay and Sansome streets. She measured nearly one hundred twenty feet long and had copper-bottom plating tacked to her oak hull. Piles driven into the mud alongside her kept her righted and "her oak hull [was] pierced with a Clay Street entrance, above which the enterprising owner had painted the ingratiating sign: 'Rest for the Weary and Storage for Trunks.'" Protected by a shingled roof, the owners divided the ship into rooms, with excellent offices on the decks. A wide balcony surrounded the deck with a veranda above reached by a broad, handsome staircase. Interestingly, the Niantic Hotel drew more income as a hotel than she would have earned hauling cargo and passengers.

The Niantic Hotel—created from a land-bound ship. —*Library of Congress*

The ship *Niantic* operated as a hotel until the fifth great fire burned through the business section of the city on May 4, 1851. The fire consumed eighteen full blocks and damaged six others. The *Niantic* burned to ground level with only the hull left to mark its passing. A new hotel quickly rose on the same site, also named the Niantic Hotel. That structure was demolished in August 1872 in order to build a larger hotel. The *San Francisco Daily* reported on August 16, 1872: "The hull of the old ship

The second Niantic Hotel, built after the first burned down in a city-wide fire. —*Author's collection*

Niantic has been exposed by the excavations for a *new* Niantic Building on the site of the old Niantic Hotel. The keel must have been fully twenty feet below the present level of the street, showing the amount of ground made over it in twenty-three years." A third Niantic building was erected in 1907 when the hull once again was uncovered but left undisturbed. A plaque mounted on the building by the Native Sons of the Golden West in 1919 gave a brief history of the Niantic Hotel.

In May 1978, during construction at 595 Sansome Street, the old hull was again "rediscovered." The construction destroyed most of the stern though the Maritime Museum salvaged some of the timbers. A portion of the bow remains undisturbed in an adjacent lot. Artifacts found included the ship's long windlass, two pistols, a rifle and derringer, thirteen bottles of champagne, stoneware ink bottles, leather-bound books, bolts of fabric, cabin doors, hundred-year-old brass paper clips, copper sheeting, and nails. It's important to remember—back in the days "when the waters came up to Montgomery Street," the *Niantic* floated to 595 Sansome Street on the high tide.

GOLD RUSH HOTELS

Christian Russ, who arrived in 1847 with his family of twelve, promptly began buying up the cheap land. He built a shanty for his family at what later became Pine and Montgomery, an area separated from the main town by a large sand dune. Following that, he and his sons began building cottages, using second-hand lumber. He did

The American Hotel—not much to look at but it beat a tent. — *Library of Congress*

this in anticipation of a population increase due to America's acquisition of California. In 1852, a fire destroyed Russ's cottages. With the Gold Rush in full swing, he built the American Hotel in their place on Bush Street. It wasn't fancy but it made a fortune for Russ.

The Parker House on Portsmouth Plaza rented rooms for as much as $1,800 to $2,400 per month. Accommodations sold for a premium encouraging a hotel-building boom. The St. Francis Hotel opened in 1849; it was a three-story wooden building located at the corner of Dupont and Clay streets. Raising the ante on services, it was the first hotel to offer bed sheets to its lodgers. Rustic by modern standards, the rooms of the St. Francis held claim as the best sleeping accommodations in California. Some customers complained that only the "thinnest of board partitions" or cloth separated the rooms. The Ward House and Graham House were located nearby and built at the same time and each came close to matching the St. Francis for luxury. Amazingly, the materials for both hotels arrived aboard ships as disassembled kits brought around the Horn from the East Coast for reassembly on site. The first St. Francis bore no relation to the twentieth-century St. Francis hotel.

At the request of some of the city's leading citizens, the St. Francis proved its respectability by staging balls and parties requiring fancy dress. Over a two-year pe-riod, its popularity increased until in July 1851 when sixty ladies attended, drawing the admiration and praise of all the local newspapers. No other venue had suc-ceeded in attracting more than twenty-five eligible ladies. Shortly thereafter, the Monumental Six, the city's first company of volunteer firemen, staged another af-

The Fremont Hotel, 1850—it sat on the eastern slope of Tele-graph Hill. —*Library of Congress*

fair at the St. Francis. That event saw five hundred ladies in attendance, though claims were made that they had ransacked the state to assemble this fine array of femininity and that some had come from as far east as Saint Joseph, Missouri, surely a gross exaggeration.

Following the June 29, 1851, city fire, the dining room of the St. Francis became the temporary Superior Court room, as well as a church on Sundays. In times of disas-ter, everyone pitched in and helped. Hotels were no exception. The St. Francis re-mained the city's most fashionable hotel until November 1851, when the Oriental Hotel opened.

The Oriental Hotel, erected on the corner of Bush and Battery streets, opened for business in February 1851 but proved to be more of a facade than a hotel. Owner Caleb Hyatt financed the building and ran out of funds before completion. The exterior looked stunning, with a four-story frame structure with an ornate set of wide balconies for each floor. Its glass pane windows and doors created an inviting look but the inte-rior told the tale of a project out of money. Hyatt furnished some of the public rooms with fine French furniture and mirrors brought over from the Leidesdorff estate, but most remained unfurnished, or, at best, looked temporary and makeshift.

The Oriental was built at the edge of the bay on piers, and tidewater rose and ebbed beneath it, giving off a terrible stench at low tide. Access required using a nar-row planked causeway from the land end to the front entryway. By day, noise from the nearby Risdon Iron Works drowned out normal speech. By night, rats scurried across the cotton ceilings stretched above the rooms, and the guests lay awake, fighting off the fleas.

Mary Faulkner Ball was managing her own boarding house in 1851, when asked by boarder Caleb Hyatt if she'd agree to manage the Oriental Hotel. Her own business wasn't doing well and, in fact, Hyatt owed her a considerable sum in back rent. She took the position with some trepidation, hoping to earn a salary and receive his back payments owed. What she found was a hotel only half completed. It took months to bring the hotel into first-class order, with Ball pleading with suppliers for the goods to furnish the hotel. The acquisition of rugs, curtain material, and dinnerware all took negotiation and pleading. As the hotel improved, more guests moved in. Yet, Hyatt's finances remained poor in spite of the improved cash flow, and Mary's back rent failed to materialize. She often didn't receive her salary. By October 1851, Mary Faulkner Ball learned of a change in management and the subsequent loss of her job. Caleb Hyatt had lost his hotel.

The change in ownership infused new money into the hotel and it soon took its rightful place, when leaders of San Francisco's fledgling society began meeting there. It had already been a gathering place for the 1851 Vigilance Committee, when Caleb Hyatt was a key member. Now it drew a more genteel crowd.

The Oriental Hotel held its position as the city's finest hotel for the next ten years.

The What Cheer House, 1866—cheap, clean, and no alcohol or women. It was built by Robert B. Woodward. —Author's collection

Robert Woodward, a grocer who came to San Francisco with a thousand dollars worth of goods, realized that housing the people coming to California might be more lucrative than selling them groceries. He began by boarding a couple of men at his store. He built a new boarding house next to the store and expanded from there, erecting houses until he had one hundred men renting his rooms. With rooms still renting at a premium, Woodward entered the hotel business. On July 4, 1852, he opened the What Cheer House on Sacramento Street. The hotel offered clean, though Spartan, rooms at a fair price and good meals and non-alcoholic beverages, ala carte. He also provided public baths in the basement.

A teetotaler, Woodward offered an alternative to the hard drinking and gambling in the town. He opened the first free lending library in the city and began collecting artifacts for a museum in the hotel, another first in San Francisco. By the mid-1860s the hotel had increased to one thousand rooms and served three thousand meals daily. His formula of temperance, cleanliness, and low prices was a great success. The What Cheer House remained in business until the 1906 earthquake and fire destroyed it.

Other hotels of the period included the Tehama House, a two-story frame structure that was a bit less luxurious and considerably more fun than the Oriental. Per Lillie Hitchcock Coit, it drew a rough-and-tumble lot, including military officers and adventurers. The brick International Hotel curried the favor of travelers. It was located on the north side of Jackson at Montgomery. The Rassette House, another wooden structure, burned to the ground in 1853. The hotel was rebuilt and renamed the Metro-

The Cosmopolitan Hotel, 1866—Corner of Sansome and Bush streets. —*Library of Congress*

politan Hotel. It was later torn down and finally replaced by the Cosmopolitan. By 1856, there were over sixty hotels and boarding houses in the city.

San Francisco's economy didn't always rocket upward. There were good times and bad, the oscillations exaggerated by the volatile nature of the people and especially the investors. The early 1850s suffered from the extension of too much credit. By 1853, there was plenty of gold, but little real currency, due to a shortage of trade outside of California. The U.S. government remedied this situation by opening private assay offices in San Francisco where gold could be minted into private coinage. The assayer certified each coin (a fifty-dollar coin was called a slug) with a stamp. A branch mint opened in 1854, setting standards for gold coinage.

By 1855, the economy had floundered. The easy pickings dried up; gold became harder to find and despondent miners drifted back to the cities. Eastern banks were drawing on California gold held in branches in San Francisco. When San Francisco businesses tried to draw out their money, it was in transit eastward in the form of gold dust and ingots. The currency that should have returned to San Francisco went into shaky investments, like the B & O Railroad. San Francisco's banks began failing on Black Friday, February 23, 1855, and a financial panic ensued. San Francisco's economy slowed down, as did the hotel-building trend. The city's focus shifted slightly, with manufacturing and trade gaining momentum. The 1859 discovery of silver in Nevada's Comstock Lode injected new life into the economy, through stock sales and speculation. The Civil War placed demands on California for gold and silver but also for produce, grains, lumber, leather, and furs. Additionally, titles on the land south of California Street had been contested earlier, but were resolved in 1860, enabling new construction to commence between Market and California.

SAN FRANCISCO'S FIRST GRAND HOTELS

The flow of new money meant opportunity, a fact not lost on a few of San Francisco's early citizens. Building again took hold with the construction of fourteen hundred new homes, and the demand for hotel rooms outstripped the available supply. Christian Russ of the American Hotel had done well, even in the hard years. A jeweler by trade, he had been burglarized in New York, an event that broke him financially and which forced him to strike out for San Francisco with the funds he had left. Russ opened a jewelry store, as well as an assay office. Taking a bit off the top in fees for gold assayed, he soon amassed his fortune again. The Comstock Lode brought new people into San Francisco and made new millionaires daily, through speculation. In 1861, Russ began to build the first of San Francisco's grand hotels, the Russ House on the site of his first home. He had moved his family to a mansion at Sixth and Harrison streets in 1853, then quickly opening the Russ Gardens there, a rollicking German beer garden designed for the pleasure of his countrymen.

Finished in early 1862, the Russ House filled the entire block on Montgomery from Bush to Pine. Its lobby and room accommodations rivaled those of the grand

The Russ House, built by Christian Russ, was arguably San Francisco's first grand hotel. —*Photo courtesy of San Francisco History Center, San Francisco Public Library*

Menu for the Russ House—1877. —*Library of Congress*

Wine List for the Russ House—1877. —*Library of Congress*

hotels in New York. Its facilities included a library, a first class restaurant, a spacious, finely appointed dining room, and a grand ballroom. The ground floor hosted the finest boutiques and shops, including Colonel A. Andrews' Diamond Palace, a massive, luxurious jewelry store with a great marble entry, glass cases, and mirrored walls. Such notables as Ambrose Bierce and Mark Twain called the Russ House home. It basked in the knowledge that it was the finest hotel west of the Mississippi River, at least for its first few months.

The Occidental Hotel soon followed the building of the Russ House, with construction beginning in 1861. Rather than proceeding as one big project, the architects, Caleb Hyatt, Thomas Johnston and William Mooser, set it up to develop in three stages, opening the hotel after the completion of the first stage. The four-story Occidental Hotel, built in an Italianate style, was completed in 1869. It took up the entire east side of Montgomery Street, from Sutter to Bush.

The Occidental also hosted the likes of Mark Twain, Robert Louis Stevenson, and Lillie Hitchcock Coit. It also became a favorite hotel for military officers visiting or based in the city. The restaurant and bar at the Occidental became a meeting place for the transaction of the city's business.

Professor Jerry Thomas claims in the 1887 edition of *Bon-Vivant's Companion, or How to Mix Drinks* to have invented the Martinez, later called the martini, at the Occi-

The Occidental Hotel—started in 1861, it was built in stages through 1869. This photo was taken in 1866. —*Library of Congress*

The Occidental Hotel was known for comfort and luxury. It hosted many notables of the time, like Mark Twain. —*Photo courtesy of San Francisco History Center, San Francisco Public Library*

dental in San Francisco. While Thomas was bartending there, a patron asked him for a cocktail while waiting to catch the ferry to Martinez. Thomas created the Martinez, starting a new trend. The town of Martinez also lays claim to the drink, but Thomas and San Francisco get the credit. New York's Knickerbocker Hotel also lays claim to the creation of the martini but that was in 1912—they'd do anything to be one up on San Francisco.

THE LICK HOUSE

James Lick, a renowned craftsman of wood products, knew opportunities must

James Lick, builder of the Lick House, and San Francisco's greatest benefactor. —*Author's collection*

be grasped. A devotee of quality, Lick began construction of the Lick House in late 1861. He'd earned fortunes on his San Francisco investments and from his farms and a mill in the Santa Clara Valley. Lick knew San Francisco stood ready for a new resurgence of growth and prosperity.

Lick House opened in August 1862. Lick designed his hotel only three stories high to account for earthquakes although it spanned to over two blocks—covering all but the corner of Montgomery and Post, which Lick deeded to the Masonic Lodge. A second-story bridge connected the two building halves over the alley between. Not interested in building the biggest hotel, Lick focused on detail and quality. Lick House offered 164 rooms, including twelve double suites with bath, six single suites with bath, forty-nine single suites, fifty-five single rooms, ten single rooms without windows, and thirty-two small single rooms. The hotel also provided a reading room, a parlor, the dining room, a kitchen, a storeroom, a bar with billiard rooms, and a barbershop, as well as the hotel's business offices.

The hotel, a true showpiece, reflected the fine craftsmanship of James Lick. The dining room was a replica of one Lick had visited at the Palace of Versailles in Paris in 1825. It dined four hundred guests in the lap of luxury. The arched ceiling began at thirty-two feet and progressed to forty-eight feet to the peak of the dome. The sixty-four- by eighty-seven-foot parquet floor consisted of 87,772 pieces of fine wood, many crafted by Lick

Barber shop inside the Lick House. —*Author's collection*

The Lick House redefined luxury, entering the field as a true grand hotel. —*Library of Congress*

himself. Sunlight streamed through the stained, ground, and cut glass ceiling by day, and two great gas-burning chandeliers illuminated the room by night. Nine- by twelve-foot French plate glass mirrors adorned the corners of the hall.

Eleven panels, painted in oils by noted landscape artist Thomas Hill decorated the walls. Rosemary Lick, Lick's great-grandniece wrote the following in *The Generous Miser*:

> The paintings represented California in 1849—a vessel coming through the Golden Gate; the Yosemite Falls; South Dome with El Capitan in the foreground; Sentinel Dome; Mount Shasta; the Redwood Forest; the Russian River Valley; a scene on the Isthmus of Panama, and others. The mirrors and the paintings were enclosed in frames designed and made in part, by James Lick. James designed his own cutting machine and sent to Washington for a patent.

The hotel opened with much fanfare and approval. The staff, many personally selected by Lick, offered the highest level of service. It became *the* place for society, yet it also catered to families and, especially, children. Lick House offered a special children's menu and began dinner for them half an hour before the appointed dinner hour should they be hungry.

Lick House dining room—James Lick crafted much of this room himself. A highly accomplished piano-maker, his work was without peer. —*Author's collection*

San Francisco suffered a strong earthquake on October 8, 1865. Lick House suffered only minor damage, its chimney shaken down, thanks to James Lick's foresight. Many buildings were left uninhabitable and the city hall was badly damaged.

Lick initially chose a simple room in the back of the hotel for his own living quarters. He brought in his books, his carpenter's tools, and his old workbench. In his latter days, he moved to room 127 on the corner overlooking Sutter and Montgomery streets. Before his death, Lick began arranging a trust to give most of his fortune to San Francisco. He also set up smaller trusts in the Santa Clara Valley. In all, he bequeathed three million dollars to its public trusts, the largest sum ever left in the State of California. Not the recluse some claimed, Lick joined the Society of California Pioneers as a charter member and served as the society's president from 1873 until 1877 when he died.

James G. Fair bought the Lick House in October 1889, renovating the aging hotel to its former beauty. The Lick House remained one of San Francisco's premier grand hotels until it burned to the ground during the 1906 earthquake and fire.

THE GRAND HOTEL

Asbury Harpending and William C. Ralston formed the Montgomery Street Land Company in 1868 with the idea of extending Montgomery Street beyond Market all the way to the bay through Rincon Hill. The tideland south of Market was to be filled in with earth dug from Rincon Hill and then sold at great profit. Harpending and Ralston acquired a critical piece of land from the Catholic church and a second piece for $150,000. Robert Woodward had originally asked $300,000 for the property but an

The Grand Hotel—first hotel built by William C. Ralston with Asbury Harpending. It was all part of a land scheme that didn't quite work out. —*Photo courtesy of San Francisco History Center, San Francisco Public Library*

earthquake unnerved him and he wanted out. Harpending and Ralston cut New Montgomery Street through their property and began construction of a new hotel. New Montgomery was to be a major boulevard, connecting Market Street to the south bay front. Two blocks down the road, New Montgomery stopped at Howard Street. The property owners there, Milton S. Latham and John Parrot, refused to sell the land on the other side. Ralston convinced the legislature to condemn the land for the public good, but Latham and Parrot convinced the governor to veto it. Over two million dollars went into creating a new street, which even today is only two blocks long.

The last of the class hotels opening in the 1860s, the Grand Hotel was completed in late 1869. The Grand was larger and more luxurious than the Russ House, Lick House, or the Occidental Hotel. Located on the southeast corner of Market and New Montgomery streets, it stood three stories tall and topped with a mansard roof. The

SENATOR SHARON AND MISS HILL AT THE GRAND HOTEL

The Grand Hotel served as the stage for a strange case that surfaced in 1883. Sarah Althea Hill, an attractive young lady, claimed that she had been secretly married to Senator William Sharon, who kept her in a suite at the Grand Hotel. Per her story, he later abandoned her. The senator owned the suite and Miss Hill claimed he removed both the furnishings and the doors in order to evict her. The pale, quiet senator, a widower worth around ten million, claimed he'd never made her acquaintance and if he had, it had been honorable and even if he had associated with her, he certainly would never have married her.

With her bases all covered, Miss Hill took her case to court, her fees covered by none other than San Francisco's mysterious Mammy (Mary Ellen) Pleasant, a freed slave with a grip on parts of San Francisco and a rumored talent with black magic. Miss Hill produced a contract, which her experts claimed was genuine, and the senator's experts claimed was a bald forgery. For sixty-one days the trial continued, with the press reporting all salaciously, including what the attractive Miss Hill wore to court. The jury reached a verdict on December 24, 1884, finding Senator Sharon guilty. The new Mrs. Sharon then began a spending spree that ended when the senator's lawyer won an appeal of the verdict. She became Miss Hill again and began her own set of appeals.

Exhausted by the process and the never-ending wrangling, Senator William Sharon died on November 13, 1885, and his funeral was held in the lobby of the Palace Hotel. Miss Hill began a new battle to gain control of his estate. She married her lawyer, David Terry, who persisted in her case, to the point of harassing the judge who had rejected her appeal. The judge's bodyguard shot the lawyer dead.

Miss Hill lost all of her appeals and her contract burned in a fire. It has been said that Mammy Pleasant paid anywhere from five thousand to one hundred thousand dollars in legal fees for Hill's case. In the end, Hill spent her last days in San Francisco on a bench in Union Square telling all who would listen that she was waiting for her next court appearance. She was committed to the state hospital in Stockton, where she died in 1937.

The Grand Hotel was the site of the Senator Sharon scandal. —*Author's collection*

hotel provided four hundred fine rooms for its discriminating guests. William C. Ralston, as part owner, financed the hotel through the Bank of California. The Grand Hotel later shared a bridge that crossed over New Montgomery to the Palace Hotel, built by Ralston on the vacant lot left over from his purchases.

THE PALACE HOTEL

By the 1870s, San Francisco considered itself a metropolis. These were the days of the Comstock's "Bonanza Kings" including the "Irish Big Four"—James C. Flood, James G. Fair, John W. Mackay, and William S. O'Brien, who made their fortunes from the Virginia City silver bonanza—and the railroad barons known as the "Big Four"— Charles Crocker, Leland Stanford, Mark Hopkins, and Collis Huntington.

The completion of the transcontinental railroad created great wealth for the railroad barons and for California. The Central Pacific and Union Pacific railroads joined on May 10, 1869, in Promontory, Utah, with the ceremonial driving of the Golden Spike into the track that joined East and West. The completion of the link made travel west by wagon train not only obsolete but also financially impractical. Families sold or shipped their goods west and rode in relative comfort to California. Both the cost to ship and the time consumed in shipping plummeted. The value of California's goods and produce increased and people flowed into the state once again.

William C. Ralston, silver king, speculator, and vice-president/cashier of the Bank of California, envisioned a hotel greater than any ever built. One of the early Comstock millionaires, Ralston purchased two and a half acres of sand dunes on Market Street in the 1860s. Gene Fowler wrote, "Europe's civilization will be judged by its churches, America's by its hotels." San Francisco had more hotel rooms per capita than any other city and already boasted four grand hotels. Ralston believed Fowler's words and wanted to build a hotel to outclass them all.

He sent his architect, John Gaynor, on a tour of the country's grand hotels, visiting the best in her great cities. On his return, Gaynor presented the plans for a hotel that would surpass them all—seven stories tall covering Ralston's entire two and a half acres on Market Street. It proposed to be the biggest hotel in America. Ralston was delighted and agreed to the project immediately, with one exception. The plan proposed bay-view windows on only the first floor. Ralston demanded bay-view windows on every floor. He would have nothing but the finest for all of his guests.

Work commenced in 1871, with a budget not to exceed $1,750,000. The digging of the basement and building of the foot-thick masonry foundations absorbed that sum and the construction of the second floor required another million. Ralston's business partner and manager of the bank's branch in Virginia City, William Sharon, realized that the hotel's building expenses would soon deplete their Comstock profits. Ralston and Sharon had organized the Union Mill & Mining Company as well as other Comstock ventures. By 1870, William Sharon controlled the Comstock through his bank position and his position in their mining company.

Sharon confronted Ralston about his side enterprises. Ralston, through the bank, financed new businesses to supply the hotel's needs. Those businesses included a ranch to provide oak planking, a furniture factory, and a foundry to forge nails and tools. Ralston demanded the best, and although Sharon complained, he backed down and the building continued as before.

Marble walls, Doric columns, large stone window openings, and, above all, a great arched roof of glass

The Palace Hotel was Ralston's passion; some say it killed him. Note the bridge on the left connecting the Palace to the Grand Hotel. No need to drop to street level. —*Courtesy of The Bancroft Library, University of California, Berkeley*

defined the exterior of the new building. The white marble came from Vermont and the black marble from Tennessee. Ten million board feet of lumber went into the construction, as did 32,000 barrels of cement, 34,000 barrels of lime, 3,500 barrels of plaster of Paris, and 3,300 tons of steel. The initial awe felt by San Franciscans soon gave way to amusement as they decided it was over-built—eight hundred rooms were four times too many and the number of elevators, thirty-four, seemed absurd. Still, Ralston pressed on and so did the bills.

The bank board soon elected Ralston as the new president of the Bank of California. Money tightened up and Ralston grew concerned over his mounting debt and the condition of the bank. He and partner Sharon sold their mines to the Irish Big Four after James Fair, a mining engineer, convinced them the mines were played out. Fair claimed sixty dollars a ton was the best they would do, a barely break-even proposition.

The Irish Big Four were determined to break Ralston, Sharon, and the Bank of California's stranglehold on the Comstock. Soon after, the mines hit as big a load as before. Ralston had originally bought stock in the mine next to the strike from Fair, hoping to cash in, but Fair hadn't disclosed that he knew the mine missed the vein. Knowing Ralston and the bank were now cash poor, Fair, Flood, and O'Brien informed Ralston they were withdrawing all of their funds from the bank.

By August 26, 1875, Ralston owed the bank $4,500,000 in loans on the hotel, although it wasn't quite finished. Word of Ralston's worthless mining stock reached San Francisco from Virginia City and depositors began a run on the bank. By 2:30 that day, the police had to push back the angry depositors. The money was gone and the bank doors closed.

The next day the board, including Sharon, met without Ralston present and fired him, blaming him for the state of the bank. Ralston was reviewing plans at the hotel, and he later returned to his office where he learned of his dismissal. He finished some paperwork, left the bank, and went down to the bay at North Beach for his daily swim. Whether it was suicide or accidental, Ralston's body was retrieved from the waters of the bay and pulled up on the beach. The completion of the hotel was two months away.

Sharon took over for Ralston at the bank and inherited the Palace Hotel. Within six weeks, the bank's debts were paid and it was solvent again. On October 2, 1875, five weeks after Ralston's death, the Palace Hotel opened—the largest hotel in the world, at least for a short while. The United States Hotel in Saratoga, New York, soon eclipsed it in size, but not in grandeur.

William C. Ralston—president of the Bank of California, Bonanza King and builder of the Grand and Palace hotels. Was it suicide? —*Courtesy of The Bancroft Library, University of California, Berkeley*

Great entrance portals led to the court inside, where carriages could deposit guests. The final structure held nearly a thousand rooms and, as proven in 1883, could accommodate twenty-five hundred guests. The great Palm Court attracted international attention for its spacious, luxurious design, where a large assembly could meet in an environment that appeared to be out-of-doors, yet it was actually indoors. Paved in alternate blocks of black and white marble, it used carved screens to isolate it from the driveway. Fruit ripened on citrus trees plants in great pots placed against the colonnades, interspersed with tropical plants and ferns.

The hotel actually had four hydraulic elevators called "rising rooms." They shone in polished glass and the finest wooden paneling and woodwork, each operated by a uniformed operator. An attendant stationed at a massive polished desk supervised

The Palace Hotel inner court—carriages entered the hotel so guests could avoid the weather. It became the Grand Court in the post-1906 hotel. —*Courtesy of The Bancroft Library, University of California, Berkeley*

The Palace Hotel dining room—there were more waiters than guests. —*Courtesy of The Bancroft Library, University of California, Berkeley*

each floor, his station complete with speaking tubes and pneumatic package tubes connected to the main office. Each room offered a view of the city through Ralston's bay windows, as well as a fireplace adorned with a mantle clock. Ralston's West Coast Furniture Company constructed its furniture from the finest California laurel trees, horsehair, goose feathers, and fabric available. The blankets and sheets originated at Ralston's Mission Woolen Mills, the blankets emblazoned with "Palace Hotel."

The seventh floor offered the crystal roof gardens complete with hanging plants; flowering shrubs, bronze, glass, and crystal chandeliers. Marble statues stood on pedestals at each corner, representing spring, summer, fall, and winter. The walk around the gardens measured one-third of a mile. The glass roof above let in the sunlight by day and reflected the light of the chandeliers and lighted globes at night.

The hotel boasted a massive kitchen that served twelve hundred guests, with a *chef de cuisine* often presenting the finest culinary skills in the city. The banquet rooms' wait staff served meals as though to royalty, standing by to meet the guests' slightest whim. Each food course had its own head chef, and the hotel was famed for it *haute cuisine*.

The hotel obtained its water from four artesian wells located beneath the floor of the Great Court. The wells fed a massive reservoir capable of supplying up to 28,000 gallons of water an hour to the hotel. The reservoir beneath the court held 630,000 gallons. Seven tanks on the roof held another 130,000 gallons. Miles of pipe carried the water through the hotel and 327 outlet valves supplied 15,000 feet of fire hose.

During its first ten years, the hotel struggled financially. Too many empty rooms, too large a staff, and too much pilfering by the staff diminished any profits that existed. European visitors now often bypassed San Francisco for easier routes to the Orient, thanks to the newly opened Suez Canal. Following Sharon's death, his son-in-law Frank Newlands took over the operation of the Palace Hotel. He trimmed the payroll, firing thirty cooks and all the dining room waiters and fourteen of the original grill-room staff of eighteen. Employees had to pay for meals eaten at the hotel and they were searched before leaving the premises. These changes helped, but the sudden world interest in the Hawaiian Islands turned the tide. All routes led through San Francisco and the hotel's trade increased markedly.

The Palace Hotel survived the repeated shocks of the great earthquake of 1906. When the fires crept toward it, the hotel's reservoir served to provide water for fighting the fires, with employees playing the hoses on the hotel's roof and on adjacent buildings. Realizing the danger from the fires, the manager began evacuating the facility, guests first, then employees. The water finally ran out and within ten minutes, the fires overtook the hotel. The foundation and walls stood strong but fire gutted the interior.

The hotel reopened in 1909, but it wasn't the same. The spacious rooms and high ceilings, as well as Ralston's great bay-view windows were lost to more compact, modern designs. One of the most beautiful buildings on Market Street had lost some of its luster. The drive-in court became the Grand Court Dining Room, said to be the finest in America. Regardless, the Palace Hotel remains a place of awe, luxury, magnificence, and remarkable history, well worth the visit.

THE BALDWIN HOTEL

Elias Jackson "Lucky"Baldwin, another of the Bonanza Kings, decided to build a hotel in San Francisco and he wanted it to be impressive. The Palace Hotel was nearing completion and Lucky Baldwin needed something that would stand in that class and turn heads. His mining operations gave him the confidence that he had "unlimited means" at his disposal. Baldwin acquired the triangular lot bounded by Market, Ellis and Powell streets, property which belonged to Thomas Maguire, and he ordered the construction of his theater and 595-room hotel. The inclusion of a theatre in the hotel set the Baldwin apart from the others. The entire complex cost Baldwin $800,000, a far cry from

The Baldwin Hotel—showpiece for "Lucky" Baldwin. —*Auth collection*

The Baldwin Hotel, 1878—the dome was reserved for ladies' recreation. —*Author's collection*

Ralston's $6 million to $7 million. However, the furnishings cost Baldwin twice the expense of the structure.

The structure was indeed impressive, but for the most part, it was a veneer, a vanity project without substance. Baldwin was a lecherous, uncultured, boisterous, and blasphemous miner, knowing or caring little for permanence or safety, and he carried almost no insurance on his personal showpiece. Still, firetrap though it was, the Baldwin Hotel attracted the highest elements of society.

The dominating feature of the hotel was the 168-foot-tall hexagonal dome, open five stories

Baldwin Hotel dining rook—the first luxury restaurant to use ambient light as well as gas light. Its windows look out onto the street. —*Author's collection*

high on the inside and raised eight stories above the pavement, with a Mansard roof studded with ornate dormer windows. The interior carpeting from W. & J. Sloan cost thirty dollars a yard, and the carpet was bought by the mile. The hotel boasted a Tiffany's office clock that Mark Twain described as telling, "not only the hours, minutes and seconds, but the turn of the tides, the phases of the moon, the price of eggs and who's got your umbrella." The Herring Brothers' ten-ton vault was "the best of its kind the firm had ever sold." All was put on for show and the city loved it.

Unique to the Baldwin, besides the theatre, was an open elevator car enclosed in glass and mirrors, framed in polished hardwoods, Parisian-style. It ascended through the center of the sweeping grand stairway to the top of the dome, allowing the passengers to "see and be seen." The dome, reserved for the ladies, included a billiard room, an aquarium, a conservatory of flowers, and a sewing room, all with a breathtaking view of the city. "Lucky" Baldwin was enamored with ladies—as many as possible.

Another feature of the hotel that caught the attention of the locals was the dining room. Hotels of the day placed their dining rooms in the center of the structure, illuminated by gas lamps. Baldwin's looked out onto Ellis Street, using the windows to provide natural light, in addition to the gaslights. The dining room, divided into three eating areas measured thirty-two feet wide and one hundred thirty-eight feet long and according, to the *Alta California*, was without equal among any of the hotels in the United States.

High stakes poker games, awash in Kentucky whiskey, commenced regularly in Baldwin's personal suites. Baldwin was a gambler, and he owned racing stables and a ranch for thoroughbred horses named Santa Anita in Southern California. That ranch was later to become the Santa Anita Racetrack. The man also couldn't control himself with the ladies. He married and divorced often, had many mistresses and lovers, and sat on the wrong end of lawsuits brought by a number of women. During one court session, he stated that his public reputation was such that every woman who came near him must have been warned about him in advance. At age fifty-six, he lost a settlement for $75,000 to a sixteen-year-old, for jilting her.

Just outside the door of his suite at the hotel, a young woman once shot and seriously wounded Baldwin, claiming he had "ruined her body and soul." Baldwin never denied the charge, and she later showed up in Denver as a successful madam, advertising her adventure with the millionaire.

While the hotel met the minimal building and fire codes, its frame construction, with gas lighting and highly lacquered woodwork, created a firetrap situation. The Baldwin Hotel and its theatre burned to the ground in the early morning hours of November 23, 1898. The fire started in the scene lofts of the theatre and spread through the theatre and hotel. Chief Dennis Sullivan, head of the San Francisco fire department quickly learned that San Francisco lacked the high-pressure water system needed to fight a large, multi-story fire. The Baldwin fire caused a great loss of life, as well as the total destruction of the hotel and theatre. The estimated loss of $2.5 million, balanced against $185,000 in insurance, broke Baldwin. He sold the land located at the corner of Powell and Market to fellow Bonanza King James L. Flood for just over $1 million.

Chief Sullivan realized the water system needed redesigning. He petitioned the city's board of supervisors to build great tanks at the top of Twin Peaks to create a high-pressure gravity-fed system. However, graft overruled common sense and need. The board rejected Sullivan's ideas. It claimed the current system was "good enough."

The great earthquake and fire of 1906 proved the officials sadly and, perhaps, criminally wrong. As with Baldwin's fire, San Francisco's firemen looked on, helpless to fight the fires, as there was no water pressure for their hoses. Chief Sullivan's unfulfilled vision had disastrous consequences. During the quake, a chimney from the California Hotel next door collapsed onto the firehouse, opening a hole down through three stories. The chief fell through that hole and was pinned to a steam register. He died four days later.

Chief Sullivan, later called the "father of the modern high pressure water system," finally received credit for his concepts. The city adopted his ideas shortly after the conflagration, marking a new era in San Francisco firefighting.

NEARLY THE END OF AN ERA

Construction began on two more grand hotels before the great disaster of 1906. The St. Francis Hotel, built by the Charles Crocker family, opened on March 21, 1904. The new hotel bore no relation to the previous hotel of the same name. Designed to rival the fine hotels of Europe, it required two years and two and a half million dollars to erect. The earthquake of April 18, 1906, put the hotel to the test and the stately St. Francis survived well. The structure remained sound and the chef prepared breakfast the next morning. The fire that ensued following the quake wasn't so kind, but again the main structure survived. Rebuilt in nineteen months, the St. Francis continues as one of the pre-1906 icons of San Francisco.

The other grand hotel was the Fairmont Hotel, built by Bonanza King James Fair, owner of the Lick House. Complete and nearly ready to open at the time of the 1906 earthquake, the Fairmont survived, though it did require structural as well as interior ornamental refurbishing. The Beaux Arts-style structure, designed by Julia Morgan (who also designed Hearst Castle in San Simeon), required a year to refurbish after the fires and reopened on April 18, 1907. Recently renovated, the Fairmont is a trip back in time. The St. Francis is...well, it is the St. Francis, and, it is always worth a visit. Since both hotels remain with us as designed, they are only mentioned for completeness.

The St. Francis Hotel, just after the earthquake and fire of 1906. It remained structurally sound. —*Library of Congress*

Bibliography

Altrocchi, Julia Cooley. *The Spectacular San Franciscans*. New York: E. P. Dutton and company, Inc. 1949.

Argonaut—Journal of the San Francisco Museum and Historical Society. "San Francisco World of Mary Ball" by Charles A, Fracchia, Vol. 11 No. 1 and 2, Summer, Winter 2000.

Argonaut—Journal of the San Francisco Museum and Historical Society. "Frenchtown In Gold Rush San Francisco" by Claudine Chalmers, Vol. 12 No. 1, Fall 2001.

Argonaut—Journal of the San Francisco Museum and Historical Society. "The Chutes: San Francisco's Unique Destination for Amusement" by John T. Freeman, Vol. 14 No. 2, Winter 2003.

Bancroft, Hubert Howe. *The Book of the Fair*. Chicago, San Francisco: The Bancroft Company, Publishers, 1893.

Barker, Malcolm E., editor. *More San Francisco Memoirs: 1852–1899—The Ripening Years*. San Francisco: Londonborn Publications, 1996.

Berger, Frances DeTalavera and John Parke Custis. *Sumptuous Dining in Gaslight San Francisco—1875–1915*. Garden City, NY: Doubleday and Company, 1985.

Bergeron, Victor. *Frankly Speaking—Trader Vic's Own Story*. Garden City, NY: Doubleday and Company, 1972.

Blaisdell, Marilyn. *San Francisciana Photographs of Three World Fairs*. San Francisco: Marilyn Blaisdell, Publisher, 1994.

Bloomfield, Arthur J. *The San Francisco Opera 1923–1961*. New York: Appleton: Century-Crofts, Inc., 1961.

Briscoe, John. *Tadich Grill—The Story of San Francisco's Oldest Restaurant, with Recipes*. Berkeley, CA: Ten Speed Press, 2002.

Brook, James, Chris Carlsson, and Nancy J. Peters. *Reclaiming San Francisco History, Politics, Culture*. San Francisco: City Lights Books, 1988.

Caen, Herb. *Herb Caen's New Guide to San Francisco*. Garden City, NY: Doubleday and Company, 1957, 1958.

Chure—San Francisco. Souvenir Brochure. San Francisco: ca. 1904.

Chutes and Its Myriad Attractions. Souvenir Brochure. San Francisco: ca. 1901.

Delkin, James Ladd. *Flavor of San Francisco—A Guide to "The City."* Stanford University, CA: James Ladd Delkin, Publisher, 1943.

Dickson, Samuel. *Tales of San Francisco*. Stanford, CA: Stanford University Press, 1947.

Dobie, Charles Caldwell. *San Francisco: A Pageant*. New York: D. Appleton-Century Company, 1939.

Dobie, Charles Caldwell. *Chinatown: A Pageant*. New York: D. Appleton-Century Company, 1936.

Duffus, R.L. *The Tower of Jewels: San Francisco Memories*. New York: W.W. Norton and Company, Inc., 1960.

Edwords, Clarence E. *Bohemian San Francisco*. San Francisco: Paul Elder and Company, 1914.

Filion, Ron. *San Francisco History*. http://www.zpub.com/sf50/sf/

Gagey, Edmond J. *The San Francisco Stage: A History*. New York: Columbia University Press, 1950.

Gilliam, Harold. *San Francisco Bay*. Garden City, NY, Doubleday and Company, 1957.

Gilliam, Harold. *The San Francisco Experience*. Garden City, NY, Doubleday and Company, 1972.

Golden Gate International Exposition. Japanese Promotional Brochure, 1940.

Goodman, Dean. *San Francisco Stages: A Concise History, 1849–1986*. San Francisco: Micro Pro Litera Press, 1986.

Gross, Alexander, editor, *Famous Guide to San Francisco and the World's Fair*. New York: "Geographia" Map Company, 1939.

Holliday, J.S. *Rush for Riches: Gold Fever and the Making of California*. Berkeley, California, University of California Press, 1999.

Library of Congress. *California As I Saw It: First-person Narratives from California's Early Years, 1849–1900*. Volume 204 [database online] Washington, D.C.: Library of Congress, 2000.

Lord, Jack, Jenn Shaw, and Lloyd Hoff. *Where to Sin in San Francisco*. First edition. San Francisco: 1939.

Lord, Jack, and Lloyd Hoff, *Where to Sin in San Francisco*. Mid-Century edition. San Francisco: Richard Guggenheim, 1953.

MacMinn, George R. *The Theater of The Golden Era in California*. Caldwell, Idaho, The Caxton Printers, Ltd., 1941.

Maradikian, George. *Dinner at Omar Khayyam's*. New York: Viking Press, 1944.

McCarty, L.P. *Statistician and Economist: 1894*, San Francisco: L.P. McCarty, 1894.

Muscantine, Doris. *A Cook's Tour of San Francisco*. New York: Charles Scribner's Sons, 1963.

O'Brien, Robert. *This Is San Francisco*. New York: Whittlesey House, McGraw-Hill Book Company, Inc. 1948.

O'Reilly, James, Larry Habegger, and Sean O'Reilly. *Traveler's Tales: San Francisco*. San Francisco: Travelers' Tales, Inc., 1996.

Palmer, John Williamson. *Gold Hunters of California. Pioneer Days in San Francisco. The Century*, vol. 43, issue 4 (Feb 1892).

Pierce, J. Kingston. *San Francisco, You're History!*. Seattle, WA: Sasquatch Books, 1995.

Purdy, Helen Throop. *San Francisco—As It Was, As It Is, and How to See It*. San Francisco: Paul Elder and Company, 1912.

"The Ship "Niantic" in San Francisco," *Quarterly of The Society of California Pioneers, vol. VI, Number 3 (October 1926)*.

Reinhardt, Richard. *Treasure Island—San Francisco's Exposition Years*. Mill Valley, CA: Squarebooks, 1978.

San Francisco Theatre Research. WPA Project 8386. *Monographs*, Vols. I–XVII; XX. (Mimeographed, San Francisco: 1938–1942).

Soule, Frank, John H. Gihon, and James Nisbet. *The Annals of San Francisco*. New York: D. Appleton and Company, 1855.

The Chapter in Your Life—San Francisco and the California It Centers. San Francisco: Californians, Inc., 1946.

Young, John P. *San Francisco—A History of the Pacific Coast Metropolis*. San Francisco: The S.J. Clarke Publishing Company, 1912.

Newspapers and Periodicals

Alta CA, San Francisco

Call, San Francisco

Chronicle, San Francisco

Critic, San Francisco

Dramatic Chronicle, San Francisco

Examiner, San Francisco

Figaro, San Francisco

Figaro and Dramatic Review, San Francisco

Morning Call, San Francisco

News, San Francisco

The Overland Monthly, San Francisco

Wide West, San Francisco

Index

About the Author

California historian **James R. Smith** is the author of the books *San Francisco's Playland at the Beach: The Early Years*, covering 1914-1939 and co-author of *The California Snatch Racket: Kidnappings in the Prohibition and Depression Eras*, as well as of a number of historical articles written for San Francisco City Guides' magazine, *Guidelines*. A well-respected authority on San Francisco history, he has spent many years researching and chronicling the stories of San Francisco and California. He is currently writing *San Francisco's Playland at the Beach: The Golden Years*, covering 1940-1972. Smith is a frequent lecturer and discussion leader at universities, historical societies, libraries and bookstores. A member of the California Historical Society, the San Francisco History Association, the San Francisco Historical Society, and the Library Fund at the University of California, Berkeley, Smith is active in the preservation and promotion of history and historical lore. A fourth-generation native of San Francisco and a sixth-generation Californian, Smith is often found haunting the libraries and archives of his native city and enjoying its social life with his wife Liberty.

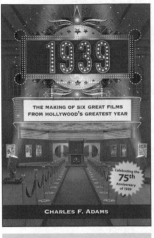
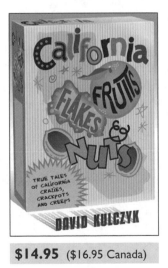